Junge Schweizer Architekten
Young Swiss Architects

Margrit Althammer / **René Hochuli**	9, 25– 37
Marc Angélil / **Sarah Graham** / **Reto Pfenninger** / **Manuel Scholl**	10, 39– 51
Bauart Architekten	11, 53– 65
Conradin Clavuot	12, 67– 79
Beat Consoni	13, 81– 93
Herbert Ehrenbold / **Barbara Schudel**	14, 95–105
Jasmin Grego / **Joseph Smolenicky**	15, 107–119
Kaschka Knapkiewicz / **Axel Fickert**	16, 121–135
Quintus Miller / **Paola Maranta**	17, 137–149
Valerio Olgiati	19, 151–161
Manfred Schafer	20, 163–173
Andi Scheitlin / **Marc Syfrig**	21, 175–185
Thomas Schregenberger	22, 187–199
Jakob Steib	23, 201–213
Vorwort	5
Preface	6

Buchkonzept, Typografie
Hans Rudolf Bosshard
Redaktion
J. Christoph Bürkle
Karin Stegmeier
Lektorat
Ernst Bommer
Übersetzung
Jori Walker
Satz, Lithografie, Druck
Heer Druck AG, Sulgen
Bindearbeit
Burkhardt AG, Mönchaltorf-Zürich

© 1997
Verlag Niggli AG, Schweiz | Liechtenstein

Printed in Switzerland
ISBN 3-7212-0303-8

Vorwort

Neue Tendenzen bei jungen Architektinnen und Architekten aufzuzeigen, ist immer ein widersprüchliches Vorhaben. Es fragt sich, ob dem Neuen auch etwas Tendenzielles innewohnt, und ob bei «jungen Arbeiten» die Stringenz für generalisierende Feststellungen bereits vorhanden ist. Aus diesem Grunde soll der vorliegenden Dokumentation keine umfassende Würdigung vorangestellt werden. Die Zusammenstellung der vorliegenden Arbeiten ist so heterogen, daß sich für eine jeweilige architektonische Position sogleich die gegenteilige finden läßt. Gerade dies ist vielleicht das Merkmal der gegenwärtigen Situation in der Schweiz. Grundlegende Tendenzen sind zudem längst festgemacht. Immer wieder wurde eine «neue Einfachheit» beschworen, ein Rückzug in die vorrangige Behandlung von Details, Materialien und ausgefeilten konstruktiven Verbindungen von beidem.

Bemerkenswert ist allerdings bei den jungen Schweizern die Sicherheit, mit der inhaltliche und formale Bilder umgesetzt werden, ebenso die Klarheit, mit der analoge Typologien zeitgemäß formuliert werden. Ebenso besticht das Interesse für die Behandlung und Handhabung von Materialien und Details, die nach der Ruchlosigkeit der sechziger und siebziger Jahre auf die Suche nach einer neuen Handwerklichkeit verweisen und nicht zuletzt auf die Beharrlichkeit, diese unbeirrt des Kosten- und Zeitdrucks auch umzusetzen. Gleichzeitig liegt dabei aber auch eine Schwäche dieses Entwurfsansatzes auf der Hand: analoge Motive bleiben gelegentlich im Bildhaften stecken, und das Entwickeln von interessanten räumlichen Architekturen, das Experimentieren mit differenzierten Geometrien oder gar mit skulpturalen Aspekten wird scheinbar durch Bauvorschriften und -zwänge verunmöglicht.

Des weiteren läßt sich eine beinahe stoische Ablehnung feststellen, sich zur Bedeutung der Architektur, der Formen und Inhalte zu äußern. Immer wieder wird das Vorhandensein «verschiedener Realitäten» konstatiert, ebenso das Thematisieren von «Dissonanzen der Provinz» oder das «Entwerfen mit polarisierten Widersprüchlichkeiten». Theoreme, die es vor einigen Jahren kaum gegeben hätte und die die Autonomie der Architektur eindeutig vor ideologische oder gar gesellschaftliche Prämissen stellen. Diese Entwicklung ist nach den siebziger Jahren mit ihren gesellschaftlichen und interdisziplinären Inhalten und nach den achtziger Jahren mit der Wiederentdeckung von Theorie und Geschichte sowie der Eigenständigkeit der Architektur nur folgerichtig. Da beide Zeiträume mit der Vermittlung und selbstbewußten, teilweise überheblichen Formulierung von Leitbildern und Doktrinen verbunden waren, ist es nicht verwunderlich, wenn heute eher das Schweigen der jungen Architekten zur Bedeutung der Architektur auszumachen ist. Damit wird Polarisierung und Positionierung vermieden – auch das waren Leitbilder der siebziger und achtziger Jahre.

Mit diesem Rückzug zur Individualisierung ist die unverkennbare Qualität der jungen Schweizer Architektur hingegen untrennbar verbunden. So wie in vielen gesellschaftlichen Bereichen das Interesse für individuelle Mythologien bereits institutionell formuliert wurde, so bewegte sich die aktuelle Architektur und deren Codes gelegentlich in Zirkeln für Eingeweihte und versagte sich bewußt gesellschaftlicher Adaption. Da der öffentliche Raum und die öffentliche Architektur mehr denn je der Privatisierung anheimgestellt ist, so ist es nicht verwunderlich, daß auch junge Schweizer Architekten sich vermehrt individuellen und regionalen Lösungsansätzen der Formfindung verschreiben.

Das geschieht in der Schweiz – wen sollte es wundern, sind doch die hier vorgestellten Architekten fast alle an der ETH (Eidgenössische Technische Hochschule) in Zürich ausgebildet – mehrheitlich vor dem Hintergrund der modernen Tradition. Das Diktum vom «Trend der einfachen Kisten» ist bereits formuliert, jedoch wird das Vokabular der Moderne differenzierter behandelt. Es werden Störungen und doppelte Kodierungen eingesetzt, oder Materialien, die bewußt dem modernistischen Repertoire zuwiderlaufen. Diese «Brüche» in Material und Form zeigen einerseits den souveränen Umgang mit dem vorhandenen Repertoire, und vermitteln, daß diese Codes verfügbar sind, andererseits bleibt es bei der Homogenität der verwendeten Bildwelten nicht aus, daß «Manierismen der Moderne» inszeniert werden, nicht zuletzt als bewußte oder unbewußte Positionierung einer gegenwärtigen Zeit des Umbruchs.

Die Auswahl der Architekten geht im vorliegenden Buch auf die Vortragsreihe «Junge Schweizer Architektinnen und Architekten» zurück, die im Architektur Forum Zürich 1995 und 1996 gehalten wurden. Diese im Sinne von Werkstattberichten geplanten Vorträge haben mittlerweile in Zürich erfreulicherweise fast institutionellen Charakter bekommen. Das Buch ist somit eine Dokumentation über die Arbeiten einiger junger Architekten in der Schweiz, die Diskussionsgrundlage und Bestandsaufnahme zugleich sein sollte und darüber hinaus den Berufsanfängern Gelegenheit bieten möchte, ihre Arbeiten in einem größeren Rahmen vorzustellen. Der Begriff «junge Architekten» – er beinhaltet in dieser Publikation selbstverständlich Architektinnen – ist nicht immer wörtlich zu nehmen. Der Auswahl liegen keine prinzipiellen Kategorien zugrunde, sie spiegelt ein Spektrum von Architekten und ihren Arbeiten wider, die zumeist noch nicht allzu viele Entwürfe realisieren konnten und diese noch nicht häufig publiziert haben. Dennoch halten wir die Zusammenstellung der vorliegenden Projekte und Bauten für interessant und repräsentativ. Die Zugehörigkeit zu bestimmten Jahrgängen spielte dabei eine untergeordnete Rolle.

Die Texte zu den einzelnen Büros wurden von Martin Tschanz (M.T.) und dem Herausgeber (J.C.B.) verfaßt und sind mit den jeweiligen Initialen versehen. Sie sind in ähnlicher Form bereits in der «Neuen Zürcher Zeitung» erschienen. An dieser Stelle sei auf Dr. Roman Hollenstein verwiesen, dessen großem Einsatz es zu verdanken ist, daß die Texte in der NZZ veröffentlicht werden konnten. Besonderer Dank gebührt Hans Rudolf Bosshard, der das Buch gestaltete und darüber hinaus mit unermüdlichem Einsatz die unterschiedlichen Ideen der Architekten zu einer Einheit verband. Redaktionelle Mitarbeit an dem Buch wurde von Karin Stegmeier durchgeführt.

Zürich, Dezember 1996   J. Christoph Bürkle

Preface

Presenting new trends of young architects is always a contradictory undertaking. It is a question whether there is indeed something of the trend inherent in the new and whether, with "young works", enough strict coherence already exists to be able to generalize about. This is why the documentation presented in the following pages should not be prefaced by a comprehensive assessment. The collection of works in this book is so heterogeneous that for each architectural position, the opposite can immediately be found. It may be exactly this that is the characteristic feature of the current situation in Switzerland. Basic tendencies have moreover long since been established. A "new simplicity" is time and again sworn to, a retreat into a priority handling of details, materials, and polished constructional combinations of the two.

Certainly noteworthy is the certainty with which images of content and form are realized by the young Swiss, just as is the clarity with which the analogous typologies are formulated within a modern context. Impressive, too, is the interest in the treatment and application of materials and details that refer, after the infamy of the sixties and seventies, to the search for a new sense of handicraft, and not least, to the determination to bring this into realization, unswayed by costs and time pressure. At the same time, though, a shortcoming of this design work is to be clearly seen: analogous motifs occasionally get hung up in graphic representation, and the development of interesting spatial architecture, experimentation with differentiated geometries or even with sculptural aspects, becomes impossible, seemingly because of building regulations and constructional dictates.

Further, an almost stoical refusal to express anything about the significance of architecture, form or content can be detected. Over and over the existence of "various realities" is declared, as in the themes taken up in "Dissonance of the Provinces" or "Designing with Polar Opposites", theorems that were hardly heard of a few years ago, and that clearly place the autonomy of the architect before ideological or even social premises. This development is only logically consistent following the seventies, with its social and interdisciplinary content, and the eighties, with the rediscovery of theory and history, and the independence of architecture. Because both time periods were linked with the conveyance and self-conscious, sometimes overbearing formulation of models and doctrines, it is not surprising that today it is rather the silence of young architects regarding the significance of architecture. In this way, polarizing and positioning – these were also models of the seventies and eighties – are avoided.

But the unmistakable quality of young Swiss architecture is inextricably bound to this withdrawal and individualization. Just as in many areas of society the interest in individual mythology has already become an institution, so has the current architecture and its codes occasionally moved in insider circles and consciously denied itself social adaptation. Because the public arena and public architecture are more than ever given over to privatization, it is not strange that young Swiss architects, too, increasingly prescribe individual and regional approaches to form-finding solutions.

This is happening in Switzerland – and no wonder, when almost all the architects presented in this collection were educated at the ETH (Swiss Technical College) in Zurich – primarily against the backdrop of modern tradition. The dictum "trend of the simple box" has already been formulated; the vocabulary of the modern, however, is brought in with a mind to differentiate. Disorder and double encoding, as it were, are employed, or materials that very consciously run counter to the modernistic repertoire. On the one hand, these "breaks" in material and form demonstrate the sovereign interaction with the existing repertoire and convey that these codes are available, while on the other, it is inevitable that "mannerisms of the modern" will be produced within the homogeneousness of the images utilized, not least as conscious or unconscious positioning in the current time of upheaval.

The selection of architects for this book refers back to the series of lectures "Junge Schweizer Architektinnen und Architekten" that was held at the Architektur Forum Zürich in 1995 and 1996. These lectures, planned in the spirit of workshop reports, have in the meantime happily assumed an almost institutional character. This book is thus a documentation of the work of a few young architects in Switzerland which should at the same time be a foundation for discussion and stock-taking and which, beyond that, would like to offer those at the beginning of their careers an opportunity to place their work in a larger context. The concept "young architects" should not always be taken literally. No categories founded on principles form the basis for the selection; it reflects a spectrum of architects and their work who, for the most part, have been able to realize far too few of their works, and of those works realized, received too little publicity. Still, we consider this collection of projects and constructions to be interesting and representative. Membership in a certain age-group has played a subordinate role in the selection.

The texts of the individual offices were written by Martin Tschanz (M.T.) and the editor (J.C.B.) and are furnished with the appropriate initials. They have already appeared in similar form in the Neue Zürcher Zeitung. At this juncture we should mention Dr. Roman Hollenstein, whose considerable contribution is to thank for the publishing of these texts in the NZZ. Special thanks are due Hans Rudolf Bosshard, who designed the book and moreover, with his unflagging efforts, brought the differing ideas of the architects together into one unified work. Editorial assistance on the book was supplied by Karin Stegmeier.

Zurich, December 1996   **J. Christoph Bürkle**

Margrit Althammer, René Hochuli, Zürich

Uhrenfabrik Corum | Corum Clock Factory | La Chaux-de-Fonds, 1992–95

Marc Angélil, Sarah Graham, Reto Pfenninger, Manuel Scholl, Zürich und Los Angeles

Überbauung Eßlinger Dreieck | Esslingen Town Center | 1989–96

Bauart Architekten, Bern

Kindergarten Morillon | Morillon Kindergarten | Wabern-Köniz, 1995

Conradin Clavuot, Chur

Anbau Haus Dr. Heinz | Residence Annex Dr. Heinz | Chur, 1995/96

Beat Consoni, Rorschach

Wohnhaus an der Seestraße | Residence on Seestrasse | Horn, 1993–95

Herbert Ehrenbold, Barbara Schudel, Bern

Studienauftrag Hauptgebäude City West | Commissioned Study for Principle Building City West | Bern, 1994

Jasmin Grego, Joseph Smolenicky, Zürich

Unterirdischer Ballettsaal, Opernhaus | Underground Ballet Hall, Opera House | Zürich, 1995

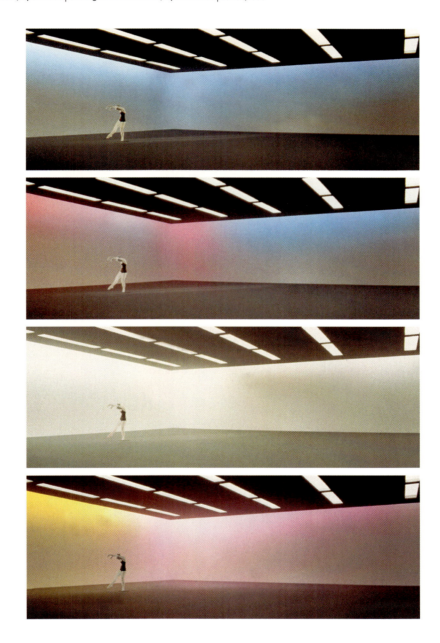

Kaschka Knapkiewicz, Axel Fickert, Zürich

Wettbewerbsprojekt | Competition Project | Wettswil, 1992

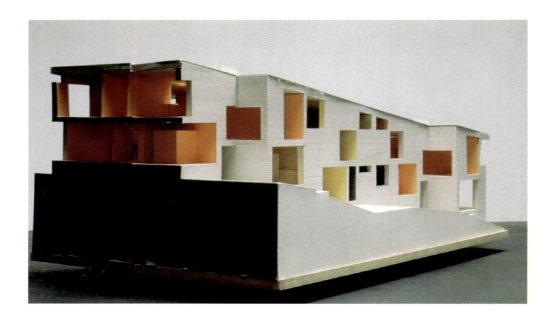

Quintus Miller, Paola Maranta, Basel und Chur

Markthalle Färberplatz | Färberplatz Market Hall | Aarau, 1996

Valerio Olgiati, Zürich

Projekt für den Wiederaufbau des Souk von Beirut | Redevelopment of the Souk of Beirut, Project | 1994

Manfred Schafer, Fribourg

Wohnüberbauung Cité du Grand-Torry | Cité du Grand-Torry Housing Superstructure | Fribourg, 1990–95

Andi Scheitlin, Marc Syfrig, Luzern

Coiffeursalon Hanin | Hairdressing Salon Hanin | Luzern, 1992

Thomas Schregenberger, Zürich

«Fabric»: Wettbewerb Fabrik am Wasser | Fabrik am Wasser, Competition | Zürich, 1995

Jakob Steib, Zürich

Mehrfamilienhaus Hinterfeld | Hinterfeld Multifamily Housing | Zwingen, 1993–95

Margrit Althammer
René Hochuli
Zürich

Uhrenfabrik Corum | Corum Company Clock Factory | La Chaux-de-Fonds, 1992–95

Mitarbeiterinnen und Mitarbeiter
Collaborators
- Stephan Popp
- Fabio Regazzoni
- Anita Reich
- Ursula Schneider
- Olga Subiros
- Jürg Thuli

Faculté des Sciences | Department of Science | Neuenburg, 1994

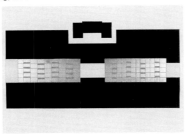

Europan 4, Schorenareal | Europan 4, Schorenareal | Basel, 1996

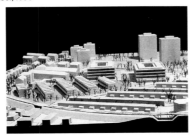

Margrit Althammer, René Hochuli

Komplexität und einfache Form.

Für Margrit Althammer und René Hochuli war es zunächst ein Glücksfall, den Wettbewerb für die Erweiterung des Sitzes der Uhrenfirma Corum in La Chaux-de-Fonds schon bald nach dem Studium zu gewinnen. Noch viel besser war es, daß sie den Auftrag auch ausführen konnten, und mittlerweile – nach der Einweihung im Juni 1995 – ist ein höchst bemerkenswertes Gebäude entstanden. Die Bauherrschaft ist immer noch so zufrieden, daß sie gleich einen weiteren Auftrag an die Architekten vergab – eine bessere Umschreibung für das Verhältnis Bauherr und Architekt kann es kaum geben.

Corum ging ganz bewußt das Wagnis ein, den Auftrag an junge Diplomarchitekten zu vergeben. Beim 1991 durchgeführten Wettbewerb, zu dem Schweizer Architekten mit Diplomabschluß zwischen August 1986 und Juli 1991 eingeladen worden waren, gab es unter 117 eingereichten Projekten sieben Prämierungen und einen Ankauf. Man ließ es sich zudem nicht nehmen, auch Max Bill in das hochrangig besetzte Preisgericht zu berufen.

Präzise wie eine Uhr sollte das neue Produktionsgebäude funktionieren – die Verbindung zum dort hergestellten Produkt Uhr ist nicht zufällig und in ihrer direkten Ablesbarkeit durchaus erwünscht. Da bei der Firma Corum die handwerkliche Tradition Verpflichtung ist und die Uhren – im Gegensatz zu anderen in industriellen Großserien produzierenden Uhrenfabriken – in kleinen Serien nahezu als Einzelstücke hergestellt werden, mußte und sollte der individuelle Arbeitsplatz der Ausgangspunkt des Entwurfes sein. Die Tradition der handwerklichen Uhrenfertigung führte in dieser Region schon früh zur Entwicklung eines bestimmten Typus von Fabrik. Es handelt sich dabei um schlanke, mehrgeschossige Gebäude mit den Uhrmacherarbeitsplätzen direkt hinter den Fenstern. Die geringe Raumtiefe ermöglicht die optimale Belichtung der Arbeitsplätze und der dahinterliegenden Maschinenräume. Selbst in den abgelegensten Dörfern trifft man auf diese typische Fabrikform bei verschiedensten Uhrenmarken.

Althammer und Hochuli haben die Herausforderung angenommen und sich voll und ganz auf die Aufgabe konzentriert. Zwar hatten sie einen örtlichen Bauleiter, darüber hinaus jedoch zeichneten sie jeden Plan und jedes Detail selbst, um die Umsetzung ihrer Vorstellungen und Ideen über den ganzen Entstehungsprozeß hinweg steuern zu können.

Das damalige Wagnis für die Firma kann sich heute sehen lassen, der scharfkantige Quader aus Sichtbeton verbindet wie selbstverständlich die bestehenden Teile der Firma zu einem einheitlichen Geviert und öffnet sich mit der freitragenden Glasfassade zu dem neu entstandenen inneren Platz. Für die Produktionsgeschosse wurde ein Montagebau aus Stahl gewählt, der in die Hülle des U-förmigen Betons hineingestellt ist. Die äußere Klarheit, die nicht zuletzt auch auf der Beschränkung der wenigen Materialien Stahl, Glas und Beton beruht, erinnert unwillkürlich an Vorbilder der klassischen Moderne.

Aus den Vorgaben der örtlichen typologischen Bautradition und der Dominanz des individuellen Arbeitsplatzes entwickelten Margrit Althammer und René Hochuli eine differenzierte Raumschichtung, wobei sich die Maßstäblichkeit der Werkräume nach der jeweiligen Nutzung richtet. An der Westfassade liegen die Ateliers der Uhrenmacher und Bijoutiers mit den Arbeitsplätzen direkt am Fenster. In der mittleren Schicht des Gebäudes befinden sich gemeinsame Nutzungen: Labors, Ebauche und die mechanischen Werkstätten. In diesen Räumen wird stehend gearbeitet; deshalb sind sie höher und, um die optimale Verbindung zu den anderen Räumen zu gewährleisten, auf einem Zwischengeschoß angeordnet, liegen also gleichsam im Mittelpunkt der horizontalen und vertikalen Ebene des Gebäudes. Die dritte Schicht ist die Erschließung. Sie ist zum Innenhof ausgerichtet und bildet mit der durchgehend verglasten Fassade die «Kommunikationsschicht» des Gebäudes zu seiner Umgebung. Von hier aus werden die Arbeitsabläufe im Inneren auch von außen sichtbar.

Das Gebäude ist aufgebaut wie eine Uhr – diese Analogie liegt bei einer Uhrenfirma nahe und wurde von den Architekten bewußt umgesetzt. Uhren bestehen aus komplexen räumlichen Gefügen von Getriebeteilen und Zwischenräumen, von beweglichen und fixierten Teilen. In eben diesem volumetrischen Aufbau entspricht das neue Haus von Corum einer Uhr: Betrachtet man den Schnitt durch eine Taschenuhr, so findet man eine ähnliche konstruktive Gliederung. In dem Gehäuse liegt die Werkplatte, auf welche das Uhrwerk und das Zifferblatt schichtweise eingelegt werden. Oberste Schicht ist das Deckglas, hinter welchem die Bewegung, der rhythmische Ablauf der Zeit, sichtbar wird. Im übertragenen Sinn wird in dem Gebäude diese Bewegung auch hinter der Glasfassade sichtbar. Es ist die Bewegung des Personals, des Arbeitsablaufs der Uhrmacher im Laufe des Tages.

Dieser metaphorische Aspekt des Gebäudes wird durchaus nicht als aufdringlich empfunden, er ergibt sich nahezu von selbst aus den übersichtlichen Funktionsabläufen der Arbeitsprozesse. Das modernistische Prinzip der räumlichen Analogie zur Präzision und Ästhetik der Maschine ist hier logisch begründet und erscheint nicht gesucht. Die Erweiterung des Firmengebäudes von Corum ist vielmehr ein gelungenes Beispiel für konzeptuelle Klarheit und formale Strenge, die als Grundidee aus der Logik des Entwurfs definiert werden. «Auch die ganzen Detaillierungsarbeiten sowie die Materialisierung des Gebäudes ordneten wir der Suche nach der Kohärenz zweckgebundener Eindeutigkeit unter», so Althammer und Hochuli. J. C. B.

Complexity and Simple Form.

For Margrit Althammer and René Hochuli it was, to begin with, a stroke of good fortune to win the competition to expand production quarters of the clock company Corum in La Chaux-de-Fonds so soon after completing their studies. Even better was the opportunity to carry the project to completion and, in the time since its consecration in 1995, a truly remarkable building has emerged. The clients were so satisfied that they immediately awarded a further commission to the architects. There can hardly be a better commentary on the architect-client relationship.

Corum went into this project totally aware of the risks involved in granting the commission to young, newly graduated architects. The invitation to enter the 1991 competition was extended to Swiss architects who had received their diplomas between August 1986 and July 1991; out of 117 submitted projects, there were seven prizes given and one purchase. The distinguished jury, moreover, included Max Bill.

As precisely as a clock – this is how the new production house was to function. The connection between the building and the product manufactured there is no accident; its immediate readability is thoroughly intended. The Corum Company is committed to the tradition of craftsmanship, and their clocks, in contrast to those from industrial mass-production factories, are assembled in small series, almost as singly created pieces. For this reason, the individual work place should be and had to be the starting point for the design. The tradition of hand-made clock production in this region led early on to the development of a very specific type of factory building: narrow, multiple-storied structures with the clock makers positioned directly beneath the windows. The shallow depth of the room allows for optimal lighting on the work stations and on the machine shop behind them. Factories have taken this form within all the various watch firms and can be seen even in the most remote villages.

Althammer and Hochuli accepted the challenge and concentrated their energy completely on the task. Although they worked with a local site manager, beyond that they drew every plan, every detail themselves, directing the realization of their concepts and ideas step-by-step throughout the entire development process.

What was once a risk for the firm is today an impressive sight: The crisp-edged block of exposed concrete naturally, almost self-evidently, connects the existing elements of the company buildings to form a unified quadrangle and opens up through a self-supporting glass façade onto the newly created inner courtyard. Steel prefabrication was selected for the production floors and installed in the U-shaped concrete shell. The external clarity of the building, due not least of all to the restricted material choice of steel, glass and concrete, reminds one involuntarily of models from classical Modernism.

From the limitations of the local, typological building tradition and the dominance of the individual work station, Althammer and Hochuli developed a differentiated stratification of space whereby the scaling of the work areas is adjusted to their respective functions. The workshops of the clock makers and jewelers are situated against the west façade with the work stations directly next to the window. Communal work space is located in the middle tier of the building: laboratories, designing rooms and the engineering workshops. The work done in these areas is done standing up; the rooms are therefore higher and, in order to ensure an optimal connection to the other areas, arranged on an *entresol* and lie more or less at the center of the horizontal and vertical planes of the building. The third floor is where the building opens up and becomes accessible. Oriented towards the inner courtyard it forms, with the continuous glazed façade, the building's "communication tier", that is, communication with its environment. Here, operations in the interior can be seen from outside.

Ultimately, the building is constructed like a clock – this analogy obviously suggests itself with a clock manufacturer and was very consciously transferred by the architects. Clocks consist of complex spatial structures of gear systems and intervals, of moving and stationary parts. It is in just this volumetric construction that the new Corum building corresponds to a clock, as in the cross-section of a watch one finds a similar constructive arrangement: Inside the watch housing is the plate upon which the clockwork and face are layered. The uppermost layer is the cover glass, behind which the movement, the rhythmic run of time, can be seen. In a figurative sense, this movement also becomes visible behind the glass façade of the building. It is the movement of the people, the day-to-day operations of the watchmakers as they go about their work.

This metaphorical aspect of the building is not at all perceived as obtrusive; it follows closely from the coherent functional flow of the work process. The modernistic principle of the analogy of space to machine precision and aesthetics is in this case logically grounded, not at all studied or forced. The expansion of the Corum Company buildings is much more a successful example of conceptual clarity and formal stringency, emerging naturally from the logic of the design and defining itself as the foundational idea. According to Althammer and Hochuli, "The entire detail work as well as the materialization of the building were subordinate to the search for the coherence of purposeful clarity."   J. C. B.

Uhrenfabrik Corum, 1992-95
Corum Company Clock Factory, 1992-95

Margrit Althammer, René Hochuli

Uhrenfabrik Corum, La Chaux-de-Fonds, 1992–95.
Der Neubau für die Uhrenfabrik Corum in La Chaux-de-Fonds geht auf einen gesamtschweizerischen Wettbewerb aus dem Jahre 1991/92 zurück. Die Aufgabe löste sich in einer metaphorischen Verknüpfung zu den soliden Tischuhren des 16. und 17. Jahrhunderts, indem ein analoges strukturelles und räumliches System entwickelt wurde. Wie das dichte und komplexe Gefüge von Getriebeteilen und Zwischenräumen präsentieren sich die Räumlichkeiten der Uhrenmacher. Dieses modernistische Prinzip der räumlichen Analogie zur Präzision und Ästhetik der Maschine wird auch in der strukturellen und konstruktiven Ausbildung des Gebäudes relevant.

Corum Company Clock Factory, La Chaux-de-Fonds, 1992–95.
The new building for the Corum clock factory in La Chaux-de-Fonds began as an entry in a 1991/92 nationwide Swiss competition. The architectural problem here was resolved through the development of an analogous structural and spatial system referring metaphorically to the reliable and durable table clocks of the 16th and 17th centuries. The work places of the clock makers are presented like the compact, complex structures of gears and intervals in a clock. This modernistic spatial analogy to machine precision and aesthetics becomes relevant also in the structural and constructive development of the building.

Südwestfassade
 Southwest façade
Längsschnitte
 Elevation section
Querschnitte
 Cross section

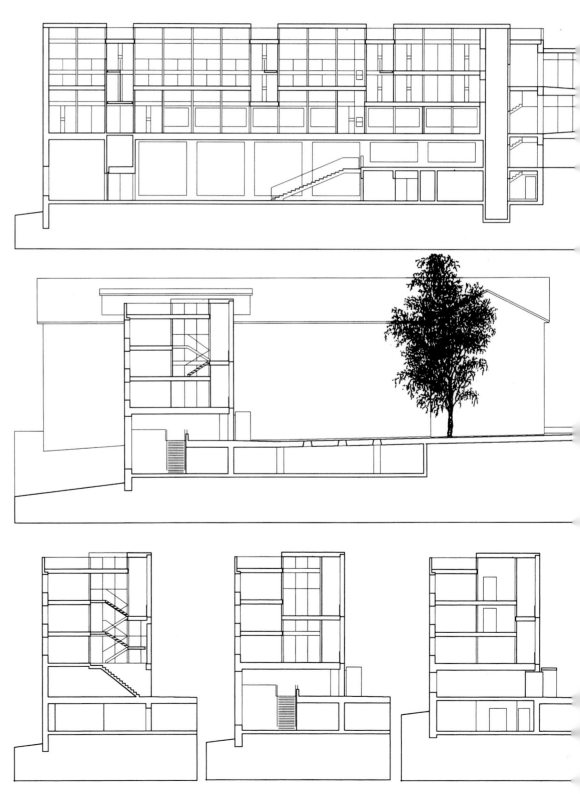

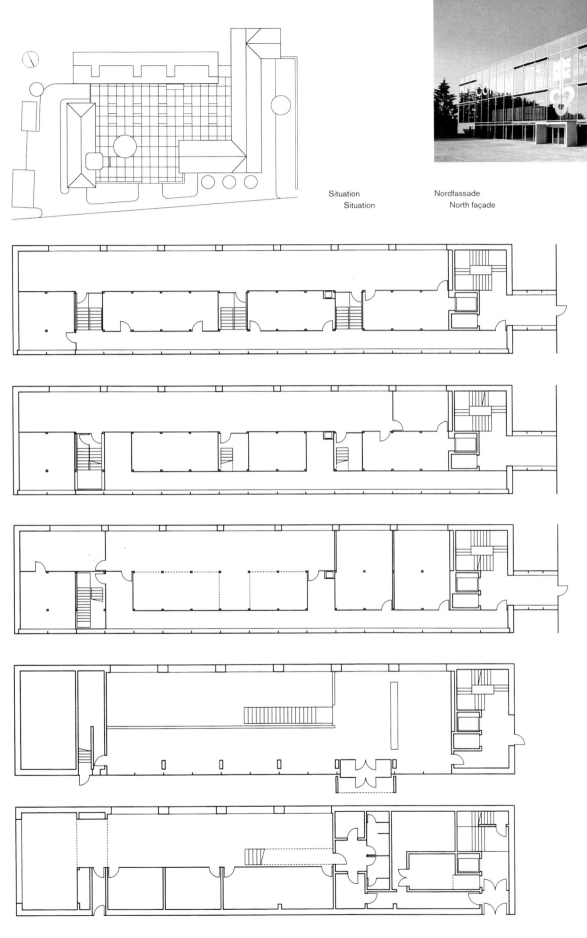

Situation
Situation

Nordfassade
North façade

Drittes, zweites und erstes Obergeschoß
Third, second and first floors above

Erdgeschoß
Ground floor

Untergeschoß
Basement level

Margrit Althammer, René Hochuli

Gestaltung der Höfe, Faculté des Sciences, Universität Neuenburg, Wettbewerb, 1994.

Das Projekt für die Gestaltung der beiden Höfe der geplanten Faculté des Sciences der Universität Unimail in Neuenburg basiert auf der typologischen Analyse der bestehenden, ambivalenten Anlage. Mit einem Belagskonzept reagiert es auf die zwei möglichen Lesarten des Gebäudes als Hoftyp oder als Doppelzeile. Materialisierung und Rhythmisierung des Belags leiten sich von der bestehenden Anlage her. Großformatige Chromstahlplatten wechseln mit Glaskörpereinlagen ab. Entsprechend dem Standpunkt des Betrachters oder der Lichtsituation verschiebt sich die Wahrnehmung der Höfe zugunsten der einen oder anderen Interpretation. Wie ein Vexierbild wirkt der einzelne Hofabschnitt somit als in sich geschlossen, oder er verbindet sich durch die transparente Wirkung des Glases mit dem Nachbarhof zu einer räumlichen Einheit.

Design of the Courtyards, Department of Science, Neuchâtel University, Competition, 1994.

The design project of the two courtyards for the planned Department of Science at Unimail University in Neuchâtel is based on a typological analysis of the existing, ambivalent complex and responds with a surface concept to the two possible readings of the building – either as a model for a courtyard or as double lines. The material and rhythmic aspects of the surface are derived from the existing complex. Large scale chromium steel plates alternate with vitreous inlays, and as the standpoint of the viewer or the source of light changes, perception of the courtyards shifts in favor of one or another visual interpretation. Like a picture puzzle, each individual courtyard section either functions as a self-contained unit or connects with the neighboring courtyard through the transparent effect of the glass to create a unity of space.

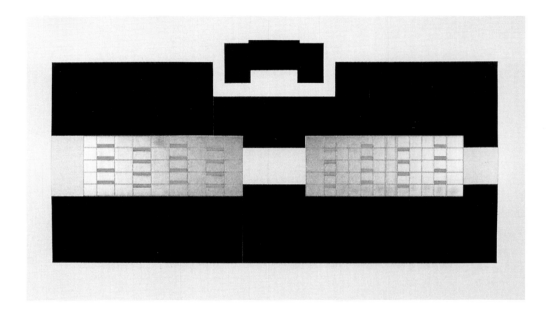

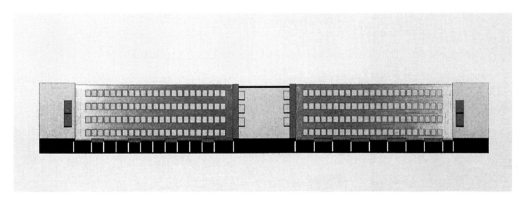

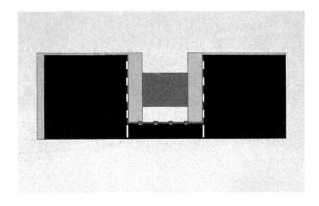

Grundriß, Ansicht Hof, Querschnitt
Ground plan, courtyard view, cross section

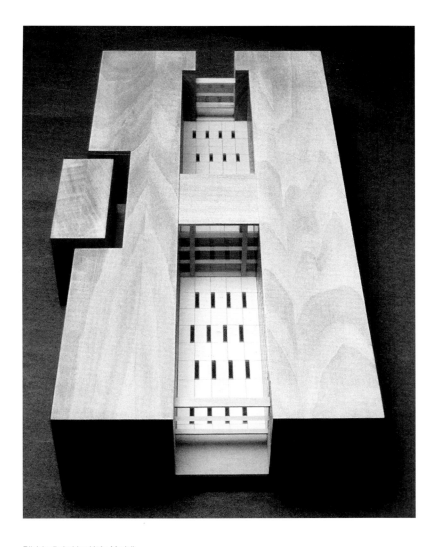

Blick in die beiden Höfe, Modell
 View into both courtyards, model
Nachtaufnahme, Modell
 Night shot, model

Margrit Althammer, René Hochuli

Europan 4, Schorenareal, Basel, mit Daniel Baumann, 1996.

Der Wettbewerb umfaßt die Umnutzung eines modernen Verwaltungsgebäudes der Ciba-Geigy AG mit Großraumbürostruktur (42×50 Meter) zu Wohnzwecken sowie die Entwicklung einer Wohnsiedlung auf dem ehemaligen Forschungsareal.

Areal A: Umnutzung des Verwaltungsgebäudes. Die chirurgische Trennung der beiden «siamesischen» Gebäudetrakte führt zu einer Öffnung und erlaubt, den von den Hochhäusern am Eglisee aufgespannten übergeordneten Landschaftsraum in das Wettbewerbsareal einfließen zu lassen. Mit der Öffnung wird eine Präzisierung der städtebaulichen Situation erreicht. Im Zusammenspiel mit den Hochhäusern definieren die beiden neu entstandenen prismatischen Wohnhäuser eine übergeordnete Konstellation analoger Gebäudegruppen in einer frei fließenden öffentlichen Parklandschaft. In den Obergeschossen der Bürogebäude wird ein Innenhof aus der bestehenden Substanz herausgeschnitten. Zwei leistungsfähige Anbauschichten auf der Längsseite des Hofs ergänzen den Altbau mit einer zusätzlichen Zimmerschicht. Zugleich übernimmt der Einbau die vertikalen und horizontalen Wohnungserschließungen sowie Steigschächte für die neu benötigte Haustechnik. Der Einbau ist so organisiert, daß an zwei Geschosse des Altbaus von 2×4,30 m drei neue Geschosse von 3×2,85 Meter angefügt werden. Die Wohnungen werden im Zwischengeschoß über einen Laubengang erschlossen und entwickeln sich jeweils darüber und darunter zu zwei unterschiedlichen Wohnungstypen.

Areal B: Nutzungsstudie für das Areal der Versuchsabteilung der Ciba-Geigy AG. Die neu geplante Siedlung ist als eigenständiges, in sich abgeschlossenes Gefüge konzipiert, das sich in seiner Maßstäblichkeit an der Umgebung orientiert. Sie läßt sich leicht in Etappen unabhängig vom bestehenden Verwaltungsbau realisieren. Die fünf südorientierten, hintereinandergeschalteten Zellenbauten mit durchgehender homogener Baustruktur weisen eine enorme Ausbauflexibilität auf, die einen differenzierten Wohnungsschlüssel zulassen.

Europan 4, Schorenareal, Basel, with Daniel Baumann, 1996.

This competition encompasses the converted uses of a modern Ciba-Geigy Corporation administration building with an open-plan office structure (42×50 meters) converted into living quarters, as well as the development of housing in the former research area.

Area A: Conversion of the administration center. The surgical separation of the two "Siamese twins" office building wings created an opening which allowed the landscape of surrounding high-rise structures spreading up and along the Egli Lake to flow into the competition area, which in turn clarified the urban development situation. In an interplay with the high-rises, the two new prismatic housing blocks define a highly developed constellation of similar corresponding building groups in a free flowing public park landscape. An interior courtyard is carved out of the existing material on the uppermost floor of each office building. Two efficient annexes on the long sides of the courtyard give the old building an additional level of rooms. At the same time, the installation appropriates the vertical and horizontal access ways to the apartments as well as the vertical shaft for the now necessary engineering system of the building. The installation is organized in such a way that three new floors of 3×2.85 meters are created from two former floors measuring 2×4.3 meters. The apartments are accessible by way of the arcade on the mezzanine and developed into two apartment types above and below, respectively.

Area B: Utilization studies for the area of the Research Department of Ciba-Geigy Corporation. The newly planned housing development is conceived as an autonomous, self-contained structure oriented in scale to its environment; it can be easily realized in stages and independently from the existing administration building. The five southward-facing units, arranged in a successive series one behind the other and united as one continuous, homogeneous construction, display an enormous flexibility for expansion that provides for differentiation in the future functional grouping of the units.

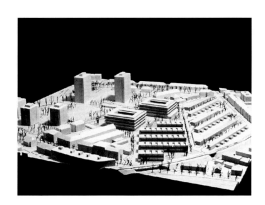

Situationsmodell, Ansicht von Norden
Situation model, view from the north

Situationsmodell, in der Bildmitte die neu geplante Siedlung auf Areal B,
rechts die zwei umgenutzten Verwaltungsgebäude auf Areal A
Situation model, in the center, the newly planned housing development on Areal B,
to the right, the two converted administration buildings on Areal A

Strukturmodelle
Structural models

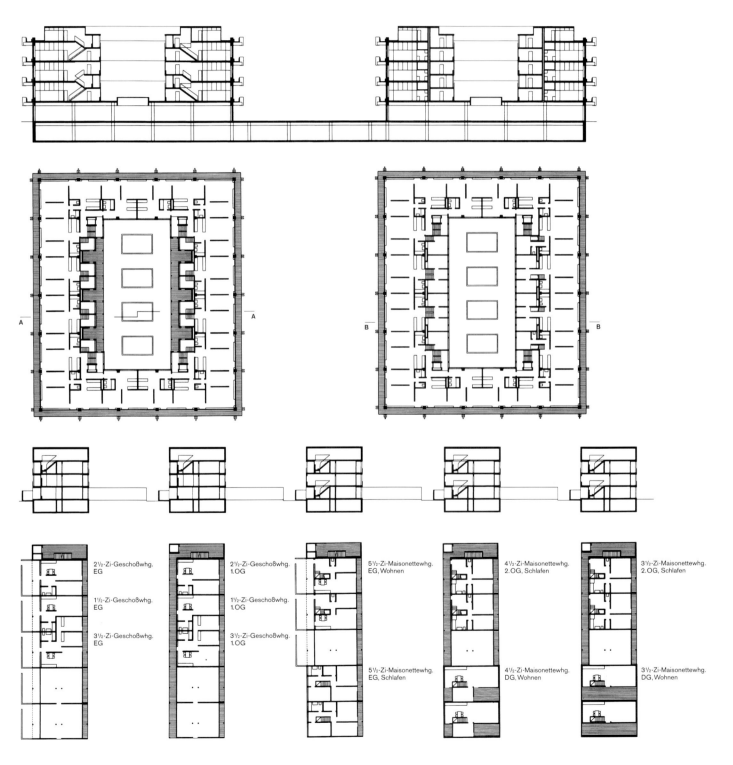

Querschnitt A–A und B–B, Erschließungsgeschoß und Wohngeschoß
Cross section A–A and B–B, access floor and residence floor
Querschnitt und Grundrisse
Cross section and floor plans

Biografien

Margrit Althammer
1962 geboren in Wettingen.
1981 Matura in Zürich.
1982-88 Studium der Architektur an der ETH Zürich.
1984 Arbeit bei Georg Gisel, Zürich.
1986 Architektin an der archäologischen Grabungskampagne Monte Jato, Sizilien.
1988 Diplom an der ETH Zürich bei Prof. Flora Ruchat.
1989/90 Arbeit im Atelier d'architecture Zurbuchen-Henz, Lausanne.
1990/91 Arbeit bei Jean-Pierre Dürig und Philipp Rämi, Zürich.
Seit 1996 Lehrbeauftragte an der Architekturabteilung des Technikum Winterthur.

René Hochuli
1962 geboren in Uster.
1981 Matura in Zürich.
1982-89 Studium der Architektur an der ETH Zürich.
1983/84 Arbeit bei Pierre Zoelly, Zürich.
1984 Arbeit bei Georg Gisel, Zürich.
1986 Architekt an der archäologischen Grabungskampagne Monte Jato, Sizilien.
1986/87 Auslandsemester an der School of Architecture in Ahmedabad, Indien.
1989 Diplom an der ETH Zürich bei Prof. Mario Campi.
1989/90 Arbeit bei Rafael Moneo und Manuel de Solà-Morales, Barcelona.
1990/91 Arbeit bei A. D. P., Zürich.
1994/95 Assistent bei Gastdozent José-Luis Mateo an der ETH Zürich.
Seit 1996 Assistent bei Gastdozent Beat Jordi.

Seit 1992 gemeinsames Büro in Zürich.

Ausstellungen, Auszeichnungen
1992 *Corum: ein exemplarischer Fall.* Wanderausstellung der prämierten Projekte im Architektur Forum Zürich sowie in den Ingenieurschulen Biel und Bern.
1994 *Spreebogen Berlin.* Eine Auswahl von Schweizer Beiträgen für ein neues Regierungsviertel in Berlin, Wanderausstellung mit Kolloquien an der ETH Zürich und am Technikum in Rapperswil.
1995 *Treffpunkt Barcelona.* Eine Ausstellung junger Schweizer Architekten, Wanderausstellung in Barcelona, Bilbao, Valencia, San Sebastian und Zürich 1995/96.

Die Besten '95. Bronzener Hase für die Uhrenfabrik Corum. Eine gemeinsam von der Zeitschrift Hochparterre und der SF-Sendung «10 vor 10» organisierte Jurierung der besten ausgeführten Bauten des Jahres 1995 in der Schweiz.
1996 Constructec '96: Europäischer Preis für Industriearchitektur, Sonderauszeichnung für die Uhrenfabrik Corum.

Werkverzeichnis

1992
Neubau des Produktionsgebäudes der Uhrenfabrik Corum, La Chaux-de-Fonds, nationaler Wettbewerb Corum, erster Preis, ausgeführt 1992-95.

1993
Spreebogen, Berlin, internationaler Ideenwettbewerb.

1994
Neue Universität in Nikosia, Zypern, internationaler Wettbewerb
Gestaltung der Höfe, Faculté des Sciences, Universität Neuenburg, nationaler Wettbewerb Unimail, zweiter Preis.

1995
Areal der Steinfabrik Pfäffikon, städtebaulicher Ideenwettbewerb, Ankauf.

1996
Umbau und Renovation der bestehenden Gebäude der Firma Corum.
Europan 4, Schorenareal in Basel, Projektwettbewerb, in Zusammenarbeit mit Daniel Baumann.
Gießereigelände, östliche Altstadt, Ingolstadt, Deutschland, Projektwettbewerb auf Einladung.

Bibliografie

Ein exemplarischer Fall, Sondernummer zur Corum-Ausstellung im Architektur Forum Zürich, in: Hochparterre 11/1992.
Der große Glasschrank, in: Hochparterre 10/1995.
Eine zeitgemäße Uhrenfabrik, in: Die Besten '95, Hochparterre-Sondernummer, 2/1995.
Natur und Abstraktion, Bde. 1+2, umfassende Publikation der Lehrstuhlveranstaltungen des Lehrstuhls José-Luis Mateo an der ETH Zürich von 1993-95, Verlag Actar, Barcelona 1995.
Treffpunkt Barcelona, Katalog zur Wanderausstellung junger Schweizer Architekten, Verlag Actar, Barcelona 1995/96.
Transparenz und Präzision: Die Uhrenfabrik Corum, in: archithese 1/1996.
Corum, in: Hangar 21, Juni 1996.
Corum, in: Werk, Bauen + Wohnen, 6/1996, Werkmaterial.
Corum, Schweizer Architekturführer 1920-95; Westschweiz, Wallis, Tessin, Bd. 3, Werk Verlag, 1996.

Biographies

Margrit Althammer
1962 Born in Wettingen.
1981 University entrance qualifying exam, Zurich.
1982-88 Studied architecture at the ETH Zurich.
1984 Worked for Georg Gisel, Zurich.
1986 Architect at archaeological excavation, Mount Jato, Sicily.
1988 Graduated from the ETH Zurich under Prof. Flora Ruchat.
1989/90 Worked in Architecture studio Zurbuchen-Henz, Lausanne.
1990/91 Worked at Jean-Pierre Dürig and Philipp Rämi, Zurich.
Since 1996 Teaching appointment in the Architecture Department of the Technikum Winterthur.

René Hochuli
1962 Born in Uster.
1981 University entrance qualifying exam, Zurich.
1982-89 Studied architecture at the ETH Zurich.
1983/84 Worked for Pierre Zoelly, Zurich.
1984 Worked for Georg Gisel, Zurich.
1986 Architect at archaeological excavation, Mount Jato, Sicily.
1986/87 Semester of study abroad at the School of Architecture, Ahmedabad, India.
1989 Graduated from the ETH Zurich under Prof. Mario Campi.
1989/90 Worked at Rafael Moneo and Manuel de Solà-Morales, Barcelona.
1990/91 Worked at A.D.P., Zurich.
1994/95 Assistant to Guest Lecturer José-Louis Mateo at the ETH Zurich.
Since 1996 Assistant to Guest Lecturer Beat Jordi.

Since 1992 joint office in Zurich.

Exhibitions, Awards
1992 *Corum: ein exemplarischer Fall*. Touring exhibition of the prize-winning projects at the Architektur Forum Zurich and in the Schools of Engineering in Biel and Bern.
1994 *Spreebogen Berlin*. A selection of Swiss contributions to a new government quarter in Berlin, touring exhibition with colloquium at the ETH Zurich and the Technikum Rapperswil (Technical School).
1995 *Treffpunkt Barcelona*. An exhibition of young Swiss architects, touring exhibition in Barcelona, Bilbao, Valencia, San Sebastian and Zurich 1995/96.

Die Besten '95. Bronze Rabbit for the Corum clock factory. A juried show organized jointly by the journal Hochparterre together with the Swiss television program "10 vor 10", honoring the best constructed buildings in Switzerland in 1995.
1996 Constructec '96: European Prize for Industrial Architecture, special award for the Corum Clock Factory.

List of Works

1992
New production buildings for the Corum clock factory, La Chaux-de-Fonds, national competition Corum, first prize, executed 1992-95.

1993
Spreebogen, Berlin, international concept competition.

1994
New university in Nikosia, Cyprus, international competition.
Design of the courtyards at the University of Neuchâtel, national competition Unimail, second prize.

1995
Area of the Stone Factory in Pfäffikon, urban development concept competition, purchase.

1996
Conversion and renovation of the existing buildings of the Corum Company.
Europan 4, Schorenareal in Basle, project competition, in collaboration with Daniel Baumann.
Giessereigelände, old city center east, Ingolstadt, Germany, project competition (upon invitation).

Bibliography

Ein exemplarischer Fall, Special edition on the Corum Exhibition at the Architektur Forum Zurich, in: Hochparterre 11/1992.
Der grosse Glasschrank, in: Hochparterre 10/1995.
Eine zeitgemässe Uhrenfabrik, in: Die Besten '95, special edition of Hochparterre, 2/1995.
Natur und Abstraktion, Vol. 1+2, comprehensive publication of the lectures of Professor José-Luis Mateo at the ETH Zurich from 1993-95, Verlag Actar, Barcelona 1995.
Treffpunkt Barcelona, catalogue for the touring exhibition on young Swiss architects, Verlag Actar, Barcelona 1995/96.
Transparenz und Präzision: Die Uhrenfabrik Corum, in: archithese 1/1996.
Corum, in: Hangar 21, June 1996.
Corum, in: Werk, Bauen+Wohnen, 6/1996, Werkmaterial.
Corum, Guide to Swiss Architecture 1920-95; Western Switzerland, Valais, Ticino, Vol. 3, Werk Verlag, 1996.

Marc Angélil

Sarah Graham

Reto Pfenninger

Manuel Scholl

Zürich und Los Angeles

Mitarbeiterinnen und Mitarbeiter
Collaborators
    Bruce Fullerton
    Michael Gräfensteiner
    Matthias Kobelt
    Mark Lee
    Anthony Paradowski
    Silvia Rüfenacht
    Susan Stevens

Weitere Mitarbeiterinnen und Mitarbeiter
Further collaborators
    Mark Adams
    Karin Baumann
    Markus Fahner
    Lukas Felder
    Sabine von Fischer
    Michael Gruber
    Sancho Igual
    Ilinca Manaila
    Mark Motonaga
    William Paluch
    Anthony Poon
    Yves Reinacher
    Cynthia Salah
    Simone Schmaus
    Thomas Schwendener
    Peter Sigrist
    Ryan Smith
    Patrick Walther
    James Woolum

Marc Angélil, Sarah Graham, Reto Pfenninger, Manuel Scholl

Offene Strukturen.

Angélil/Graham/Pfenninger/Scholl Architecture steht für Teamarbeit. Die Dynamik des Arbeitsprozesses ist für die Gruppe eindeutig formuliertes Programm. Folgerichtig versucht das Team, mit seinen Projekten «Prozesse zu entwerfen, und nicht Lösungen zu fixieren». Das Arbeiten mit unfertigen Zuständen ist für sie eine stärkere Herausforderung als das Entwerfen und Gestalten von festgelegten Abläufen oder Objekten.

Das Architekturbüro wurde 1982 von Marc Angélil und Sarah Graham in den Vereinigten Staaten gegründet. Neben den ersten Bauten in Boston, einem Ferienhaus in Aspen, Colorado (1987–89), der Platzüberdachung eines School District in Los Angeles (1988–91) und einem Ladengebäude für Fixel Corporation, ebenfalls in Los Angeles (1989–92), wurde 1989 aufgrund mehrerer Planungs- und Architekturaufträge ein Büro in Zürich eröffnet.

Bislang größtes Projekt in der Schweiz ist das «Stadtzentrum für Eßlingen», für welches das Büro 1989 mit dem ersten Preis ausgezeichnet worden war und dessen erster Bauabschnitt, der Bahnhof für die Endstation der Forchbahn, im Frühjahr 1995 in Betrieb genommen wurde. Eßlingen liegt am Rande des Pfannenstils, zwischen Zürichsee und Greifensee. Es war die Aufgabe gestellt, am hangseitigen Rand der kleinen Stadt, zwischen Landschaft und Bebauung ein Gebiet zu schaffen, in welchem Raum für Wohnhäuser, den Bahnhof, eine Post, ein Restaurant, eine Laden- und Geschäftszone strukturiert und geplant werden sollte. Das Projekt der Architektengemeinschaft versucht nicht, die einzelnen Bereiche kontextuell einzufügen, vielmehr ist jede funktionelle Einheit typologisch anders formuliert. Dennoch setzt sich der Entwurf dezidiert mit der vorhandenen Situation und Topographie auseinander. Die Formation des kleinen Wasserlaufes bildet die Kontur für die fünfzig Hauseinheiten, die mit ihrer einheitlichen Reihung und den schrägen Solardächern eine eigenständige Textur bilden. Das Projekt versucht auch sinnfällig, eine Verbindung zwischen der umgebenden Natur und den eher städtischen Forderungen der Verdichtung herzustellen. Mit ganz bewußt eingesetzten unterschiedlichen Bildern oder architektonischen Codes – die Architekten selbst sprechen von offenen Geometrien –, die den jeweiligen Funktionsbereichen entsprechen, ergibt sich das Bild einer differenzierten Collage, deren Teilbereiche sich wie selbständige molekulare Strukturen zu einer Gesamtheit der kleinstädtischen Mitte verbinden. Zusammen mit der Ingenieurfirma Basler & Hofmann wurde das Projekt als Fallstudie entwickelt, um verdichtetes Bauen mit effizienter Ausnützung des Grundes, sparsamem Umgang mit Energie und Verwendung kreislauffähiger Materialien im Sinne eines «zukunftgerichteten Bauens» zu erproben.

Das sind die «Offenen Strukturen», die die Architekten zur Grundlage ihrer Arbeit erklären. Gemeint ist damit die Suche nach Strategien, die einen Dialog zwischen den konstituierenden Elementen der jeweiligen Entwurfsaufgabe und der architektonischen Substanz herstellen. Das Experimentieren mit Materialien, das Untersuchen unterschiedlicher Strukturen, die sich aus dem jeweiligen Kontext ergeben und die Verbindung von verschiedenen Berufsdisziplinen charakterisieren das Arbeitsfeld der Gruppe. Dabei fließen Erfahrungen aus der Lehre – alle vier Büropartner sind in der Lehre tätig – als «experimentelles Feld» in den Bereich des Entwurfs und der Realisierung mit ein. Auch hier werden keine ausschließlichen Wahrheitsgehalte vermittelt, sondern es wird der strukturelle Gehalt einer Entwurfsaufgabe gesucht und keine determinierenden Formen. Das heißt, in einem Entwurf unterschiedliche Bilder und Zeichen zu verwenden, verschiedene Ordnungen wirksam werden zu lassen. So wie der Bahnhof von Eßlingen mit seinen leichten, gleichsam fliegenden Dächern städtische Assoziationen weckt – die Forchbahn bringt schließlich den Städter aufs Land –, so soll die Mauerformierung der Bürobauten die dahinterliegende Bebauung vor dem Verkehrslärm schützen, allerdings mit ganz anderen syntaktischen Zeichen. Diese wiederum unterscheiden sich von den dahinterliegenden, eng zusammengerückten Wohnhäusern, die ihren Siedlungscharakter nicht verleugnen und mit den Solardächern eine neue Typologie andeuten. Es ist diese Ordnung, die das «Mannigfaltige und Mehrdeutige pflegt», wie es aus dem Büro Angélil/Graham/Pfenninger/Scholl Architecture verlautet: «Es ist eine Ordnung, die sich gegen jeden Versuch des Totalisierens stellt …» J.C.B.

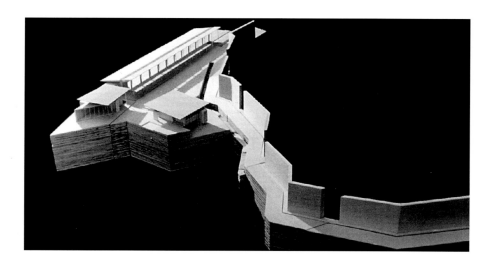

Eßlinger Dreieck, 1989–96
Esslingen Town Center, 1989–96

Open Structures.

Angélil/Graham/Pfenninger/Scholl Architecture stands for teamwork. The dynamic of the work process within the group is one of clearly formulated program. The team aims consistently "to design processes, not to prescribe solutions". They find working in unresolved situations to be a greater challenge than the plotting and designing of fixed projects or objects.

The office was founded by Marc Angélil and Sarah Graham in the United States in 1982, but following the first construction in Boston, a vacation house in Aspen, Colorado (1987–89), courtyard roofing for the Los Angeles School District (1988–91) and a store building for Fixel Corporation in Los Angeles (1989–92), they opened their Zurich office in 1989 to accommodate the increase in planning and architectural commissions.

Their largest project to date in Switzerland is the "Esslingen Town Center", which earned the office first prize in 1989. The project's first completed construction sector, the end station for a small inner-city train line in Zurich, the Forchbahn, was open for operation in Spring 1995. Esslingen lies on the border of the Pfannenstil, a long hill situated between Lake Zurich and a smaller Lake, the Greifensee. The task at hand was to create a building tract on the sloping outskirts of the small town between the hilly landscape and the development of the town which would ultimately contain residences, a train station, post office, restaurant, and shopping and business zone. The project submitted by this architectural team does not attempt to insert itself contextually into the individual zones; rather, each functional unit is formulated in yet another typological fashion, and still the design decidedly tackles the existing situation and topography. The course of a small waterway forms the contour for the fifty housing units, whose unified rows and their slanting solar roof panels in turn form an autonomous texture. The project obviously aims at producing a connection between the surrounding natural environment and the demands of the rather compressed town. With entirely conscious employment of various images or architectonic codes – the architects themselves speak of open geometry – that correspond to the various functional zones, the picture surrenders itself to a differentiated collage whose own partial zones connect to the whole of the small town's center like independent molecular structures. Together with the engineering firm Basler & Hofmann, the project was developed as a "future-oriented building" case study for the testing of compact construction with efficient use of ground space, economic use of energy and the application of recyclable materials.

These are the "Open Structures" that the architects interpret as the basis of their work, indicating the search for strategies that produce a dialogue between the essential elements constituting the respective designing tasks and the architectural substance. Experimentation with material, investigation of the various structures resulting from the various contexts, and the conjunction of differing professional disciplines characterize the group's working sphere. Experiences from active teaching – all four partners are actively teaching – flow together into the designing and realization process in the form of an "experimental field". Yet even here no exclusive truth is conveyed; rather, the structural content of a designing task, not a determined form, is sought. This means utilizing a variety of signs and images in one design, allowing a variety of orders to exert their effect. Just as the train station in Esslingen, with its light, virtually flying roofs, awakens urban associations – the Forchbahn carries the city-dweller finally into the countryside – so should the formation of the walls of office buildings protect the development behind it from the noise of the traffic, certainly with completely different syntactic symbols. And these in turn differ from the various narrow residence homes clustered together behind them, not denying their housing development character, their solar roofs suggesting a new typology. This is the order that "cultivates the diverse and the ambiguous", as characterized by Angélil/Graham/Pfenninger/Scholl Architecture: "It is an order that opposes any attempt to totalize..." J. C. B.

Marc Angélil, Sarah Graham, Reto Pfenninger, Manuel Scholl

Theorie und Praxis.

Wir sind interessiert an der Verbindung von Theorie und Praxis, an der Wechselwirkung von Idee und Form. Erkenntnisse aus anderen Wissensgebieten und die Theorie der Architektur gehören ebenso zu unserem Fundus wie Entwicklungen der Baubranche und die eigene Bautätigkeit. In diesem sehr weit gespannten Feld ist das Abstrahieren und Konkretisieren wichtiges Werkzeug, um sich produktiv darin bewegen zu können. Die sprachliche Formulierung von Absichten ist ebenso ein Mittel dazu wie zeichnerische Darstellungen oder bauliche Umsetzungen.

Theory and Practice.

We are interested in the connection between theory and practice, in the interaction of idea and form. Knowledge from other areas of learning and the theory of architecture belong just as much to our store of knowledge as the development of the building industry and its construction activity. The process of abstraction and conceptualization is an important tool enabling movement within this extremely wide-ranging field. Verbal formulation of intentions is just as much an instrument of this process as graphic representation or constructive realization.

Gartenpavillon | Garden Pavilion | Pfaffhausen, 1996

Eßlinger Dreieck | Esslingen Town Center | 1989-96

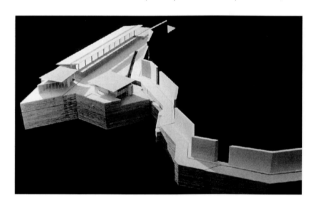

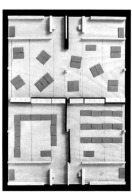
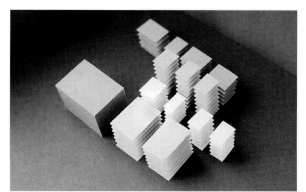

Schulhaus «Schützenareal» | School Complex «Schützenareal» | Zürich, 1993

Zusammenarbeit/Transfers.

Die Zusammenarbeit im Team ist Teil unseres Selbstverständnisses. Die Zusammensetzungen der Teams in Zürich und Los Angeles überschneiden sich, wechseln mit der Zeit, wechseln mit den Aufgaben. Wir sind überzeugt, daß ein Team Leistungen erbringen kann, die über die Summe aller Einzelleistungen hinausgehen. Dies bedingt die Pflege der Kommunikationskultur. Projektieren, Diskutieren, Konsolidieren, Weiterentwickeln bilden einen wichtigen Ablauf in der Entwicklung von Projekten. Kein Erzeugnis unseres Büros läßt sich somit auf bestimmte Autoren fixieren.

Wie unsere Arbeitsgemeinschaft, verstehen wir auch Architektur als Zusammenwirken verschiedenster Fachbereiche. Wir suchen nach fachübergreifenden Ansätzen. Wir versuchen, mit dem Entwurf des Gebäudes nicht über die Architektur zu beginnen. Zur Ideensammlung oder auch zur Überprüfung von Ansätzen organisieren wir Seminarien, Fachgespräche, Workshops. Aus der Frage anläßlich des Wettbewerbs für die Berufsschule Zürich, wie eine Schule für die heutige Zeit und die absehbare Zukunft aussehen sollte, konnten wir erst aufgrund der Zusammenarbeit mit einem Pädagogikwissenschaftler neuartige Schulraumideen und ungewohnte Schulhauskonzepte entwickeln.

Cooperation/Transfers.

The cooperation in our team is a part of our understanding of ourselves. The composition of the teams in Zurich and Los Angeles overlap, shift over time, change according to the task. We are convinced that a team can achieve results greater than the sum of all the individual achievements. This requires the cultivation of a communication culture. Formulation of projects, discussion, consolidation and development all form the vital course of a project's development. There is thus no one definite author of any product that issues from our office.

Our understanding of architecture corresponds to our understanding of our own working pool; they are both the interplay of various areas of expertise. We look for interdisciplinary approaches. When we design a building, we try not to begin with the architecture. We organize seminars, discussions in different specialties and workshops to collect ideas or review approaches. At the time of the competition for the Berufsschule Zurich, we were faced with the question of how a school of today and the foreseeable future ought to look. We could develop our novel ideas for schoolrooms and our unusual concepts for a schoolhouse only by basing them on our collaboration with educational specialists.

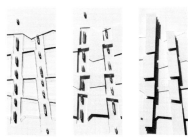

Areal «Steinfabrik» | Housing Fabric | Pfäffikon, 1995

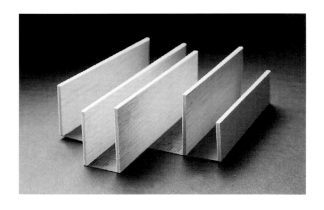
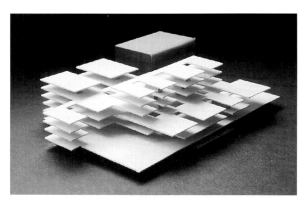

Marc Angélil, Sarah Graham, Reto Pfenninger, Manuel Scholl

Offenheit.

Eindeutigkeit und ausschließliche Zuordnung sind im kulturellen Rahmen heute nicht mehr hinreichende Kriterien. Offenheit schafft Raum für andere Perspektiven. Verschiedene Vorstellungen können in mehrschichtigen Projekten verbunden werden, welche wiederum vielfältige und auch neuartige Interpretationen zulassen sollen. Offenheit kann sich in formaler, räumlicher Art zeigen mittels mehrfacher Raumbezüge, Durchlässigkeit, Transparenz oder nicht abgeschlossener Geometrien. Sie kann aber auch inhaltlich oder bezüglich des Vorgehens umgesetzt werden. So gelang es uns in einem Beispiel, anhand von Ausschnitten abstrakter Bilder mit Bauherren eine gemeinsame Absicht bezüglich des ästhetischen Charakters zu formulieren, ohne uns auf konkrete Teillösungen zu fixieren.

Openness.

Definitiveness and exclusive classification are no longer adequate criteria for today's cultural framework. Openness creates room for other perspectives. Various conceptions can be joined in multi-layered projects which in their turn allow for diverse and even novel interpretations. Openness can display itself in formal, three-dimensional ways by means of multiple spatial relations, permeability, transparency or non-self-contained geometries. It can also, however, be realized in relation to the content or procedure. We have been successful, for example, in formulating, with the help of extracts from abstract images, a common intent concerning the aesthetic character of the project, without having to fix firmly on partial concrete solutions.

Zahnarztpraxis | Dental Clinic | Zürich, 1995

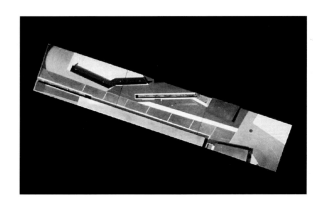

(Parkgarage | Parc Garage)

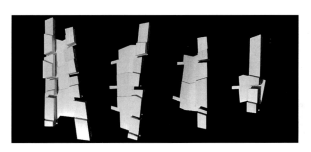

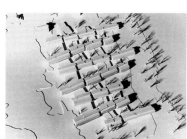

Prozeß/Arbeitsmodus.

Der Faktor Zeit spielt eine bestimmende Rolle beim Planen und Bauen. Wir versuchen, Abläufe miteinzubeziehen, sichtbar werden zu lassen. Die Art des Prozesses beeinflußt sehr stark das resultierende Produkt. Dementsprechend leisten auch die zur Realisation eines Projektes eingesetzten Methoden einen großen Beitrag zur Definition des Resultates. Wir versuchen deshalb vielmehr, Vorgehensweisen zu entwerfen, anstatt Lösungen zu fixieren. Aus der Wechselwirkung von Vorstellungen, Anforderung und Prozeß entstehen neue Zusammenhänge. Die in solchen Abläufen auftretenden unfertigen Zustände ermöglichen uns, auf neue Aspekte anders zu reagieren.

Process/Work Mode.

The factor of time plays a definite role in planning and building. We try to incorporate the currents of the work flow, allow them to become visible. This kind of process very strongly influences the resulting product. The methods employed towards the realization of a project contribute largely to the definition of the result. We therefore try much more to design with the progression in mind, rather than to determine solutions. From the interplay of preconditions, requirement and process new connections emerge. Such unresolved situations occurring within the progression of the work make it possible for us to react to new aspects in an entirely other way.

(Forchbahn | Train Station)

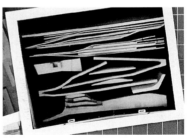

Städtebauliche Entwicklungs-Strategien | Urban Development Strategies | Neuenburg, 1994

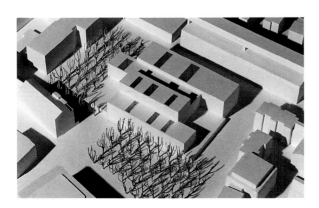

Marc Angélil, Sarah Graham, Reto Pfenninger, Manuel Scholl

Experiment.

Das Experiment ist ein wichtiger Teil unserer Arbeit. Es schafft einen Freiraum, in welchem wir unabsehbare Richtungen aufnehmen können. Experimente lassen Unvorhergesehenes entstehen, bringen die gewohnte Wahrnehmung durcheinander, zwingen zur Auseinandersetzung und ermöglichen, neue Systeme zu etablieren. Wir bewegen uns zwischen Bricolage und Forschung und lassen uns vom Interesse an erweiterten Betrachtungsweisen leiten.

So entstand zum Beispiel aus der Schichtung verschiedener Planungsprojekte für den gleichen Ort ein dreidimensionales Gefüge, welches einen Ansatz für ein weiteres architektonisches Projekt bildet. Oder die Verbindung von Darstellungsmethoden für Oberflächen mit einem amerikanischen Holzbausystem führte zu einer ungewohnten Raumkonstruktion. Ferner führte der Wunsch, Front und Dach optisch zu verbinden, zu einer erweiterten Anwendung eines gängigen Fassadenmaterials.

Experiment.

Experimentation is an important part of our work. It creates a free space in which we can take off in unforeseen directions. Experiments let the unpredictable happen, turn familiar perceptions upside down, force confrontations and make it possible to establish new systems. We move between hand-crafted assembly and research and let ourselves be led by our own interest to expanded modes of reflection.

Out of the layers of various planning projects for the same site, for instance, a three-dimensional structure was developed that formed the departure for a further architectural project. Combining methods of surface presentation with an American wooden structural system led to an unusual spatial construction. The wish to optically connect front and roof, moreover, led us to an expanded application of a popular façade material.

(Postgebäude | Post Office)

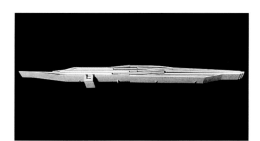
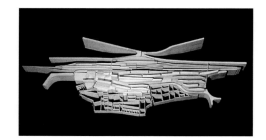

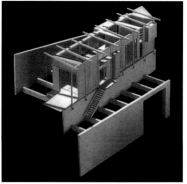

Wohnhaus in Hollywood | Experimental House | Los Angeles, 1990-93

Text/Lesen/Schreiben.

Wir sind interessiert an der Bedeutung des Lesens und der Notation. Lesen als das Vermögen, sich Sach- und Sinnzusammenhänge zugänglich zu machen. Notation als die lesbare Aufzeichnung von wesentlichen Merkmalen mittels Zeichen. Physisch nur schwach oder nicht wahrnehmbare Eigenheiten einer Situation, seien es Geländeneigungen, Wasserläufe, Immissionen oder Sichtbeziehungen, verstärken sich in Plänen und können zu Ausgangspunkten für verschiedenste architektonische Elemente werden. Wir verstehen Architektur auch als Text und versuchen ihn zu lesen, umgekehrt verstehen wir das Entwickeln von Projekten als Schreiben eines Textes.

Text/Reading/Writing.

We are interested in the meaning of reading and notation. Reading as the power to create connections between facts and between meanings. Notation as the readable recording of essential characteristics by means of symbols. Physically weak or not at all perceivable peculiarities of a situation, be it land inclinations, waterways, emissions or relationships within the field of vision, strengthen when drawn up in plans and can become starting points for the most diverse architectonic elements. We also understand architecture as text and try to read it; conversely, we understand the development of a project as the writing of a text.

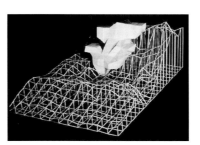 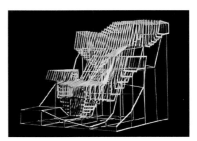

Experimenteller Wohnbau | Hillside Housing and Work Space | Tokio, 1993

 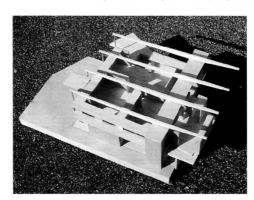

Experiment St. Jakobsplatz | Experiment St. Jakobsplatz | München, 1994

Marc Angélil, Sarah Graham, Reto Pfenninger, Manuel Scholl

Schichtungen/Strukturen.

Schichtungen und Überlagerungen bringen neue Qualitäten und Potentiale zum Vorschein. Durch deren Verbindungen entstehen neue Gefüge, die verschiedene Auslegungen eröffnen und eigene Strukturen entwickeln können. Im Gegensatz zu Objekten zeichnen sich Strukturen dadurch aus, daß sie, ohne ihre grundlegenden Eigenschaften zu verlieren, sich weiterentwickeln oder neue Beziehungen aufnehmen können. Wir suchen Strukturelles auf verschiedenen Abstraktionsstufen.

Stratifications/Structures.

Layers and overlappings bring new qualities and potential to light. Through their connections, new structures arise which open up various interpretations and can in turn develop their own structures. In contrast to objects, structures distinguish themselves by their ability to develop further or to enter into new relationships without losing their fundamental characteristics. We search for the structural on different levels of abstraction.

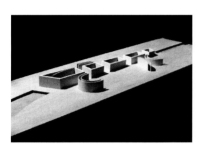

Architektur und Infrastruktur | West Coast Gate Way | Los Angeles, 1990

(Bürohaus | Office Building)

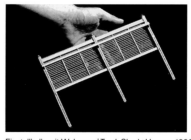 

Einstellhalle mit Wohnung | Truck Shed Horgen, 1996

Bezüge/Kontexte.

Jede Tätigkeit entsteht in einem Umfeld. Der architektonische Kontext erschöpft sich nicht in der physischen Situation, im funktionellen Programm oder in persönlichen Bildern. Von vielen Möglichkeiten werden nur einzelne wahrgenommen und davon nur wenige gewählt. Wird der Kontext bewußt zur Sache der Wahl oder der Anschauung, erweitern sich die möglichen Bezüge. Wir wählen den eigenen Kontext. Unsere Bezüge können wir in Bachläufen, Sichtbeziehungen, bestehenden oder neuen Fertigungstechnologien oder auch in einer Kiste von Dentalwerkzeugen und -materialien finden. Der Umgang mit den verschiedenartigsten Phänomenen kann sehr direkt sein oder aber sich auch der späteren Wahrnehmung entziehen.

References/Contexts.

Every activity arises within an environment. The architectonic context is not limited to the physical situation, the functional program or personal images. From many possibilities only a few are perceived, and from these fewer are chosen. If one becomes conscious of the context through choice or personal view, the number of possible references grows. We choose our own context. We can find our references in the running of a stream, in optical relationships, in existing or new manufacturing technology, or in a case of dental tools. The dialogue with the various types of phenomena can be very direct, or it can even escape later perception.

Wohnhaus | Environmental House | Topanga, Kalifornien, 1992-94

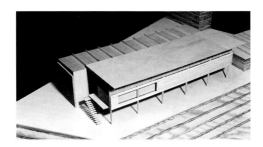

Platzüberdachungen | 50 Lunch Shelters | Los Angeles, 1989

Marc Angélil, Sarah Graham, Reto Pfenninger, Manuel Scholl

Biografien	**Werkverzeichnis**	**Bibliografie**

Marc Angélil
1954 geboren.
1973-79 Architekturstudium an der ETH Zürich.
1987 Doktor der Technischen Wissenschaften an der ETH Zürich.
1982-87 Professur an der Harvard University.
1987-94 Professur an der University of Southern California, Los Angeles.
Ab 1994 Professur an der ETH Zürich.

Sarah Graham
1951 geboren.
1970-74 Bachelor of Arts an der Stanford University.
1979-82 Master of Architecture an der Harvard University.
Ab 1987 Professur an der University of Southern California, Los Angeles.

Reto Pfenninger
1963 geboren in Zürich.
1980-84 Hochbauzeichnerlehre in Zürich.
1984-87 HTL Winterthur.
1990-92 Akademie der Bildenden Künste, München.
1988-90 Architekturbüro: Atelier Cube, Lausanne.
Ab 1994 Assistent bei Prof. Marc Angélil, ETH Zürich.

Manuel Scholl
1962 geboren in Zürich.
1982-88 Architekturstudium an der ETH Zürich.
1988-90 Architekturbüro Campi & Pessina, Lugano.
1990/91 Architekturbüros Gallego & Fernandez und Sanmartin & Muñoz, Barcelona.
Ab 1994 Assistent: Lehrstuhl für Architektur und Entwurf, Marc Angélil, ETH Zürich.

Ausstellungen, Auszeichnungen
1995 *Haus-Geburt, Architektur zwischen Idee und Wirklichkeit,* Museum für Gestaltung, Zürich.
1995 *Urban Revisions, Current Projects for the Public Realm,* Museum of Contemporary Art, Los Angeles.
1996 *Bauten Projekte,* Architekturgalerie München.

1994 *AIA Honor Award Los Angeles, AIA California Council,* House Dr. Rodgerton, Los Angeles.
1996 *Honor Award, AIA California Council,* Urban Design Esslingen Town Center.

1986
Laboratorium Harvard Universität.

1988
Lunch Shelters Los Angeles.
West Coast Gateway Los Angeles, Wettbewerb.
Amerika-Gedenkbibliothek Berlin, Wettbewerb.

1989
Experimental House Los Angeles.

1990
Gestaltungsplan Eßlinger Dreieck.
Platz der Auslandschweizer, Brunnen, Wettbewerb.

1991
Topanga House Los Angeles.
SZU-Areal Gießhübel Zürich, Studienauftrag.
Bahn- und Busstation Eßlingen.
Postgebäude Eßlingen.
Park + Ride-Garage Eßlingen.
Bürogebäude Eßlingen.

1992
Schulhaus Los Angeles, Wettbewerb.

1993
Experimenteller Wohnungsbau Shinkenshiku-sha, Japan, Wettbewerb.

1994
Bahnhofgebiet Neuchâtel, Studie.
Berufsschule Schütze Zürich, Wettbewerb.
Zahnarztpraxis Tessinerplatz Zürich.
St. Jakobsplatz München, Studie.

1995
Steinfabrik Pfäffikon, Wettbewerb.
Werkhof Horgen.
Umbau Einfamilienhaus Küsnacht.

1996
Gaswerkareal Zug, Wettbewerb.
Pavillon Pfaffhausen.
Midfield-Dock Flughafen Kloten, Wettbewerb, in Zusammenarbeit mit Martin Spühler, dipl. Arch. ETH/SIA/BSA, Weiterbearbeitung.
Umgebung Camp Nou Barcelona, Wettbewerb, erster Preis.

Ernst Hofmann, *Zukunftsgerichtetes Bauen,* in: Schweizer Ingenieur und Architekt, 8/1992.
V. M. Lampugnani, *Casa sperimentale nei collini di Hollywood,* in: Domus, Dezember 1994.
Barbara Lamprecht, *Framing a Question,* in: The Architectural Review, July 1994.
Urban Revisions, Current Projects for the Public Realm, Katalog des Museum of Contemporary Art of Los Angeles, MIT Press, May 1994.
E. Hubeli und Ch. Luchsinger, *Ausschöpfen, was Architektur leisten kann,* in: Werk, Bauen + Wohnen, April 1994.
Shinkenshiku-sha Residential Design Competition, in: The Japan Architect, April 1994.
A Topological Study, in: Global Architecture, März 1995.
Topanga Canyon House, in: Korean Architects, February 1995.

Eigene Veröffentlichungen
M. van Norman, M. Angélil, S. Graham, *Study of Effects of Office Automation on Design Criteria for Office Furniture,* Harvard University 1986.
M. Angélil, *Technique and Formal Expression in Architecture, Theory in Architectural Technology from the Renaissance to the Age of Reason,* Dissertation 1987.
M. Angélil und andere, *Architecture, Technology, and the City,* Butterworth-Heinemann 1991.
M. Angélil, *Violated Perfection: Geschichtsschreibung «sous rature»,* in: Werk, Bauen + Wohnen, September 1991.
M. Angélil, *Topos 0-9: An Exploration of the Process of Design,* in: Semiotext(e) Architecture, 1992.
M. Angélil, *La mégalopole, une forme d'écriture automatique,* in: L'architecture d'aujourd'hui, Dezember 1993.
M. Angélil, S. Graham, *Konstruktive Grammatologie,* in: archithese, April 1994.
M. Angélil, M. Scholl, R. Pfenninger, *Prozessorientiertes Projektieren: Entwerfen als interdisziplinäre Teamarbeit,* in: SZS, Bauen in Stahl, 1996.

Biographies

Marc Angélil
1954 Born.
1973-79 Studied architecture at the ETH Zurich.
1987 Doctor of Technical Science at the ETH Zurich.
1982-87 Professor at Harvard University.
1987-94 Professor at the University of Southern California, Los Angeles.
From 1994 Professor at the ETH Zurich.

Sarah Graham
1951 Born.
1970-74 Bachelor of Arts at Stanford University.
1979-82 Master of Architecture at Harvard University.
From 1987 Professor at the University of Southern California, Los Angeles.

Reto Pfenninger
1963 Born in Zurich.
1980-84 Architectural drafting apprenticeship in Zurich.
1984-87 HTL Winterthur.
1990-92 Academy of Fine Arts, Munich.
1988-90 Architecture office: Atelier Cube, Lausanne.
From 1994 Assistant to Prof. Marc Angélil, ETH Zurich.

Manuel Scholl
1962 Born in Zurich.
1982-88 Studied architecture at the ETH Zurich.
1988-90 Architecture office Campi & Pessina, Lugano.
1990/91 Architecture offices Gellego & Fernandez and Sanmartin & Muñoz, Barcelona.
From 1994 Assistant: Chair for Architecture and Design, Marc Angélil, ETH Zurich.

Exhibitions, Awards

1995 *Haus-Geburt, Architektur zwischen Idee und Wirklichkeit,* Museum für Gestaltung, Zurich.
1995 *Urban Revisions, Current Projects for the Public Realm,* Museum of Contemporary Art, Los Angeles.
1996 *Bauten Projekte,* Architekturgalerie, Munich.

1994 *AIA Honor Award Los Angeles, AIA California Council,* House Dr. Rodgerton, Los Angeles.
1996 *Honor Award, AIA California Council,* Urban Design Esslingen Town Center.

List of Works

1986
Laboratory, Harvard University.

1988
Lunch Shelters, Los Angeles.
West Coast Gateway, Los Angeles, competition.
American Commemorative Library Berlin, competition.

1989
Experimental House, Los Angeles.

1990
Design plan for Esslingen Town Center.
Platz der Auslandschweizer, Brunnen, competition

1991
Topanga House, Los Angeles.
SZU-Areal Giesshübel, Zurich, commissioned study.
Train and bus station, Esslingen.
Post office building, Esslingen.
Park + Ride Garage, Esslingen.
Office buildings, Esslingen.

1992
Schoolhouse, Los Angeles, competition.

1993
Experimental residence building, Shinkenshiku-sha, Japan, competition.

1994
Train station grounds, Neuchâtel, study.
Berufsschule Schütze, Zurich, competition.
Dental Clinic, Tessinerplatz, Zurich.
St. Jakobsplatz, Munich, study.

1995
Housing Fabric, Pfäffikon, competition.
Work yard, Horgen.
Conversion of residence home, Küsnacht.

1996
Gas Company grounds, Zug, competition.
Pavilion, Pfaffhausen.
Midfield Dock, Kloten Airport, competition, in collaboration with Martin Spühler, dipl. Arch. ETH/SIA/BSA, further development work.
Camp Nou environs, Barcelona, competition, first prize.

Bibliography

Ernst Hofmann, *Zukunftsgerichtetes Bauen,* in: Schweizer Ingenieur und Architekt, 8/1992.
V. M. Lampugnani, *Casa sperimentale nei collini di Hollywood,* in: Domus, December 1994.
Barbara Lamprecht, *Framing a Question,* in: The Architectural Review, July 1994.
Urban Revisions, *Current Projects for the Public Realm,* catalogue, Museum of Contemporary Art, Los Angeles, MIT Press, May 1994.
E. Hubeli and Ch. Luchsinger, *Ausschöpfen, was Architektur leisten kann,* in: Werk, Bauen + Wohnen, April 1994.
Shinkenshiku-sha Residential Design Competition, in: The Japan Architect, April 1994.
A Topological Study, in: Global Architecture, March 1995.
Topanga Canyon House, in: Korean Architects, February 1995.

Publications by the Architects

M. van Norman, M. Angélil, S. Graham, *Study of Effects of Office Automation on Design Criteria for Office Furniture,* Harvard University 1986.
M. Angélil, *Technique and Formal Expression in Architecture, Theory in Architectural Technology from the Renaissance to the Age of Reason,* Dissertation 1987.
M. Angélil and others, *Architecture, Technology, and the City,* Butterworth-Heinemann 1991.
M. Angélil, *Violated Perfection: Geschichtsschreibung "sous rature",* in: Werk, Bauen + Wohnen, September 1991.
M. Angélil, Topos 0-9: *An Exploration of the Process of Design,* in: Semiotext(e) Architecture, 1992.
M. Angélil, *La mégalopole, une forme d'écriture automatique,* in: L'architecture d'aujourd'hui, December 1993.
M. Angélil, S. Graham, *Konstruktive Grammatologie,* in: archithese, April 1994.
M. Angélil, M. Scholl, R. Pfenninger, *Prozessorientiertes Projektieren: Entwerfen als interdisziplinäre Teamarbeit,* in: SZS, Bauen in Stahl, 1996.

Bauart Architekten
Bern

Büropartner
Office partners
- Reto Baer
- Willi Frei
- Peter C. Jakob
- Matthias Rindisbacher
- Marco Ryter

Mitarbeiterinnen und Mitarbeiter
Collaborators
- André Erard
- Rahel Fiechter
- Gabriel Guth
- Martine Kull
- Corinne Reinhard
- Andres Schenker
- Noël Schneider
- Bettina Spang
- Sandra Vogel
- Marie-Hélène Weber
- Cédric Zbinden

Bundesamt für Statistik | Federal Department of Statistics | Neuenburg, 1993–98

Bahnhof Aarau, Wettbewerb | Aarau Railway Station, Competition | Aarau, 1991

Provisorisches Mehrzweckgebäude | Provisional Multipurpose Building | Neuenburg, 1993

Parlamentsgebäude, Umbau | Parliament House, Conversion | Bern, 1993–95

Kindergarten Morillon | Morillon Kindergarten | Wabern-Köniz, 1995

Baukunst und Ökologie.

In einem glasüberdeckten Innenhof mit trapezoider Grundfläche schwingt sich ein schwarzglänzender Körper über mehrere Geschosse: Eine Treppe, geformt aus einem bloß einige Millimeter starken Stahlblech, bei der die geschlossenen Brüstungen mit dem Lauf zusammen einen U-förmigen, wannenartigen Träger bilden. Auf den Stufen spielt Licht, das seitlich einfällt, wo schmale Streifen des Bleches zur Aussteifung nach außen gefaltet sind. Je nach Standort und Lichtreflexion wirkt der Körper fast schwerelos leicht oder aber massiv und schwer.

Dieses Gebäude, das in unmittelbarere Nähe zum Bahnhof in Neuenburg entsteht, ist das bislang größte und bedeutendste Werk der Bauart Architekten: das neue Bundesamt für Statistik. Im über zweihundert Meter langen schlanken Baukörper löst sich im Süden eine Raumschicht vom ruhigen Rücken ab, um in elegantem Schwung der Rue du Cret Taconnet zu folgen. So entsteht eine spitz zulaufende Zwischenzone, die durch Spezialräume und Lichthöfe mit Verbindungsbrücken und Nebentreppen gegliedert wird. Die Länge und Horizontalität des Baukörpers wird nach Süden zusätzlich durch schmale Balkone betont, die ihm ein Gesicht verleihen, das weit über die Altstadt auf den See blickt. Die Nordfassade dagegen, auf das Gleisfeld des Bahnhofs gerichtet, ist kühl und zurückhaltend, aber um so komplexer gestaltet. Vor einer Schicht mit konventionellen Bandfenstern und isolierten Brüstungen liegt eine Haut aus Profilitglas, in der lediglich Lochfenster für einen punktuellen Ausblick ausgespart sind. Die leicht grünlichen Gußglaselemente lassen die dahinterliegende Zeichnung der Fenster, der roten Stoffstoren und der grün-grauen Brüstungselemente noch durchschimmern und bilden einen Schleier, der je nach Lichteinfall stärker oder schwächer wirkt. Dadurch entsteht ein gleichzeitig homogenes und flächiges, wie auch sehr lebendiges, sich veränderndes Fassadenbild.

Im Gespräch über dieses Gebäude streichen die Architekten allerdings nicht zuerst seinen formalen Reichtum heraus, sondern Aspekte der Ökologie. Die Balkone im Süden erhalten so ihren Sinn als Schattenspender und Vordach, die Haut im Norden erlaubt helle Büros und ermöglicht gleichzeitig, die dahinterliegenden Lüftungsfenster auch bei Wind und Regen offenzulassen, wobei ein ausgeklügeltes System natürlicher Belüftung eine aufwendige Klimatechnik weitgehend überflüssig macht. Selbst die eingangs beschriebenen Treppen werden zuerst mit ökologischen Argumenten erklärt: die Konstruktion ist technisch einfach und materialsparend, zudem erlaubt die Homogenität des als Baustoff eingesetzten Stahls eine problemlose Wiederverwertung.

Das Umweltbewußtsein der Architekten spielt schon seit der Gründung des Büros im Jahre 1987 eine wichtige Rolle. Es führt weder zu spektakulär technoiden Lösungen, noch zu einer Architektur, der etwas Handgestricktes anhaftet. Die Minimierung des Aufwandes und die verantwortungsvolle Verwendung der Ressourcen scheint eher beiläufig, beinahe selbstverständlich zu geschehen. Entsprechende Ansatzpunkte werden auch auf ihr formales Potential hin untersucht und entsprechend weiterentwickelt. Daß dabei konstruktiven Fragen eine zentrale Bedeutung beigemessen wird, versteht sich schon beinahe von selbst.

Die Bauten und Entwürfe der Bauart Architekten zeichnen sich nicht durch eine einheitliche Formensprache aus, vielmehr wird der architektonische Ausdruck jeweils aus den Gegebenheiten des Programms, des Ortes und nicht zuletzt des Budgets spezifisch entwickelt. Eine solche Arbeitsweise kommt dem Entwurfsprozeß im Team entgegen, wo die fünf Partner Reto Baer, Willi Frei, Peter C. Jakob, Matthias Rindisbacher und Marco Ryter sowie die mittlerweile rund zehn Mitarbeiter ihre jeweils spezifische Erfahrung einbringen können. Auch wenn kompositorische Aspekte dabei nicht im Vordergrund stehen, wird ihnen doch die nötige Aufmerksamkeit geschenkt. Deutlich wird dies etwa beim Kindergarten Morillon (1994), wo in der als unwirtlich empfundenen Umgebung eines Berner Vorortquartiers eine introvertierte Hofanlage geschaffen wurde, deren weitgehend geschlossene Hülle aus Holz um so sorgfältiger gestaltet ist. Die Kohärenz von Entwurfsgedanken und fertigem Bau bei sorgfältiger, ökologisch verantwortungsbewußter Detaillierung und hoher formaler Qualität ist wohl mit ein Grund, weshalb die Architekten trotz des nicht sehr umfangreichen Werks bereits zweimal mit dem «Bernischen Kulturpreis für Architektur, Technik und Umwelt», ATU-prix, ausgezeichnet wurden. M. T.

Architecture and Ecology.

In a glass-covered inner courtyard with a trapezoidal base, a glossy black unit swings up over the height of several floors: a staircase molded from one sheet of steel just a few millimeters thick forms, together with the closed parapet, a U-shaped, tub-like support. Light plays on the steps, entering from the side where slender strips of steel have been folded toward the outside to lend rigidity. According to location and light reflection, the unit seems to be almost weightlessly light or else massively heavy.

This building, in direct proximity to the train station in Neuchâtel, is the largest and most significant work yet produced by the Bauart Architects: the new Federal Department of Statistics. A slice of the narrow building, itself more than 200 meters long, peels off on the south side to follow the Rue du Cret Taconnet in an elegant curve of reposing underlying layers. This creates a long, sharply-pointed middle zone that has been sectioned into special-use rooms and open-air inner courtyards connected by passageways and secondary staircases. The length and horizontality of the body of the building is additionally emphasized by narrow balconies which lend the south side a face that looks out far over the old part of the city and the lake. In comparison, the north façade, directed towards the train station's field of railway tracks, is cool and reserved, yet just as complexly designed. On this side, in front of a stratification lined with conventional strip windows and insulated parapets, lies a skin of textured glass dotted with single windows, each giving a puzzle piece of the view. The light green cast glass components still let the pattern from behind the windows – the red fabric curtains and the gray-green parapet elements – shimmer through and form a veil either weak or strong depending on the changing incidence of light. The result is an image of a façade homogenous and flat, and at the same time alive and ever-changing.

To be sure, in conversations about the building, the architects do not praise its formal richness but rather its ecological aspects. The balconies on the south side retain their purpose as providers of shade and as canopy while on the north side the glass skin allows for bright offices and makes it possible for the ventilation windows to be left open even during wind and rain; this natural air-circulation cooling system renders costly air-conditioning largely unnecessary. Even the staircase itself is explained first in terms of ecology: the construction is technically simple and material-efficient; because of the homogeneity of the steel building material, the whole thing is easily recycled and reutilized.

The architects' environmental consciousness has played a role in their work since the founding of the office in 1987. It leads neither to spectacular technoid solutions nor to an architecture with a home-made feel. The minimalization of expenditure and the responsible application of resources seem to happen rather casually, naturally. Respective departure points are explored to the limit of their potential and correspondingly developed. It is understandable from this that structural questions are ascribed a central significance.

The buildings and designs of the Bauart Architects do not single themselves out by their uniform formal language; the architectonic expression develops much more specifically from the given situations of programs, sites and, not least of all, the budget. This method of working complements the team's design process, whereby the five partners – Reto Baer, Willi Frei, Peter C. Jakob, Matthias Rindisbacher and Marco Ryter – along with approximately ten colleagues and collaborators, can each contribute their own specific experience. Compositional aspects are given the necessary attention even when they are not obviously in the foreground. This becomes clear when we look at the Morillon Kindergarten (1994). In an inhospitable vicinity of a Bern suburb, an introverted courtyard complex has been created whose wooden shell was designed and put together with great care and attention. The coherence of the design ideas and the finished construction, with its careful ecological and responsibility-conscious detailing and high formal quality, make it clear why the architects, despite their not yet voluminous body of work, have already been twice distinguished with the Bern Cultural Prize for Architecture, Technology and Environment. M.T.

Kindergarten Morillon, Wabern-Köniz, 1995
Morillon Kindergarten, Wabern-Köniz, 1995

Bundesamt für Statistik, Neuenburg, Wettbewerbsergebnis 1990, Bauzeit 1993–98.

Der für 400 ständige sowie 300 temporäre Arbeitsplätze konzipierte, 240 Meter lange Baukörper dieses Verwaltungsgebäudes zeichnet auf der Talseite die geschweifte Kante des Bahnhofplateaus nach und beschließt mit einer schnurgeraden Bergfassade die Gleistrasse. Eleganz bestimmt die markante Großform und Transparenz die innere Anlage. Zwei Stränge von Büros schließen im breiteren Kopfteil eine Mittelzone ein, die zwischen Lichthöfen die zentrale Erschließung sowie Sitzungszimmer und andere Funktionen enthält. Im separat erschlossenen schmalen Schwanzteil liegen die Großraumbüros mit temporären Arbeitsplätzen. Restaurants und ein Konferenzsaal profitieren von Seesicht, Licht und Sonne der Attikazone.

Reduktion der Elemente und Farben prägen die Fassade. Die geschweifte Südfassade ist durch die schattenspendenden Betonplatten gebändert, die zudem Witterungsschutz für die der Belüftung und der Nachtauskühlung dienenden Oberlichtzone bieten. Bei der geraden Nordfassade übernimmt ein Vorhang aus Glaslamellen diese Aufgabe. Die Ökobilanz war bei der Materialwahl ausschlaggebend, die Grundlagen dazu erarbeitete das Institut für Baubiologie. Nachhaltigkeit bestimmte den Entscheid, Sonnenkollektoren und einen riesigen Wärmespeicher einzubauen.

Federal Department of Statistics, Neuchâtel, Competition Result 1990, Construction Period 1993–98.

The 240-meter-long administration building was conceived to house 400 permanent and 300 temporary work stations. It traces the valley side of the train station plateau's curving edge and hems the railway grounds like an unswerving wall of mountains. Elegance defines the marked overall form and transparency the inner complexes. In the wider main section, two strands of offices enclose a central zone containing, between open-air courtyards, the central accessway as well as sitting rooms and other functional areas. In the separately developed narrow tail section lie the open-plan offices with temporary work places. Restaurants and a conference hall have the advantage of a view of the lake, of light and of sun shining into the attic region above.

Reduction of elements and colors characterize the façades. The curving south façade is banded by the shade-providing concrete plates that offer weather resistance for the air circulation and night cooling systems that service the skylight zone. On the straight northern façade, this function is provided by a curtain wall of glass slats. Ecological balance was the deciding factor in the choice of material, the ground work for which was done by the Institute for Building Biology, just as durability and effectiveness weighed in favor of the installation of sun collectors and a huge heat storage unit.

Gesamtsituation, Modell
View of the total site, model
Nordfassade, Modell
North façade, model
Südfassade, Modell
South façade, model

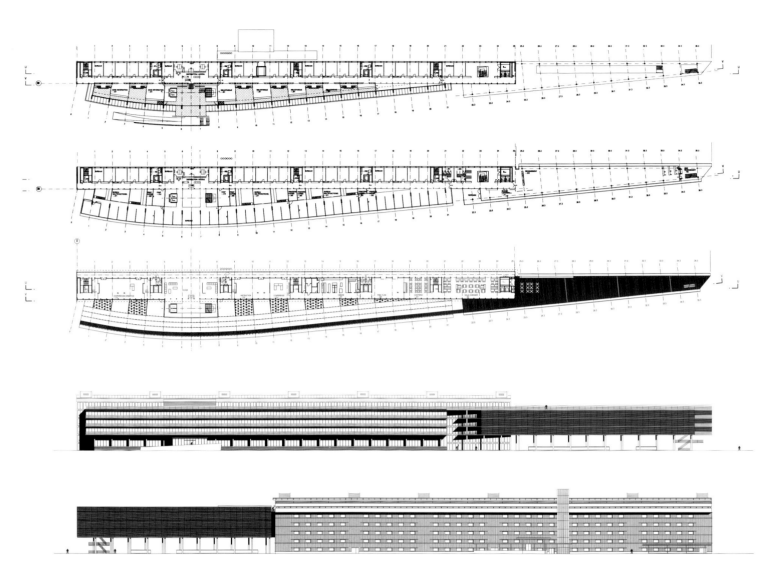

Eingangsgeschoß, Obergeschoß, Dachgeschoß, Südfassade und Nordfassade
 Entrance level, upper floor, attic floor, south façade and north façade
Querschnitte
 Cross sections

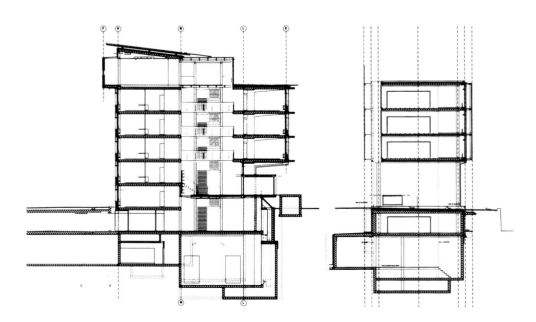

Wettbewerbsprojekt Bahnhof Aarau, 1991.

Aus dem Bericht des Preisgerichts: «Das Projekt zeichnet sich durch seine Schlichtheit und durch die Bescheidenheit der angewendeten Mittel aus. Das Bahnreisezentrum ist ebenerdig angeordnet; zwei offene, gut ersichtliche Treppen führen zu den Personenunterführungen. Der lange, einheitlich gestaltete Baukörper verdeutlicht die Schneise des Bahngleises. Die öffentlichen Elemente werden leicht hervorgehoben: Der Bahnhof, das Restaurant, das Reisebüro und das Schulungszentrum. Einziger öffentlicher Raum von städtischer Bedeutung bleibt der Bahnhofplatz. Der Baukörper wirkt durch seine Einheit als ruhiger Hintergrund zum nördlich direkt angrenzenden Wirrwarr (Gebäude und Außenräume verschiedenster Dimensionen). [...] Die Gliederung der verschiedenen Außenräume ist klar und einfach. Die Bepflanzung des Platzes zwischen dem ‹Aarauerhof› und dem Bahnhofgebäude soll deutlich machen, daß sich dieser Platz vom Bahnhofplatz unterscheidet. [...] Das Projekt zeichnet sich durch die Einfachheit und die Angemessenheit der baulichen Eingriffe aus und ist städtebaulich von guter Qualität.»

Aarau Railway Station, Competition Project, 1991.

From the jury report: "The project is singular in its simplicity and in the frugality of the material applied. The passenger departure area is arranged at street level; two open, clearly visible stairways lead to the pedestrian underpasses. The long uniformly designed building makes the aisles of train platforms plain. The public elements are gently brought to one's attention: the train station, the restaurant, the travel bureau, the educational center. The railway plaza remains a single public space with urban significance. The body of the building works through its uniformity as a restful background for the confusion directly against its northern border (buildings and exterior spaces of greatly differing dimensions) [...] The organization of the various exterior spaces is clear and simple. The plaza is planted between the 'Aarauerhof' square and the railway station building; this location should make it clear that this square is distinct from the railway plaza [...] The project is remarkable for its simplicity and the suitability of the structural operations, and is of high quality in the realm of city planning."

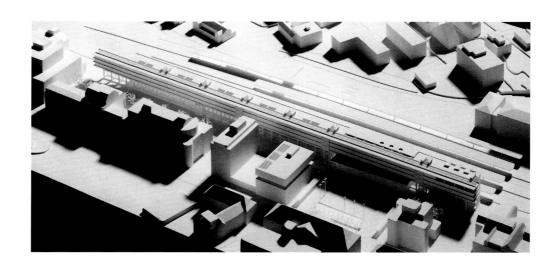

Gesamtsituation, Modell
Situation, model
Nordwestfassade
Northwest façade

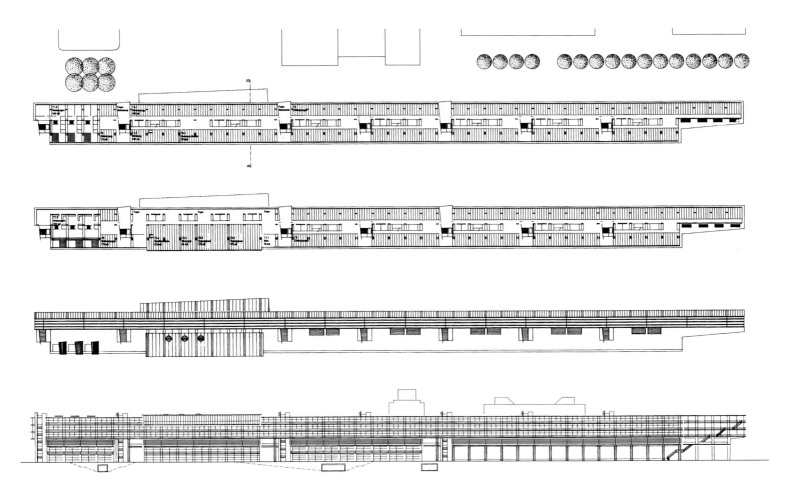

Viertes und fünftes Obergeschoß, Dachaufsicht, Südostfassade
Fourth and fifth floors, view of the roof, southwest façade
Querschnitt B–B
Cross section B–B

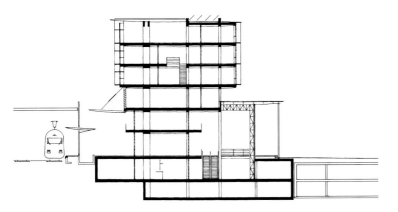

Provisorisches Mehrzweckgebäude, Neuenburg, 1993.

Das Provisorium beherbergt das Baubüro für den Neubau des Bundesamtes für Statistik sowie für Büros und Werkstätten der SBB über einer Verladerampe für Camions der PTT. Auf die Aufgabenstellung, die kurze Aufbau- und Abbruchzeiten sowie eine günstige Konstruktionsweise einschließt, reagierten die Architekten mit einer vorfabrizierten stapelbaren Raumzelle aus Holz. Sie ist dank winkelförmiger Rahmenprofile in sich und als Raumgitter stabil. Sie kann als allseitig umwandete Kiste wie auch mit offenen Seiten verbaut werden, wodurch sich eine Vielfalt von räumlichen Möglichkeiten eröffnet. Der Modulor-T genannte Prototyp von Neuenburg mißt rund 3×4 Meter und ist 3 Meter hoch. Über einer Stahlständerkonstruktion wurden insgesamt 57 Elemente zu drei Obergeschossen aufgesetzt. Zwei Außentreppen und ein Lastenaufzug bewerkstelligen die Vertikalerschließung. Die in Zusammenarbeit mit dem Schweizerischen Institut für Baubiologie und dem Brandverhütungsdienst entwickelte Holz-Raumzelle wird in variablen Maßen produziert. Sie ist unter anderem für temporäre, rasch zu erstellende Schulhaus-Ergänzungsbauten in Thun vorgesehen. Auch die Verwendung für preisgünstige Hotelbauten wird studiert.

Provisional Multipurpose Building, Neuchâtel, 1993.

This provisional arrangement accommodates the construction office for the new building of the Federal Department of Statistics, plus the offices and workshops of the Swiss Federal Railways (SBB), mounted over a loading platform for post office trucks. The specifications of the commission include short periods allotted for setting up and tearing down, as well as an inexpensive construction system. The architects responded with a prefabricated, stackable wooden building block unit. Thanks to angular frame sections, it is sturdy in and of itself and is also stable as a room frame. It can be built up as boxes with walls on all or some sides, which opens up a multitude of spatial possibilities. The so-called Modular-T prototype from Neuchâtel measures approximately 3×4 meters and is 3 meters high. Altogether 57 elements are attached to a steel post construction up to three stories tall. Two outside staircases and a freight elevator handle the vertical access. The wooden building block unit, developed in cooperation with the Swiss Institute for Building Biology and the Fire Prevention Service, is produced in variable sizes. Among other things, it is intended for temporary replacement schoolhouses in the city of Thun that need to be assembled quickly. Possible application as inexpensive hotel construction is also being studied.

Die Stahlständerkonstruktion, zu drei Obergeschossen aufgesetzt
The steel post construction, set up for three floors

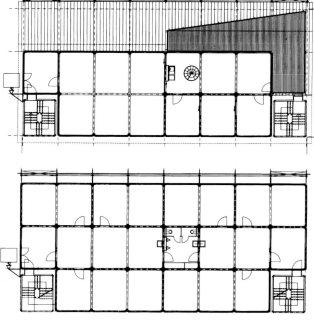

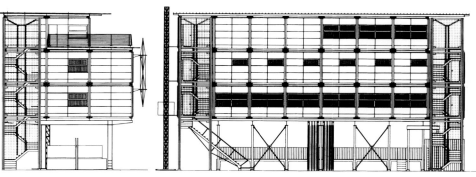

Erstes und zweites Obergeschoß, Querschnitt und Längsschnitt
First and second floors, cross section and elevation section

Bauart Architekten

Bundeshaus Bern, Parlamentsgebäude, Umbau der Untergeschosse, 1993–95.

Ehemalige Haustechnik- und Magazinräume sind in vollwertige Arbeitsräume umgewandelt worden. Dabei wurde die großzügige Raumstruktur des Hauses beibehalten beziehungsweise geklärt. In der segmentförmig geschweiften Bogenhalle unter der Bundeshausterrasse, die über zwei Geschosse offen und durch mächtige Stützpfeiler regelmäßig gegliedert ist, wurden 42 Arbeitsplätze für den Dienst für das amtliche Bulletin der Bundesversammlung eingebaut. Die Architekten ließen den großzügigen, von Süden mit Licht durchfluteten Raum offen. Eine Holzstruktur für Teilzeitarbeitsplätze, die auf kleinstem Raum alle nötigen Funktionen gewährleistet, aber auch Intimität vermittelt, wurde entlang der Innenwand der Bogenhalle und an den Pfeilerwänden dicht gereiht. In den Fensterkammern an der Außenmauer sind ständig belegte Büros eingerichtet. Im Keller unter der Kuppelhalle, durch die Stützpfeiler und -bogen der Subkonstruktion rhythmisch gegliedert, wurde eine Handbibliothek mit Arbeitsplätzen für Parlamentarier eingerichtet. Hier, wo kein Tageslicht einfällt, wurde mit ähnlichen Mitteln ein gegensätzliches Raumkonzept verwirklicht: Die Bibliothek, ein zweigeschossiger, geschlossener Bau aus Massivholz, bildet das zentrale Herzstück des ruhigen, introvertierten und mit edlem Mobiliar ausgestatteten Großraums.

Federal Building, Bern, Parliament House, Conversion of the Basement Floors, 1993–95.

Rooms housing the former engineering services and technical equipment for the building, plus storerooms, have been transformed into fully functional work areas. The generous spatial structure of the building has in the process been maintained, even clarified. In the segmented curving *Bogenhalle* under the Federal Building terrace, open to the height of two stories and divided by the regular placement of hefty support pillars, forty-two work places have been built to service the official bulletin of the Swiss Parliament. The architects have left the generous space open to the southern light that floods the room. A wooden structure for part-time work allows all necessary functions to be attended to in the smallest space, yet still imparts intimacy. A close row of these structures has been set along the inner wall of the *Bogenhalle* and on the pillared walls. Permanently occupied offices are set up in the windowed chambers of the outer wall, while in the cellar under the domed hall, a reference library with workspaces for the members of Parliament has been rhythmically arranged among the support pillars and arches of the substructure. Here, where no daylight falls, an opposite spatial concept has been put into effect using a similar means: the library, a compact two-story building made from solid wood, introverted and equipped with aristocratic furniture, forms the heart of this large, tranquil room.

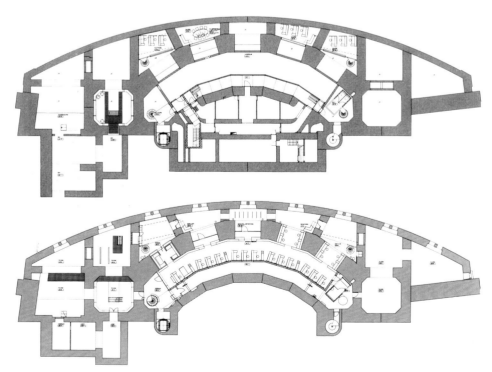

Handbibliothek für Parlamentarier
Reference library for Members of Parliament
Die Holzstrukturen der Teilzeitarbeitsplätze in der Gangzone
The wooden structures of the part-time work places in the passageway
Erstes und zweites Untergeschoß
First and second basement floors

Kindergarten Morillon, Wabern-Köniz, 1995.

Inmitten eines großräumigen, von Hochhäusern, weiten Rasenflächen und breiten Straßen geprägten Quartiers wurde ein allseitig umwandeter, introvertierter Hofraum ausgeschieden. Darin sind Kindergarten und Spielhof sowie ein Gartenhaus in einem Maßstab realisiert, den Kinder begreifen und in Besitz nehmen können. Der Hofbereich, bestimmt durch eine einfache Struktur und Materialisierung, ist eine eigene kleine Welt, die sich dezidiert von der gebauten Umgebung unterscheidet. Die eingeschossigen Gebäude nehmen die beiden Schmalseiten des rechteckigen Hofbereichs ein. An der Eingangsseite steht das gegen den Spielhof und das eigentliche Kindergartenhaus hin offene Garten- und Gerätehaus. Dem mit einer verglasten Front zum zentralen Spielhof hin geöffneten Kindergartenhaus vorgelagert ist eine Laube, Sonnenschirm und Regen-Außenspielplatz zugleich. Eine einfache, leicht nachvollziehbare Konstruktionsweise ergänzt das klare Raumkonzept: Ein Holzskelettbau mit naturbelassener Bretterverschalung aus Lärchenholz, das an den ausgesetzten Stellen rasch verwittert und gut wahrnehmbar Farbe und Oberfläche ändert. Auch im Innenraum wurden möglichst schadstoffarme Materialien aus umweltgerechter Produktion eingesetzt.

Morillon Kindergarten, Wabern-Köniz, 1995.

In the center of a wide-open quarter marked by high-rises, vast lawns and wide streets, an all-around convertible and introverted wooden space has been carved out. Inside, a kindergarten, playground and garden house have been realized in a scale that the children can comprehend and possess. The yard area is its own little world, defined through simple structure and materialization, and distinct from its developed surroundings. The one-story buildings occupy the two short sides of a rectangular courtyard. The open garden and equipment house stands on the entrance side across the playground from the actual kindergarten building. Directly before the kindergarten house, whose glass front opens onto the central playground, is a covered walk, sun shade and play area protected from the rain. A simple, easily duplicated method of construction complements the clear spatial concept: a wooden skeletal structure of natural larch wood slats that wear quickly in the weather at their exposed locations and noticeably change in color and surface. In the interior, too, the most non-toxic materials possible from environmentally friendly production processes have been employed.

Situationsmodell
Situation model

Das Kindergartenhaus
The kindergarten building
Übereckansicht des Garten- und Gerätehauses
Diagonal view of the garden and equipment house
Erschließungsweg entlang einer Betonmauer
Access way along a concrete wall

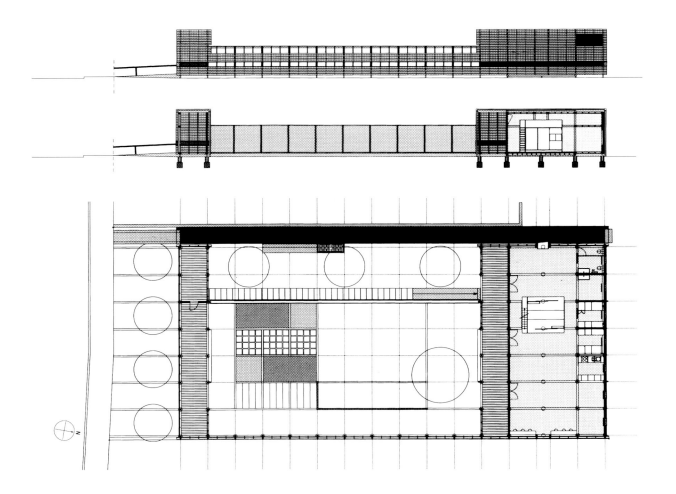
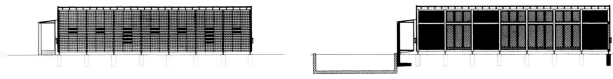

Ansicht von Osten, Längsschnitt und Grundriß
 View from the east, cross section, floor plan
Südfassade Geräte- und Gartenhaus
 Southwest equipment and garden house
Südfassade Kindergarten
 South façade of kindergarten

Bauart Architekten

Biografien

Reto Baer
1955 geboren in Zürich.
1972-76 Lehre als Hochbauzeichner in Langenthal.
1978-81 Ingenieurschule HTL in Burgdorf.
1981-85 Mitarbeit im Büro Rausser + Clémençon in Bern.
1985 Eigenes Büro in Bern mit Matthias Rindisbacher.
1987 Gründung Büro Bauart Architekten mit Matthias Rindisbacher und Peter C. Jakob.
1996 Aufnahme in den Bund Schweizer Architekten, BSA.

Willi Frei
1949 geboren in La Chaux-de-Fonds.
1969 Matura Typ C.
1969-75 Architekturstudium an der ETH Zürich.
1975 Diplom bei Professor Dolf Schnebli an der ETH Zürich.
1975/76 Assistenz bei Professor Franz Oswald an der ETH Zürich.
1977-81 Mitarbeit im Büro Ernst Gisel in Zürich.
1981-88 Mitarbeit im Büro Itten + Brechbühl in Bern.
Seit 1988 Partner im Büro Bauart Architekten in Bern.

Peter C. Jakob
1954 geboren in Seftigen.
1971-74 Lehre als Hochbauzeichner in Seftigen.
1975-78 Ingenieurschule HTL in Burgdorf.
1979-83 Mitarbeit im Büro Atelier 5 in Bern.
1983 Eigenes Büro in Bern.
1987 Gründung Büro Bauart Architekten mit Reto Baer und Matthias Rindisbacher.
1991-93 Co-Präsident Schweiz. Werkbund SWB, Ortsgruppe Bern.
1991 Mitgründer Architekturforum Bern.
1996 Aufnahme in den Bund Schweizer Architekten, BSA.

Matthias Rindisbacher
1955 geboren in Thun.
1971-75 Lehre als Hochbauzeichner in Thun.
1976-79 Ingenieurschule HTL in Biel.
1979-85 Mitarbeit im Büro Rausser + Clémençon in Bern.
1985 Eigenes Büro in Bern mit Reto Baer.
1987 Gründung Büro Bauart Architekten mit Reto Baer und Peter C. Jakob.

Marco Ryter
1954 geboren in Biel.
1969-73 Lehre als Hochbauzeichner in Biel.
1973-77 Ingenieurschule HTL in Biel.
1977-82 Mitarbeit im Büro Rausser + Clémençon in Bern.
1982-84 Projektleiter-Wiederaufbau für die Caritas-Schweiz in Süditalien.
1984-88 Mitarbeit im Büro Itten + Brechbühl in Bern.
Seit 1988 Partner im Büro Bauart Architekten in Bern.

Auszeichnungen
1989 ATU-Prix, Anerkennung, Stiftung Bernischer Kulturpreis für Architektur, Technik und Umwelt (Wohnhaus Zuber-Stähli in Mühlethurnen).
1989 Nomination für den Internationalen Eternitwettbewerb.
1995 ATU-Prix, Auszeichnung, Stiftung Bernischer Kulturpreis für Architektur, Technik und Umwelt (Kindergarten Morillon, Wabern-Köniz).

Werkverzeichnis

1986
Umbau Zahnarztpraxis Dr. Balsiger in Wattenwil BE.
Umbau Wohnhaus Feldeck, Bolligenstraße, Bern.

1987
Doppeleinfamilienhaus Stähli und Zuber in Mühlethurnen BE.
Quartierplanung Stadtbach, Bern.
Umbau Wohnhaus Stadtbachstraße, Bern.

1988
Unterstände für Zweiradfahrzeuge in Köniz BE.
Zentrumsüberbauung Gemeindeverwaltung und Dienstleistung in Baar ZG, Wettbewerb, dritter Preis.
Wohnhaus Gilliéron in Bern-Felsenau.

1989
Wohnhaus Kornhausgasse in Burgdorf BE, Wettbewerb, Ankauf.
Wohnüberbauung Sagi-Areal in Oberbipp BE, Wettbewerb, zweiter Preis.

1990
Umbau Haus Aebnit in Wattenwil BE.
Umbau Haus Schürch in Chabrey VD.
Bundesamt für Statistik in Neuenburg, Wettbewerb, erster Preis, Ausführung 1993-98.
Wohn- und Dienstleistungsbauten, Bern-Marzili, Wettbewerb, zweiter Preis.

1991
Gebäudeerhebung der bundeseigenen Bauten in der Region Bern.
Bahnhof und Dienstleistungsbauten in Aarau, Projektwettbewerb, zweiter Preis, Überarbeitung, Ideenwettbewerb, zweiter Preis.

1992
DIANE-Öko-Bau des Bundes, Forschungsprojekt.
Umbau Forsthaus in Schüpfen BE.
Bauprovisorium und Bahnwerkstätte in Neuenburg.

1993
Bahnhof Bümpliz-Süd BE, Nutzungsstudie.
Wohnüberbauung Etzmatt in Urtenen-Schönbühl BE, Wettbewerb, zweiter Rang, Ankauf.
Umbau Bundeshaus/Parlamentsgebäude in Bern, Büroarbeitsplätze für die Parlamentsdienste und Parlamentarierbibliothek (1993-95).

1994
Wohnüberbauung und Altersheim Roost in Zug, Wettbewerb.
Umbau Wohnhaus Brunnadernstraße Bern.

1995
Kindergarten Morillon in Wabern-Köniz BE.
Umbau Büroräumlichkeiten Dietiker und Jakob in Lenzburg AG.
Neubauten mit vorgefertigten Raumzellen in Thun BE: Schulhauserweiterung Länggasse, Kindergarten Aaremätteli, Kindergarten Bostudenzelg, Jugendtreff Lerchenfeld; Ausführung 1996/97.
Regionaltheater in Neuenburg, Wettbewerb.
Sanierung Kasernenareal in Bern, Wettbewerb.

1996
Umbau und Ausstellungsgestaltung einer Verkaufsstelle für Sanitärartikel in Bern.

Bibliografie

Jürg Burri, *So gut wird im Kanton Bern gebaut*, in: Der Bund, 30. Mai 1989.
Wohnbauten 2, in: Holz Bulletin 22/1989.
Zweifamilienhaus in Mühlethurnen, in: AS, Dezember 1989.
Werner Lehmann, *Modulares Holzskelett als Lösung*, in: Das Einfamilienhaus 6/1989.
Prototyp Velounterstand, in: AS, Mai 1990.
Wettbewerbe, Bundesamt für Statistik in Neuenburg, in: SIA 11/1990.
Zweifamilienhaus in Mühlethurnen, in: Zeitgemäßes Gestalten und Konstruieren mit Holz, 1991.
Vorstösse, zum Beispiel Bern, Umbau Haus Feldeck, in: archithese 2/1991.
Dossier Bahnhof, in: Werk, Bauen + Wohnen 3/1991.
Benedikt Loderer, *Nächster Halt: Aarau*, in: Hochparterre 3/1992.
Wettbewerbe, Bahnhofgebiet Aarau, in: SIA 8/1992.
Christoph Allenspach, *Berner Architektur im Banne der Moderne?*, in: Berner Zeitung, 21. Oktober 1994.
Christoph Allenspach, *Neue Bären, Berner Architekturszene*, in: Hochparterre 10/1994.
Christoph Allenspach, *Ein ungewöhnliches Reich für Kinder*, in: Berner Zeitung, 6. Februar 1995.
Katharina Matter, *Das Bäbihus ist das Liebste*, in: Der Bund, 8. April 1995.
Robert Walker, *Der Kindergarten in der Raumkiste*, in: Hochparterre 4/1995.
Christoph Allenspach, *Junge Architekten-Generation erntet erste Früchte*, in: Berner Zeitung, 27. Mai 1995.
Eine Welt für Kinder, in: Der Bund, 6. Februar 1995.
115 Bauten im Kanton Bern, Benteli Verlag, 1995.
Martin Tschanz, *Zur Architektur von Bauart Architekten*, in: Neue Zürcher Zeitung, 2. Februar 1996.
Andres Janser, *Raumzellen für Modul-Holzbausystem*, in: SIA 13/1996.
Christoph Allenspach, *Nationalräte und Ständeräte finden im Keller neue Oase der Ruhe*, in: Berner Zeitung, 8. Juli 1996.
Katharina Matter, *Parlamentarier ins Tiefparterre versetzt*, in: Der Bund, 8. Juli 1996.

Biographies

Reto Baer
1955 Born in Zurich.
1972-76 Apprenticeship as architectural drafter in Langenthal.
1978-81 Engineering school HTL in Burgdorf.
1981-85 Worked at office of Rausser + Clémençon in Bern.
1985 Own office in Bern with Matthias Rindisbacher.
1987 Founding of Bauart Architects with Matthias Rindisbacher and Peter C. Jakob.
1996 Admission into the Federation of Swiss Architects, BSA.

Willi Frei
1949 Born in La Chaux-de-Fonds.
1969 University entrance qualifying exam Type C.
1969-75 Studied architecture at the ETH Zurich.
1975 Graduated from the ETH Zurich under Professor Dolf Schnebli.
1975/76 Assistant to Professor Franz Oswald at the ETH Zurich.
1977-81 Worked in office of Ernst Gisel in Zurich.
1981-88 Worked in office of Itten + Brechbühl in Bern.
Since 1988 Partner in office of Bauart Architects in Bern.

Peter C. Jakob
1954 Born in Seftingen.
1971-74 Apprenticeship as architectural drafter in Seftingen.
1975-78 Engineering school HTL in Burgdorf.
1979-83 Worked in office of Atelier 5 in Bern.
1983 Own office in Bern.
1987 Founding of Bauart Architects with Reto Baer and Matthias Rindisbacher.
1991-93 Co-president Schweiz. Werkbund SWB, local chapter Bern.
1991 Co-founder Architekturforum Bern.
1996 Admission into the Federation of Swiss Architects, BSA.

Matthias Rindisbacher
1955 Born in Thun.
1971-75 Apprenticeship as architectural drafter in Thun.
1976-79 Engineering school HTL in Biel.
1979-85 Worked in office of Rausser + Clémençon in Bern.
1985 Own office in Bern with Reto Baer.
1987 Founding of Bauart Architects with Reto Baer and Peter C. Jakob.

Marco Ryter
1954 Born in Biel.
1969-73 Apprenticeship as architectural drafter in Biel.
1973-77 Engineering school HTL in Biel.
1977-82 Worked in office of Rausser + Clémençon in Bern.
1982-84 Project supervisor, reconstruction for Caritas, Switzerland in southern Italy.
1984-88 Worked in office of Itten + Brechbühl in Bern.
Since 1988 Partner in office of Bauart Architects in Bern.

Awards
1989 ATU-Prix, Acknowledgment, Foundation for the Bern Culture Prize for Architecture, Technology and Environment (residence home Zuber-Stähli in Mühlethurnen).
1989 Nomination for the International Eternit Competition.
1995 ATU-Prix, Award, Foundation for the Bern Culture Prize for Architecture, Technology and Environment (Morillon Kindergarten, Wabern-Köniz).

List of Works

1986
Conversion of Dental Practice Dr. Balsiger in Wattenwil.
Conversion of residence home Feldeck, Bollingenstrasse.

1987
Duplex residence home Stähli and Zuber in Mühlethurnen.
Town quarter plan, Stadtbach, Bern.
Conversion of residence home, Stadtbachstrasse.

1988
Bicycle and motorcycle shelter in Köniz.
Central superstructure for Community Administration and Services in Baar, competition, third prize.
Residence home Gilliéron in Bern-Felsenau.

1989
Residence home on Kornhausgasse in Burgdorf, competition, purchase.
Residential superstructure Sagi-Areal in Oberbipp, competition, second prize.

1990
Conversion of house Aebnit in Wattenwil.
Conversion of house Schürch in Chabrey.
Federal Department of Statistics in Neuchâtel, competition, first prize, construction 1993-98.
Residence and service buildings, Bern-Marzili, Competition, second prize.

1991
Survey of the federal buildings in the region of Bern.
Railway and service buildings in Aarau, project competition, second prize, revision, concept competition, second prize.

1992
DIANE-Öko-Bau des Bundes, research project.
Conversion of forest ranger house in Schüpfen.
Provisional building and railway workshops in Neuchâtel.

1993
Bümpliz South train station, utilization study.
Residence superstructure Etzmatt in Urtenen-Schönbühl, competition, second place, purchase.
Conversion Federal Building/Parliament House in Bern, office work places for Parliamentary Services and Parliamentary Library (1993-96).

1994
Residence superstructure and retirement home Roost in Zug, competition.
Conversion of residence home Brunnadernstrasse, Bern.

1995
Morillon Kindergarten in Wabern-Köniz.
Conversion of office premises of Dietiker and Jakob Corporation in Lenzburg.
New building with prefabricated units in Thun: expansion of Länggasse Schoolhouse, Aaremätteli Kindergarten, Bostudenzelg Kindergarten, Lerchenfeld Youth Center: construction 1996/97.
Regional theater in Neuchâtel, competition.
Redevelopment and renewal of Kasernenareal in Bern, competition.

1996
Conversion and exhibition design for retail outlet for hygenic articles in Bern.

Bibliography

Jürg Burri, *So gut wird im Kanton Bern gebaut,* in: Der Bund, May 30 1989.
Wohnbauten 2, in: Holz Bulletin 22/1989.
Zweifamilienhaus in Mühlethurnen, in: AS, December 1989.
Werner Lehmann, *Modulares Holzskelett als Lösung,* in: Das Einfamilienhaus 6/1989.
Prototyp Velounterstand, in: AS, May 1990.
Wettbewerbe, Bundesamt für Statistik in Neuenburg, in: SIA 11/1990.
Zweifamilienhaus in Mühlethurnen, in: Zeitgemässes Gestalten und Konstruieren mit Holz, 1991.
Vorstösse, zum Beispiel Bern, Umbau Haus Feldeck, in: archithese 2/1991.
Dossier Bahnhof, in: Werk, Bauen + Wohnen 3/1991.
Benedikt Loderer, *Nächster Halt: Aarau,* in: Hochparterre 3/1992.
Wettbewerb, Bahnhofgebiet Aarau, in: SIA 8/1992.
Christoph Allenspach, *Berner Architektur im Banne der Moderne?,* in: Berner Zeitung, October 21 1994.
Christoph Allenspach, *Neue Bären, Berner Architekturszene,* in: Hochparterre 10/1994.
Christoph Allenspach, *Ein ungewöhnliches Reich für Kinder,* in: Berner Zeitung, February 6 1995.
Katharina Matter, *Das Bäbihaus ist das Liebste,* in: Der Bund, April 8 1995.
Robert Walker, *Der Kindergarten in der Raumkiste,* in: Hochparterre 4/1995.
Christoph Allenspach, *Junge Architekten-Generation erntet erste Früchte,* in: Berner Zeitung, May 27 1995.
Eine Welt für Kinder, in: Der Bund, February 6 1995.
115 Bauten im Kanton Bern, Benteli Verlag, 1995.
Martin Tschanz, *Zur Architektur von Bauart Architekten,* in: Neue Zürcher Zeitung, February 2 1996.
Andres Janser, *Raumzellen für Modul-Holzbausystem,* in: SIA 13/1996.
Christoph Allenspach, *Nationalräte und Ständeräte finden im Keller neue Oase der Ruhe,* in: Berner Zeitung, July 8 1996.
Katharina Matter, *Palamentarier ins Tiefparterre versetzt,* in: Der Bund, July 8 1996.

Conradin Clavuot
Chur

Mitarbeiterinnen und Mitarbeiter
Collaborators
    Paula Deplazes
    Norbert Mathis

Anbau Haus Dr. Heinz | Residence Annex Dr. Heinz | Chur, 1995/96

Unterwerk Vorderprättigau | Power Substation Vorderprättigau | Seewis, 1993/94

Schulanlage | School Complex | St. Peter, 1994-98

Lapidar und intelligent.

In einem Unterwerk wird Strom aus dem Netz der Fernleitungen heruntertransformiert, um regional verteilt zu werden. Das Unterwerk für das Vorderprättigau steht in Seewis unmittelbar am Ende der ersten Schlucht nach Landquart, hart an der Landstraße, umfaßt von der Schlaufe einer abzweigenden Straße. Es wurde bereits mehrfach mit Architekturpreisen ausgezeichnet und doch dürfte es den meisten Passanten, trotz seiner prominenten Lage, kaum aufgefallen sein. Conradin Clavuot hat für die bescheidene Bauaufgabe eine wahrlich lapidare Architektur geschaffen. Wie ein mächtiger Felsbrocken liegt das Gebäude aus Sichtbeton in der Verkehrsinsel: ein Denkstein für die weitgehend unsichtbare Infrastruktur der Stromversorgung. Seine Form ist aus den exakten Raumbedürfnissen der umhüllten Maschinen entwickelt, um die sich der Beton «wie eine Tüte unter Vakuum» (Clavuot) schließt. Der Baukörper erhält so eine charakteristische Form, die zwingend wirkt, obwohl ihre Gesetzmäßigkeit nicht unmittelbar erkennbar ist. Er gleicht darin jenen eindrucksvollen Räumen, die in den Bauten der Kraftwerke oft quasi beiläufig und als Nebenprodukte der Ingenieurskunst entstehen.

Clavuot nutzt alle architektonischen Mittel, um diese Charakteristik zu stärken. Kein Dachblech und keine Tropfnase stört die Kubatur, die mit ihren Versprüngen als monolithisch, aber auch als zusammengesetzt gelesen werden kann. Im hohen Teil stehen die mächtigen Transformatoren, im niedrigen auf zwei Geschossen, zum Teil im Hang liegend, die Schalter und Verteiler. Eine zwar regelmäßige und sorgfältig ausgeführte, aber betont rohe Betonschalung und tief eingeschnittene Lüftungs- und Fensterschlitze unterstreichen die Massivität und Schwere des Körpers. Schwer sind auch die Türe und die Tore: bündig in die Fassade eingesetzt, sind sie ebenfalls aus Beton. Sie werden von einem verdeckten Stahlrahmen gehalten, so daß von außen nur ein schmaler Spalt und die Beschläge sichtbar sind. Besonders die zwei riesigen, mehr als dreieinhalb mal fünf Meter großen Tore für die Transformatoren wirken dadurch trotz ihres Gewichts von je etwa vier Tonnen wie Tapetentüren und lassen den massiven und groben Beton plötzlich als feine Membrane erscheinen. Für einen Moment ist man erstaunt, wie enorm schwer sie sind, wo man doch verblüfft sein müßte, daß sie sich überhaupt mühelos von einer Person bewegen lassen.

In diesem Unterwerk sind in exemplarischer Weise die architektonischen Themen des Umhüllens und der Körperhaftigkeit aufgenommen, doch ansonsten hat es mit üblicher Architektur nur wenig gemein. Dies hängt mit der Aufgabe des Baus zusammen, der praktisch ausschließlich Maschinen beherbergt und nur gelegentlich von Menschen für Kontroll- und Unterhaltsarbeiten aufgesucht wird. Entsprechend fehlen auf den Menschen zugeschnittene Räume und somit auch der menschliche Maßstab, wobei diese Fremdheit durch den Verzicht auf vertraute Formen zusätzlich betont wird.

Ganz andere Anforderungen stellen sich bei der Schulanlage für St. Peter, die nach einem gewonnenen Wettbewerb in der Projektphase steht. In dem relativ intakten Dorf, das nebst einer steinernen Kirche ausschließlich Holzbauten aufweist, soll neben den Schulräumen ein Mehrzwecksaal als Versammlungsort für die ganze Region entstehen. Clavuot führt mit zwei Baukörpern, die zusammen mit dem alten Schulhaus einen offenen Hof bilden, das bestehende Bebauungsmuster weiter. Als Holzbauten mit Giebeldach fügen sich die neuen Teile ein, wobei eine ruhige, relativ großmaßstäbliche Fassadengestaltung jegliche Anbiederung vermeidet. Wie die traditionellen Häuser sollen sie zudem als Strickbauten – aus gemeindeeigenem Holz – ausgeführt werden. Die massive Konstruktion, aus der auch das Dach geformt wird, soll dabei allerdings nicht außen, sondern innen zu liegen kommen, während an den Fassaden eine leichte, aber kompakte Schalung die zusätzlich notwendige Isolation schützt. Auf die Raumwirkung dieser schweren Massivkonstruktion darf man gespannt sein.

Clavuot gehört zu einer Reihe jüngerer Bündner Architekten, von denen sich viele an der Eidgenössischen Technischen Hochschule (ETH Zürich) im Traditionalismus der «analogen Architektur» geübt und zudem einige Zeit im Atelier von Peter Zumthor gearbeitet haben. Sie sind nicht auf eine bestimmte Formensprache fixiert und zeichnen sich durch einen behutsamen und bewußten, gleichzeitig aber völlig unsentimentalen Umgang mit der Tradition aus, die sie weiterentwickeln, anstatt sie erstarren und ersterben zu lassen. Basis dafür ist eine genaue Kenntnis der Materialien und ein innovativer Umgang mit oft traditionellen Konstruktionsweisen, worin sie von findigen Ingenieuren unterstützt werden. Erfreulicherweise schaffen die Behörden für diese Entwicklung ein günstiges Klima, so daß das Bündnerland derzeit zu den interessantesten Architekturregionen der Schweiz gehört. M. T.

Succinct and Intelligent.

In a power substation, electrical current from the transmission network is transformed to a lower voltage and distributed over the entire district. The substation for the Vorderprättigau region in Switzerland is located in Seewis, immediately at the end of the first ravine after Landquart, directly on the main country road, encircled by the loop of a branching exit. It has already been distinguished more than once with architectural prizes and still, despite its prominent location, it is hardly noticed by most passersby. Conradin Clavuot has created a truly succinct architecture for this construction task. The exposed concrete building sits like a powerful hunk of rock on an island in the traffic: a memorial to the largely invisible power supply infrastructure. Its form develops out of the exact spatial requirements of the machines encased in the concrete, as if the concrete were "like a bag in a vacuum" (Clavuot). The body of the building thus takes on a characteristic form that works compellingly, although its legitimacy is not immediately recognizable. In this respect it is like all other impressive spaces that often come about in the course of building power stations, almost in passing and as byproducts of the engineering.

Clavuot utilizes all architectonic elements to strengthen this characteristic. No sheet metal roofing, no pointed rain gutter disturbs the cubature, which can be read with its slits either as monolithic or as compound. The powerful transformers are located in the upper part; in the lower are two floors which lie partly in the incline, the control floor and the distribution floor. A truly regular and carefully executed, yet accented, raw concrete facing plus deeply cut ventilator and window slits underline the massiveness and weight of the building. The doors and gates are also heavy: set flush into the façade and made as well from concrete, they are held by concealed steel frames so that from the outside only the narrow fissure and fittings are visible. The two gigantic portals for the transformers, more than 3.5 × 5 meters in size, act, despite their weight of more than four tons apiece, as jib doors and allow the coarse solid concrete to suddenly appear as a fine membrane. For a moment, one is astounded at how enormously heavy they are; while actually one should be dumbfounded that they can be effortlessly manipulated by one person.

The architectural themes of sheath and solidity are taken up in the facility in an exemplary way, but the facility itself has little in common with more general architecture. This has to do with the function of the building, which almost exclusively houses machines and is visited only occasionally by people for control and maintenance work. Missing, therefore, are the rooms tailored to human beings and consequently also the human scale. This feeling of alien strangeness is additionally emphasized through the renunciation of familiar forms.

Entirely other demands needed to be met for the St. Peter school complex, in the project phase of construction as the result of winning a competition. With the exception of the stone church, the relatively intact village boasts almost exclusively wooden buildings. Next to the church, a multipurpose hall was to be built as the gathering place for the whole region. Clavuot carries on the existing pattern of development with two building units that join with the old schoolhouse to form an open courtyard. Wooden structures with gabled roofs, the new sections fit with the old in a calm, relatively large scale façade design that avoids ingratiation. They are to be constructed from the community's own wood like the traditional houses, in *Strickbau,* an extremely strong method of frameworking. The solid construction, out of which the roof is also formed, is thereby to be seen on the inside, certainly not on the outside, where a light but compact covering offers the façade protection from the elements. The three-dimensional effect of this massive construction is dramatic.

Clavuot belongs to a series of young Grisons architects, many of which practiced the traditionalism of *analoge Architektur* at the Swiss Technical University (ETH Zurich) and some of which worked for a time at the atelier of Peter Zumthor. They are not fixated on a definite formal language but are noted instead for a careful and deliberate, fully unsentimental interaction with tradition, which they would rather develop further than leave to atrophy and die out. The basis for this is an exact knowledge of materials and an innovative dealing with often traditional construction methods, in which endeavor they are supported by resourceful engineers. Happily, the authorities create a favorable climate for this development. As a result, the canton of Grisons belongs to one of the most interesting architectural regions of Switzerland. M. T.

Schulanlage St. Peter, Werkraum, 1994-98
St. Peter School complex, workroom, 1994-98

Anbau Haus Dr. Heinz, Chur (Bauingenieur: Jürg Conzett), 1995/96.

Ausgangslage war ein Einfamilienwohnhaus, welches zu Beginn der sechziger Jahre gebaut worden war. Das Erdgeschoß steht auf einem betonierten Untergeschoß und wird oben durch eine Ständerbaukonstruktion zu einem zweistöckigen Haus mit Giebeldach ergänzt. Das Erdgeschoß ist gemauert und innen und außen weiß gegipst oder verputzt. Das Obergeschoß ist innen weiß ausgekleidet und außen durch palisanderbraun gebeizte Fichtenholzbretter geschützt. Die Fenster sind aus Holz, sprossenlos und weiß gestrichen. Im Jahre 1980 wurde nordseitig in unauffälliger Weise angebaut.

Die Aufgabe bestand darin, das Einfamilienhaus in ein Zweifamilienhaus umzubauen. Die zwei Wohnungen sollten dabei auf je ein Geschoß zu liegen kommen. Platz für eine Erweiterung fand sich – topographisch und parzellengeometrisch bedingt – nur auf der Ostseite, auf einer kleinen, ebenen Fläche. Durch das Aufteilen des Einfamilienhauses ergab sich im Erdgeschoß der Bedarf an Schlafzimmern und im Obergeschoß der Bedarf eines Wohnzimmers mit Außenraum. Entscheidend für den Entwurf war der Ansatz, das Schöne des Altbaus zu respektieren und ihn mit dem Neubau in einen Zusammenhang zu stellen – gewissermaßen mit dem Altbau zu flirten. Dafür wurden – auf sehr direkte Weise – Oberflächen und Farben des bestehenden Baus übernommen. Der Neubau wird dabei sehr nahe an den Altbau gestellt. Es entsteht ein Neben- und Miteinander; Übergänge werden gelesen, sind aber klar getrennt; Volumen werden zusammengesetzt, sind aber total verschieden. Der Neubau ergänzt das Bestehende und führt dies zu einem neuen Ganzen – zu einer neuen Einheit.

Residence Annex Dr. Heinz, Chur (Construction Engineer: Jürg Conzett), 1995/96.

The departure point was a one-family residence home built at the beginning of the 1960's. The ground floor stands over a cast concrete basement and will be converted into a two-story house with gabled roof by means of an added story post and beam construction. The ground floor has been masoned and plastered or finished white inside and out. The upper floor has a white surface inside and is protected by palisander brown stained spruce wood boards outside. The windows are wooden with no sash bars and painted white. In 1980, the north side was inconspicuously annexed.

The task consisted of converting the one-family house into a two-family house. In the process, the apartments were to be placed on one floor. Allowing for topographic and geometric needs relating to the parcel, there was room for expansion only on the east side, on a small flat plain. Through the allocation of space, it was requested that the bedrooms be placed on the ground floor and a livingroom with an outer extension on the upper. It was emphatic for the design to respect the beauty of the old building and to place it in a correlation with the new building – to let the new flirt with the old, so to speak. To this end, surfaces and colors from the existing building were – in a very direct way – adopted. In so doing, the new building was brought close to the old. A situation of "next to one another and together" arises; transitions can be read but are clearly separate, volumes are placed together but are totally different. The new building complements the existing building and leads it to a new whole – to a new unity.

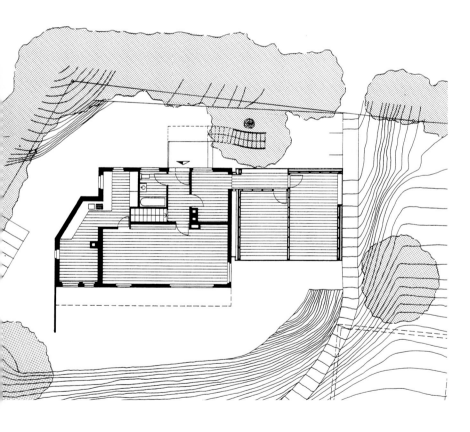
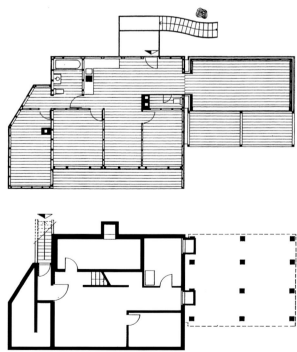

Erdgeschoß, Obergeschoß und Untergeschoß
Ground floor, upper floor, basement

Der Übergang zwischen dem bestehenden Haus und dem Anbau an der Rückseite (Ostfassade)
　The transition between the existing house and the annex from the back (east façade)
Ansicht vom Garten
　View from the garden

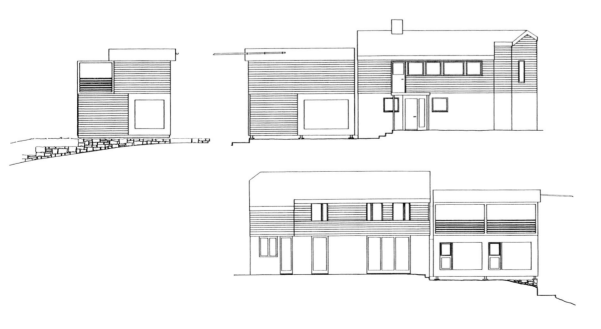

Südfassade, Ostfassade und Westfassade
　South façade, east façade and west façade

Unterwerk Vorderprättigau, Seewis (Bauingenieur: Jürg Conzett), 1993/94.

Für die Übertragung der elektrischen Energie vom Erzeuger (Kraftwerkzentrale) bis zum Verbraucher sind aus wirtschaftlichen Gründen verschiedene Spannungsebenen notwendig. Die Funktion eines Unterwerkes besteht nun darin, diese elektrische Energie von einer Spannungsebene auf eine andere – zumeist niedrigere – zu transformieren. Im Unterwerk befinden sich Schaltanlagen und Transformatoren, die diese rein technische Funktion ausführen. Die elektrische Energie erreicht nun mit einer hohen Spannung das Unterwerk und verläßt dieses mit einer niedrigeren Spannung in Richtung Versorgungsgebiet. Die Maschinen werden allesamt von einer weit entfernt liegenden Kraftwerkzentrale aus ferngesteuert.

Im Bereich Grüsch-Seewis/Station-Valzeina mußte ein geeigneter Standort gefunden werden. Das gewählte Bauland liegt ideal unter der 50-KV-Leitung und ebenfalls in einem Knotenpunkt der 10-KV-Leitung (Regionalversorgung). Dieser Punkt befindet sich im Niemandsland zwischen den Fahrbahnen einer vielbefahrenen Kreuzung der Prättigauerstraße. Die Bedingungen der Bauherrschaft, der AG Bündner Kraftwerke, Klosters, waren optimaler Schutz der Maschinen vor äußeren Einflüssen (Wasser, Schnee, Straße) und Übersichtlichkeit im Verkehrsknotenpunkt.

Power Substation Vorderprättigau, Seewis (Construction Engineer: Jürg Conzett), 1993/94.

In the transfer of electrical energy from the producer (the main power station) to the user, various voltage levels are necessarily employed for economic reasons. The function of a substation lies in the transformation of this electrical energy from one voltage to another, primarily to the next lower, and there, one finds switch systems and transformers that carry out this purely technical function. The electricity reaches the substation at a high voltage level and leaves at a lower voltage in the direction of its service zone. The machines are all remote-controlled from the distant main power station.

In the region Grüsch–Seewis/Station–Valzeina, a suitable location had to be found. The selected site lies ideally under the 50-KV main and likewise at an intersection point with the 10-KV main (for regional service). This point is located in a no man's land between the roadways of a heavily travelled intersection of Prättigauerstrasse. The requirements of the clients, the Graubünden power utility company in Klosters, were optimal protection of the machines against seepage from the outside (water, snow and street) and clarity of the traffic intersection point.

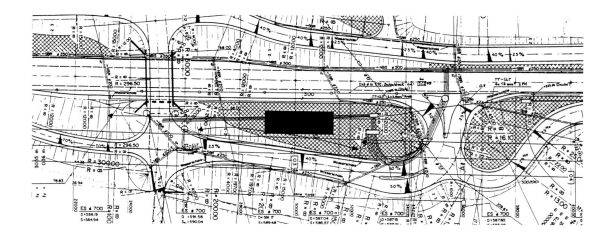

Situation
Situation
Ansicht von der Prättigauerstraße
View from Prättigauerstrasse

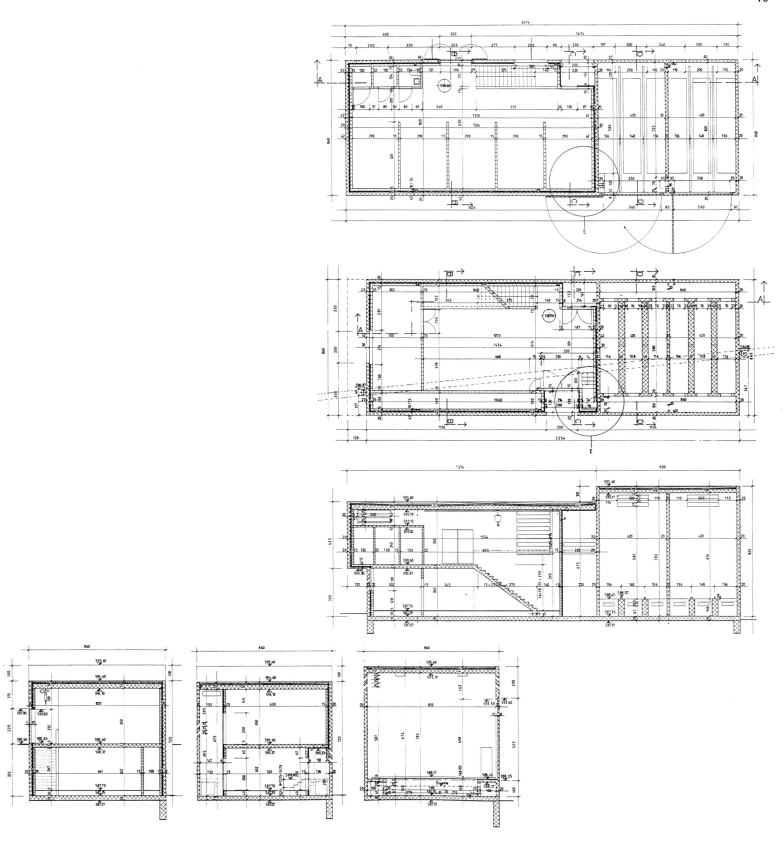

Grundrisse Obergeschoß und Erdgeschoß
　Floor plans, upper floor and ground floor
Längsschnitt
　Elevation section
Querschnitte
　Cross sections

Ansicht von der Ausfahrtsstraße
View from the exit road
Ansicht von der Kantonsstraße; die Türen aus Eisenbeton wirken in geöffnetem Zustand trotz ihrer Dimensionen (5,25 m × 3,60 m × 10 cm) leicht und beweglich
View from Kantonsstrasse; the iron concrete doors are light and easy to swing despite their Size (5,25 m × 3,60 m × 10 cm)

Conradin Clavuot

Schulanlage in St. Peter GR (Bauingenieur: Jürg Conzett), 1994–98.

Wenn man Chur Richtung Arosa verläßt, tritt man schon bald in eine sehr bäuerliche, weite Talschaft ein: das Schanfigg. Verschiedene kleinere Dörfer säumen den Weg bis zum Talschluß. Die Topografie der Talhänge zeigt eine rege Abfolge von tief eingefressenen, engen Schluchten zu leicht abfallenden, milden Wiesen. Diese wiederum werden von beinahe rhythmisch auftretenden, mit dem Berg fallenden Hangrippen eingefaßt. Auf diesen Rippen und den dazwischen sich ausbreitenden fruchtbaren Flächen wurden die Dörfer errichtet. Oberhalb der Waldgrenze liegen auf wiesenreichen Terrassen die Alpweiden mit den Maiensässen.

Es ist doch sehr erstaunlich, daß hier, in so kurzer Distanz zur Stadt, zur Autobahn und so weiter, sich ganze Siedlungen zeigen, die sich in ihrer baulichen Struktur noch genau gleich wie vor dreihundert Jahren befinden. Mit wenigen Elementen, wie der präzisen Stellung der Gebäude zueinander, zur Sonne und zum Tal, oder der einfachsten und sehr stark das bauliche und materialhafte Volumen betonenden Aufbauart in Strickbau, werden die raumbildenden Bedürfnisse erfüllt. Die Schönheit und die Kraft dieser baulichen Tradition soll in der nun geplanten und vor der Ausführung stehenden Mehrzweckanlage umgesetzt werden.

School Complex in St. Peter, Grisons (Construction Engineer: Jürg Conzett), 1994–98.

Leaving Chur in the direction of Arosa, one soon enters a wide, very rustic valley community, the Schanfigg. A variety of small villages line the way to the end of the valley. The topography of the incline shows a vivid succession from deeply cut narrow ravines to mild, gently sloping meadows. These in turn are framed by nearly rhythmically arranged ribs leading vertically down the side of the mountain incline. On these ribs and on the spreading fertile plains in between, the villages are situated. Above the forest line on terraces rich with meadows lie pastures with fields for Spring grazing.

It is amazing, though, that here, such a short distance from city, highway, and so on, whole settlements appear the same in their architectural structure as were found three hundred years ago. With few elements, such as the precise positioning of the buildings in relation to one another, to the sun and to the valley, or the simplest and extremely strong framework construction method, *Strickbau*, with its stress upon the constructive and material volumes, the three-dimensional requirements are met. The beauty and strength of this building tradition is to be realized in a planned and a soon-to-be executed multipurpose complex.

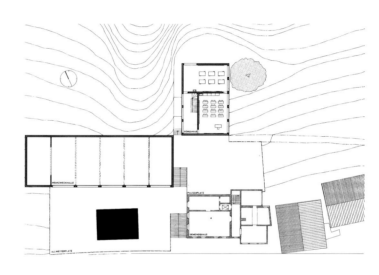

Grundriß, Perspektiven der Mehrzweckhalle und Situation
  Ground plan, perspectives of multipurpose hall and situation

Perspektive der Schulanlage:
links die Mehrzweckhalle mit dem Allwetterplatz,
dahinter das Schulhaus mit dem Pausenplatz,
rechts das bestehende Gemeindehaus
  Perspective of the school complex:
    on the left, the multipurpose hall with all-weather area,
    behind, the schoolhouse with recess yard,
    on the right, the existing community center

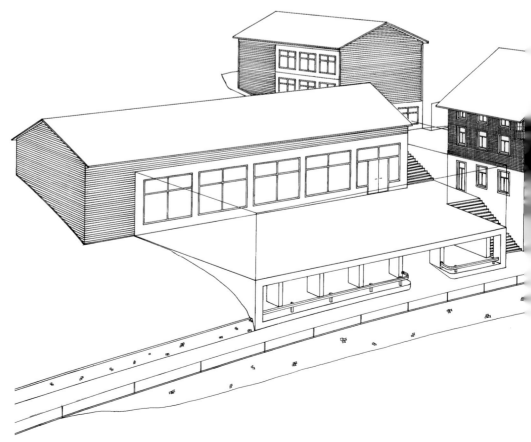

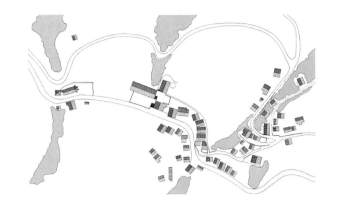

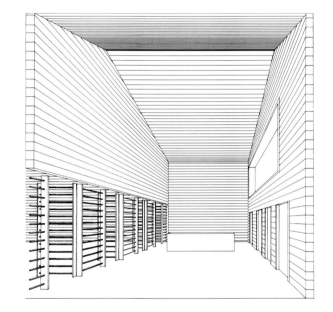
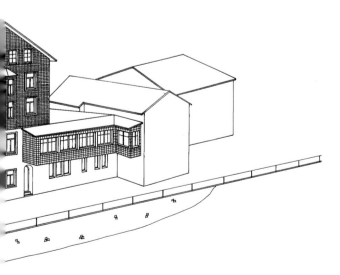

Conradin Clavuot

| **Biografie** | **Werkverzeichnis** | **Bibliografie** |

Conradin Clavuot
1962 geboren in Davos.
Seit 1964 wohnhaft in Chur.
1982-87 Architekturstudium an der ETH Zürich.
1988 Diplom bei Prof. Fabio Reinhart.
Seit 1988 eigenes Büro in Chur.

Auszeichnungen
1994 *Gute Bauten im Kanton Graubünden,* Unterwerk Vorderprättigau.
1996 *Neues Bauen in den Alpen,* Unterwerk Vorderprättigau.

1988
Wohnhaus in Rhäzüns, Projekt.

1989
Fitnesscenter in Le Prese GR.
Autohaus in Chur, I + II + III, Projekt, 1989-96.

1990
Gartenhaus in Chur GR.

1991
Autowaschanlage in Chur GR.
Wohnhaus im Fextal, Oberengadin GR, Umbau/Sanierung.

1993
Wohnhaus in Cortébert BE, Umbau.
Coiffeursalon in Andeer GR, in Zusammenarbeit mit Christian Kerez.

1994
Unterwerk Vorderprättigau in Seewis GR.
Mehrzweckanlage in St. Peter GR, Wettbewerb, erster Preis, Weiterbearbeitung und Baubeginn im Herbst 1996.

1995
Sieben-Familien-Wohnhaus in Chur, Umbau.

1996
Zweifamilienwohnhaus Dr. Heinz in Chur, Anbau/Umbau.
Sportzentrum St. Moritz, Wettbewerb, erster Preis, in Zusammenarbeit mit Lorenzo Giuliani und Christian Hönger, Zürich.
Zweifamilienwohnhaus in Klosters, Anbau/Umbau, Projekt.

Conradin Clavuot, Jürg Ragettli, *Die Kraftwerkbauten im Kanton Graubünden,* Chur 1991.

Biography	**List of Works**	**Bibliography**

Conradin Clavuot
1962 Born in Davos.
Resident of Chur since 1964.
1982-87 Studied architecture at the ETH Zurich.
1988 Graduated under Professor Fabio Rheinhart.
Since 1988 own office in Chur.

Distinctions
1994 *Gute Bauten im Kanton Graubünden,* Power Substation Vorderprättigau.
1996 *Neues Bauen in den Alpen,* Power Substation Vorderprättigau.

1988
Residence in Rhäzüns, project.

1989
Fitness Center in Le Prese, Grisons.
Auto garage in Chur, I + II + III, project, 1989-96.

1990
Garden house in Chur, Grisons.

1991
Car wash in Chur, Grisons.
Residence in Fextal, Oberengadin, Grisons, conversion/renewal.

1993
Residence in Cortébert, Bern, conversion.
Hair salon in Andeer, Grisons, in collaboration with Christian Kerez.

1994
Power Substation Vorderprättigau in Seewis, Grisons.
Multipurpose complex in St. Peter, Grisons, competition, first prize, further development and beginning of construction in Fall 1996.

1995
Seven-Family Residence in Chur, conversion.

1996
Two-family residence, Dr. Heinz in Chur, annex/conversion.
Sport center, St. Moritz, competition, first prize, in collaboration with Lorenzo Giuliani and Christian Hönger, Zurich.
Two family residence in Klosters, annex/conversion, project.

Conradin Clavuot, Jürg Ragettli, *Die Kraftwerkbauten im Kanton Graubünden,* Chur 1991.

Beat Consoni

Rorschach

Wohnhaus Sonderegger | Sonderegger Residence | Frasnacht, 1989–94

Sanierung Wohnhaus Gnädinger | Renewal Gnädinger Residence | St. Gallen, 1992/93

Wohnhaus an der Seestraße | Residence on Seestrasse | Horn, 1993–95

Wettbewerbe | Competitions | 1990–96

Mitarbeiterinnen und Mitarbeiter seit 1980
Collaborators since 1980
- Hansjörg Affolter
- Philipp Bienz
- Teodor Biert
- Ralph Büsser
- Ivana Consoni
- Christian Dill
- Karl Dudler
- Daniel Engler
- Lukas Imhof
- Daniel Keiser
- Matthias Keller
- Manfred Kunz
- Elisabeth Merkt
- Andy Senn
- Gioni Signorell
- Veronika Summerauer
- Toni Thaler
- Daniel Walser
- Johannes Wick

Starke Körper.

Das berühmteste Haus von Beat Consoni steht in Frasnacht, im Kanton Thurgau: ein Einfamilienhaus, das wie eine Skulptur in die liebliche Landschaft gesetzt ist. Die Komposition aus drei sich durchdringenden Kuben bildet einen markanten Grenzpunkt zum anschließenden Siedlungsgebiet, auf das sie zwar mit gewissen Strukturmerkmalen reagiert, von dem sie sich in ihrer Architektursprache dafür um so deutlicher abhebt. Der Bau erinnert trotz Sichtbeton und anderen «brut» verwendeten Materialien in seiner geometrischen Klarheit an Objekte des russischen Suprematismus oder in seiner Eleganz und räumlichen Differenziertheit an Villen des International Style und erreicht gerade in dieser Mischung von Kargheit und Großzügigkeit seinen eigenständigen Ausdruck.

Es ist nicht selbstverständlich, daß Beat Consoni heute vorwiegend in der Bodenseeregion tätig ist. Nach der Bauzeichnerlehre in Rorschach und nach Studien in Burgdorf, Salzburg und Brugg-Windisch begann er seine Tätigkeit im Engadin, mit dem er seit seiner Schulzeit verbunden ist. In Scuol errichtete er 1984–86 das Center Augustin, einen größeren Komplex mit Läden, einer Bank und Wohnungen. Der Bau, der mit seiner städtischen Haltung an die älteren Hotelbauten im Ort anknüpft, wurde zwar 1987 mit dem Preis «Gute Bauten im Kanton Graubünden» ausgezeichnet, löste jedoch im Ort heftige Polemiken aus.

Während das Center Augustin noch aus verschiedenen Elementen besteht, die addiert auf die spezifische Situation reagieren, sind die jüngeren Bauten und Projekte von Beat Consoni einfacher und volumetrisch klarer. Consoni geht von schlichten, wohlproportionierten Kuben aus, die den spezifischen Gegebenheiten von Ort und Programm entsprechend angepaßt werden, ohne dabei jedoch ihre Ganzheit zu verlieren. Außenräume entstehen dabei durch die Spannung zwischen den einzelnen Körpern.

Beim Haus Gnädinger in St. Gallen beispielsweise etabliert ein quadratischer Garagenpavillon eine völlig neue Beziehung des sanierten Wildhüterhauses zur Umgebung. Die Ausrichtung zum nach Norden hin sanft abfallenden Gelände wird verstärkt, und im Westen bildet sich ein Vorplatz, der den Zugang auf der ehemaligen Rückseite des Hauses aufwertet. Wie das alte Gebäude hat auch der Pavillon eine geschlossene Wetterfront, die ihn von Westen als einen schweren Köper erscheinen läßt. Nur andeutungsweise ist hier die starke Auskragung erkennbar, die das Volumen nach Norden zur offenen Landschaft hin ausrichtet. Die Orientierung der Fenster schließlich und die Ausbildung der Deckenplatte, die mit der Westwand einen Winkel aus Beton bildet, öffnen den Pavillon nach Osten und schaffen einen starken Bezug zum Wildhüterhaus. Aus der ungerichteten quadratischen Grundform entsteht so ein komplexes Gebilde, das auf allen Seiten präzise auf die Gegebenheiten des Ortes reagiert. Die Materialisierung in Sichtbeton, grau schimmerndem Aluminiumblech und Glas hilft dabei mit, daß die Einheit nicht verlorengeht.

An der Sanierung des Wildhüterhauses bestätigt sich Consonis Sensibilität für Materialien, für einmal nicht im Zusammenhang mit seinem bevorzugten Baustoff Sichtbeton. In Übersetzung des alten Zustandes differenziert er die ehemaligen Wohn- und Wirtschaftsteile, wobei das Material Holz, einmal in Form einer feinen Horizontallattung, einmal als rechteckige, bakelisierte Sperrholzplatten verwendet, den Zusammenhang garantiert. Die Wetterfront wird wie bei üblichen Sanierungen mit einem günstigen, wetterfesten Material verkleidet. Nicht Eternit oder Blech jedoch kommen zur Anwendung, sondern transluzente Stegplatten aus Polycarbonat, wie man sie als Glasersatz bei Gewächshäusern oder Industriebauten verwendet. Sie lassen die dahinterliegende, tiefblau gefärbte Bretterverschalung durchschimmern und schaffen mit ihrem Glanz und ihrer Farbigkeit, die sich je nach Lichtverhältnissen stark verändert, einen Bezug zu den Materialien des Pavillons. Die Eigenschaften des Produktes erlauben es zudem, hinter der Schutzschicht die bestehenden Öffnungen zu belassen, ohne die typische Geschlossenheit solcher Westfronten zu zerstören. Zusammen mit einem einzelnen echten Fenster bildet sich so bei aller flächigen Homogenität eine differenzierte Fassade.

Obwohl die wenigen Bauten von Beat Consoni mit ihren skulpturalen, räumlichen und haptischen Qualitäten in der Fachwelt Anerkennung finden, waren sie aufgrund anfänglichen Widerstands seitens der Behörden oft nur mit etlichen Schwierigkeiten realisierbar. Für Bauherren, Architekt und letztlich auch die Öffentlichkeit hat sich der oft schwierige Weg jedoch gelohnt. M. T.

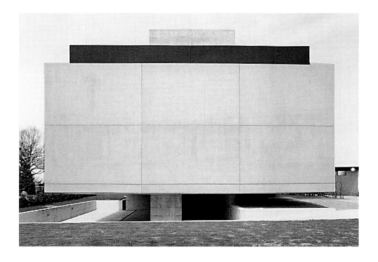

Wohnhaus an der Seestraße, Horn, 1993-95
Residence on Seestrasse, Horn, 1993-95

Powerful Elements.

Beat Consoni's best-known house stands in Frasnacht, in the Canton of Thurgau: a one-family residence set in the lovely landscape like a sculpture. The composition of three intersecting cubes forms a distinct border to the adjacent housing development, to which the composition, in fact, responds with certain structural characteristics, but to which it even more strongly contrasts in its architectural language. Despite exposed concrete and other *brut* materials, the building's geometric clarity recalls objects of Russian Suprematism; its elegance and spatial differentiation remind one of villas in the International Style. And it is exactly this combination of sparseness and generosity that achieves its independent expression.

It is not self-evident that Beat Consoni is predominantly active today in the region of Lake Constance. Following his apprenticeship in constructional drafting in Rorschach and his studies in Burgdorf, Salzburg and Brugg-Windisch, he began practicing his profession in the Engadine, with which he has had a connection since his school years. In Scuol from 1984–86 he erected the Center Augustin, a larger complex with shops, a bank and apartments. The building, which has an urban bearing and takes off on the older hotel buildings in the town, was awarded the "Good Building in Canton Grisons" prize in 1987, but has nevertheless stirred up hefty controversy in the area.

While the Center Augustin is composed of various elements that respond as a whole to the specific location, later buildings and projects by Consoni are simpler and volumetrically clearer. Beat Consoni proceeds from plain, well-proportioned cubes that are correspondingly designed to suit the specific existing situation of the location and program without losing their wholeness in the process. Exterior spaces arise through the tension between the individual elements.

At the Gnädinger House in St. Gallen, a quadrangular garage pavilion establishes a fully new relationship between the upgraded gamekeeper's house and its surroundings. The orientation of the house toward the terrain gently sloping away towards the north is strengthened, and in the west a forecourt is formed that upgrades the approach to the house from what was once the rear. The pavilion has a closed weather front, as does the old building, that looks from the west like a heavy twill weave. The powerful cantilever is only hinted at from here. Its volume faces out toward the open countryside in the north. Ultimately, the orientation of the windows and the development of the floor panel, which forms an angle of concrete with the west wall, opens the pavilion up to the east and creates a strong relationship with the gamekeeper's house. Out of a non-directional quadrangular ground space a very complex structure arises that responds precisely to the location on all sides. The material choice of exposed concrete, shimmering gray aluminum sheeting and glass supports the unity of the composition.

The renewal of the gamekeeper's house confirms Consoni's sensitiveness to materials, for once not in connection with his preferred building material, exposed concrete. In translating the old situation, he has differentiated between former living and working areas; wood, here in the form of horizontal lathing, there as square bakelite impregnated plywood panels, guarantees the continuity. The weather front has been covered with an inexpensive weatherproofing material, as in standard renewals. Neither Eternit nor metal sheeting was used, but rather translucent polycarbonate web panels as can be seen on greenhouses or industrial buildings as a replacement for glass. They let the deep blue wooden shutters shimmer through from behind and their gloss and their color, which alters dramatically according to the light intensity, create a relationship with the material of the pavilion. The properties of the products, moreover, allow the existing openings to be left behind the protective layers without disturbing the typical closed appearance of such weather fronts. Together with a single genuine window, a differentiated façade is thus formed out of each flat homogeneity.

Although Beat Consoni's few buildings, with their sculptural, spatial and tactile qualities, have found recognition in professional circles, they were, due to resistance on the part of officials, often actually built only with some difficulty. For the clients, the architect and ultimately also the public, however, the difficult path to realization has paid off. M. T.

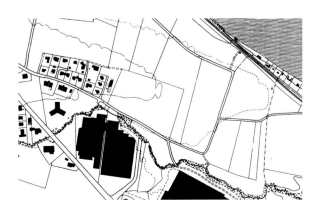

Fassade zum See
　Lakeside façade
Ansicht von Süden
　View from the south
Situation
　Situation

Wohnhaus Sonderegger, Frasnacht, 1989-1994.

Das Wohnhaus Sonderegger ist Teil eines Gesamtprojektes am Siedlungsrand in Frasnacht. Es bildet städtebaulich den Abschluß des Siedlungsgebietes gegen eine Landschaftsschutzzone. Der Baukörper weist in der Lage die gleiche Geometrie auf wie die bestehende Bebauung im Westen und steht senkrecht zum leicht abfallenden Südhang. Der kubische Aufbau setzt sich aus einem stehenden und einem liegenden Körper sowie einem Sockelgeschoß zusammen. Beim stehenden Körper sind die Innenräume über eine raumhohe, zweigeschossige Glasfront zur freien Landschaft und zum See hin orientiert. Der räumlich geschlossene, liegende Körper bildet im Inneren mit dem stehenden zusammen eine zweigeschossige Eingangshalle, von der aus eine Treppe ins Erdgeschoß führt. Ein Bandfenster im Erdgeschoß mit Ausblick auf die freie Landschaft belichtet die Kinderzimmer und die Wohndiele. Auf dem liegenden Volumen befindet sich eine Sonnenterrasse, die dem Wohn- und dem Elternschlafzimmer vorgelagert ist. Im Sockelgeschoß sind die Garage, die Technik und ein Gästezimmer mit einem Außenhof angeordnet. Auf der Südseite des Hauses befindet sich ein Schwimmbad und ein Außenspielplatz. Eine Gartenhalle schließt diesen Außenraum ab.

Sonderegger Residence, Frasnacht, 1989-1994.

The Sonderegger Residence is part of a larger project on the border of a housing development in Frasnacht and forms the developmental border between the housing and a landscape protection zone. The building exhibits the same geometry of location as the existing development to the west and stands vertically above a gently sloping southern incline. One standing and one reposing element, plus a basement, make up the cubic structure. Inside the vertical element the interior spaces are oriented over a floor-to-ceiling, two-story glass front facing the open countryside and the lake. Inside, the spatially closed horizontal element, together with the vertical, forms a two-story entrance hall with stairs leading to the ground floor where a band of windows brightens the children's rooms and the entrance hall with light from the wide open view. A sun terrace on the horizontal unit is placed directly in front of the livingroom and master bedroom. The garage, the house engineering room, and a guest room with an outer courtyard are arranged on the basement floor. On the south side of the house is a swimming-pool and outer play area complete with garden hall.

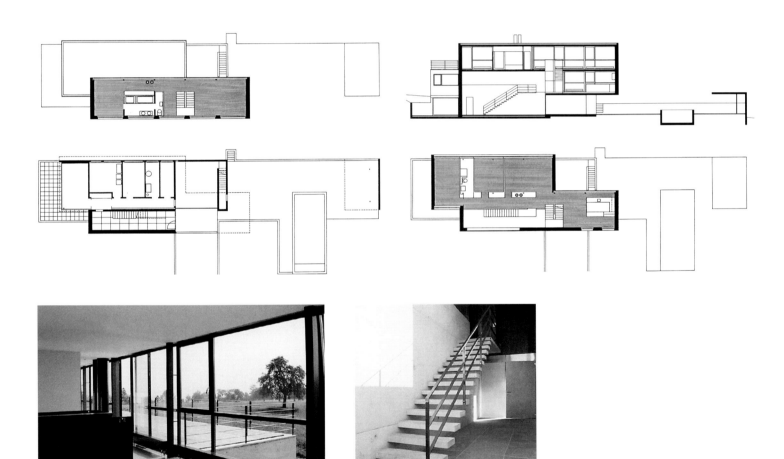

Dachgeschoß, Längsschnitt, Erdgeschoß und Obergeschoß
  Attic, elevation section, ground floor and upper floor
Blick vom Wohnzimmer im Dachgeschoß
  View from the attic livingroom
Treppe in der Eingangshalle
  Stairway in the entrance hall

Sanierung Wohnhaus Gnädinger, St. Gallen, 1992/93.

Das Wohnhaus mit kleinem Stall in einer Waldlichtung unweit von St. Gallen ist für einen Wildhüter um die Jahrhundertwende erstellt worden. Da das Objekt außerhalb der Bauzone und innerhalb des Waldabstandes liegt, konnte die Nutzung nur um ein Bad mit WC und eine Küche erweitert werden. Damit der Wohnanteil in seiner Grundstruktur belassen werden konnte, sind die neuen Nutzungen in einem vom bestehenden Objekt statisch unabhängigen Baukörper in das Stallgebäude eingebaut worden. In einem neuen, würfelförmigen Nebengebäude ist eine Doppelgarage sowie eine Heizungsanlage realisiert. Der Neubau begrenzt gegen Norden die Zugangsebene. Mit den geschlossenen Sichtbetonwänden wurde das Gefälle des Hanges aufgenommen. Die Konstruktion ist ein Skelettbau in Beton und Stahl. Die Ausfachung der Wände im Erdgeschoß ist in feuerverzinktem Blech und Glas ausgeführt. Die Außenwand des Heizungsraums ist eine Leichtkonstruktion aus Duripanelplatten. Die bestehenden Texturen und Materialien an den Fassaden des Hauptgebäudes sind mit neuen Materialien neu interpretiert worden. Stall und Schopf sind anstelle von Holzbrettern mit bakelisierten Sperrholzplatten und der Wohnteil anstelle von Schindeln mit feinen Latten verkleidet. An der Westfassade schützt eine Makralonverkleidung die dahinterliegende, dunkelblau gestrichene Holzbretterwand.

Renewal Residence Gnädinger, St. Gallen, 1992/93.

This house with a small stall in a forest glade not far from St. Gallen was built around the turn of the century for a gamekeeper. Because it is located outside the development zone and inside the buffer zone intended to protect the forest, utilization of the house could be expanded only with a bathroom and a kitchen. So that the living quarters in the basic structure could be left as they were, the new facilities were installed in an element constructed independently of the existing object. In one new cube-shaped accessory building a double garage as well as a heating system have been built. The new building borders the flat access area to the north. The grading of the slope is held by a closed exposed concrete wall. The building construction is a skeleton of concrete and steel. The infilling of the walls on the ground floor has been done in hot-dipped galvanized sheet metal and glass while the outer wall of the heating room is a light-weight construction of Duripanel. The existing textures and materials of the main building façade have been newly interpreted in new materials. Stall and roof hip are covered with bakelite impregnated larch wood panels instead of wooden boards, and the living area of the house with fine lathing instead of shingles. On the west façade, a Makralon covering protects the dark blue painted wooden board wall.

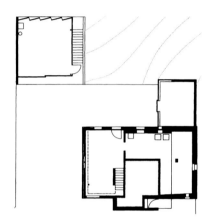

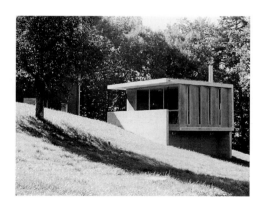
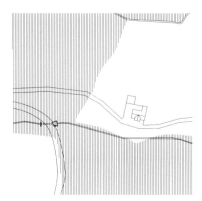

Untergeschoß, Erdgeschoß, Längs- und Querschnitt Wohnhaus
  Basement, ground floor, elevation and cross section of residence
Eingang zum Wohnhaus
  Residence entrance
Nebengebäude
  Accessory building
Situation
  Situation

Nebengebäude und Wohnhaus
　Accessory building and residence
Nebengebäude
　Accessory building

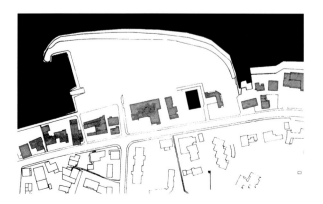

Ansicht von Südost
    View from the south east
Ansicht von der Straße
    View from the street
Situation
    Situation

Wohnhaus an der Seestraße, Horn, 1993-95.

Dieses Wohnhaus liegt in der Kernzone zwischen der Durchgangsstraße und einer öffentlich nutzbaren Aufschüttung am See. Die Außenwände des Untergeschosses bilden eine Wanne, in die ein Kern gestellt ist, der Platz für Parkplätze bietet. In den Obergeschossen sind im Kern das Treppenhaus sowie die Naßzellen der einzelnen Wohneinheiten untergebracht. Die Flachdecke über dem Untergeschoß ist zum Teil frei auskragend und nimmt am Rand die Lasten der darüberliegenden Stockwerke auf. Das statische Konzept mit Kern und Stützen an der Fassade ermöglicht einen leichten, fast schwebenden Baukörper und in den Wohneinheiten eine flexible Raumeinteilung. Im Süden, gegen die Straße hin, liegt eine zweigeschossige Maisonettewohnung, die je nach Bedarf auch der einen oder anderen Wohnung zugeschlagen werden kann. Anstelle einzelner Balkone wurden raumhohe Fensterfronten mit Hebeschiebefenstern konstruiert, die den Blick zum See hin öffnen. Die Dachterrasse kann in einzelne private Bereiche unterteilt werden. An der Westfassade schützen Schiebeläden die Fensterfront vor extremer Witterung.

Residence on Seestrasse, Horn, 1993-95.

This residence home lies in the heart of a zone between the throughway and a publicly accessed lake fill. The outer walls of the basement form a tub-like container that is placed inside a core and provides parking places. In the upper floors, the stairway and bathroom units of the individual living compartments are lodged in the core. The flat ceiling over the basement is in part freely cantilevered and takes the weight of the above floors onto its rim. The construction concept of façade supports and core allows for a light, almost airborne body and a flexible partitioning in the living units. In the south, against the street to the back, lies a two-story maisonette apartment that can be added on to one or the other of the larger apartments according to need. In place of single balconies, floor-to-ceiling window fronts with lifting windows have been constructed that open onto the lake view. The roof terrace can be partitioned into private areas. On the west façade, sliding shutters protect the window fronts from extreme weather.

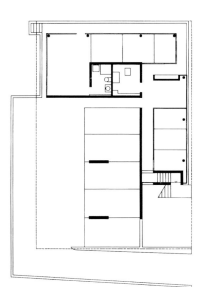
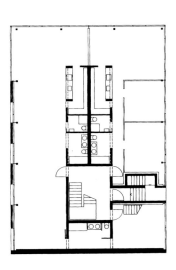
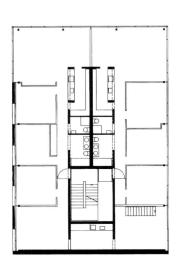
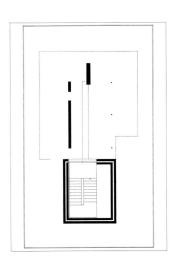

Untergeschoß, Erdgeschoß, Obergeschoß und Dachterrasse
  Basement, ground floor, upper floor and roof terrace
Dachterrasse
  Roof terrace
Wohnraum im Obergeschoß
  Livingroom on the upper floor

Ideenwettbewerb Zentrum Buchs, 1990.

Die Neugestaltung des Zentrums klärt die Lage von Buchs am Eingang des landschaftlichen Korridors nach Sargans durch seine langgestreckte Form. Die historisch bedingte Richtung und Lage der Bahnhofstraße als Verbindung alter Dorfkern–Bahnhof–Rheinbrücke wird durch die Raumkontinuität wieder in den ursprünglichen Zustand versetzt. Im Zentrum ist eine gemischte Nutzung mit hohem Wohnanteil, am westlichen Rand sind öffentliche Einrichtungen wie ein Stadtsaal und die Bibliothek und am östlichen Rand die Infrastruktur für Bahn, Post und Zoll vorgesehen.

Ideenwettbewerb Schloßbergareal Romanshorn, 1991.

Das Gebäude ersetzt in gleicher geometrischer Ordnung ein abgebranntes Bauernhaus in einem von historischen Gebäuden umgebenen Grünraum am Bodenseeufer von Romanshorn. In seiner Ausrichtung klärt es das alte Fußwegnetz, wertet die Ebene der alten Friedhofanlage auf, formuliert die Hangkante zum See hin und demonstriert Offenheit zum gegenüberliegenden deutschen Ufer. Im Sockelgeschoß befindet sich das Ortsmuseum, in den Obergeschossen eine Bibliothek und Ausstellungsräume. Die Grundfläche des abgebrannten Bauernhauses wird als Freilichtbühne im öffentlichen Raum genutzt.

Wettbewerb Raiffeisenbank Gossau, 1996.

Ein wichtiges städtisches Merkmal Goßaus ist die Straßenbebauung entlang der Hauptstraße und der Herisauerstraße. Mit der Verlegung des Bahnhofs an die Peripherie sind Freiflächen entlang dem Dorfbach und vereinzelt Gebäude zwischen diesem und dem Friedhof entstanden. Der Baukörper reagiert auf diese Situation, indem er den Rhythmus der Einzelbebauung aufnimmt und den Straßenraum gegen die Herisauerstraße schließt. Neben der Bank sind Läden, Büros und Wohnungen vorgesehen.

Concept Competition Buchs Center, 1990.

The long, extended form of the new design for the center clarifies the site location of Buchs, which lies at the entrance of the scenic corridor to Sargans. The continuity of space places the direction and site of the Bahnhofstrasse, historically the connection between the old village center, train station and bridge over the Rhine, again in its original situation. In the center is an area of multiple uses with a large amount of space for residential quarters; public facilities, such as a town auditorium and library, are located on the western edge, and on the eastern a train station, post office and customs office infrastructure is planned.

Concept Competition Schlossbergareal Romanshorn, 1991.

The building replaces with the same geometrical order a farmhouse once destroyed in a fire. The site is in one of the green lawns surrounded by historical buildings on the shore of Lake Constance in Romanshorn. It clarifies the old network of footpaths with its orientation, upgrades the plateau of the old cemetery complex, defines the edge of the slope to the water, and opens itself to the German shoreline on the other side of the lake. The local museum is located in the basement floor, a library and exhibition space in the upper floors. The floor space of the burned farmhouse will be used as an open-air theater in the public area.

Competition Raiffeisen Bank Gossau, 1996.

The street development along Hauptstrasse and Herisauerstrasse is an important characteristic of Gossau. The positioning of the train station on the periphery of this area has created open areas along the village brook and scattered buildings between these areas and the cemetery. The body of the new building responds to this situation; it takes up the rhythm of the individual development and hems the street area on Herisauerstrasse. Shops, offices and apartments are intended to be built next to the bank.

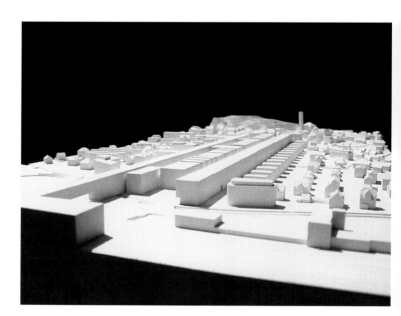

Zentrum Buchs
Buchs Center

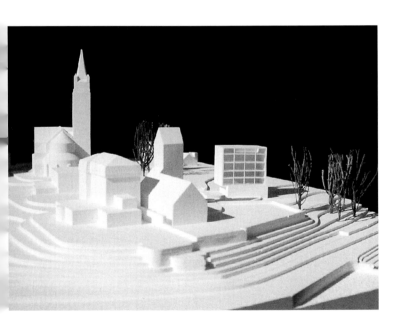

Schloßbergareal Romanshorn
Schlossberg site Romanshorn

Raiffeisenbank Goßau
Raiffeisen Bank Gossau

Beat Consoni

Biografie

Beat Consoni
1950 geboren im Horn.
1966-69 Lehre als Hochbauzeichner.
1969-71 Mitarbeit bei Lienhard und Strasser, Bern.
1971-74 Architekturstudium HTL Burgdorf.
1974/75 Mitarbeit bei Hans Jörg Affolter, Romanshorn.
1975 Sommerakademie Salzburg.
1975/76 Nachdiplomstudium Raumplanung Brugg-Windisch.
1977/78 Mitarbeit bei Hans Peter Menn, Chur.
Seit 1980 eigenes Büro in Rorschach.
Mitglied des Bundes Schweizer Architekten und des Schweizerischen Werkbundes.

Auszeichnungen, Vorträge
1987 *Gute Bauten in Graubünden 1987,* Chasa Center Augustin, Scuol.

1994 *Zwischen Engadin und Bodensee,* SIA Sektion Thurgau und BDA Konstanz Werk- und Erfahrungsbericht Kreisgruppe Bodensee.
1994 an der Liechtensteinischen Ingenieurschule Vaduz.
1995 *Das Ungebaute, das Gebaute,* Zentralschweizerisches Technikum Luzern.
1995 *Starke Körper,* Architektur Forum Zürich.
1995 an der ETH Zürich, Lehrstuhl Peter Quarella.
1995 am BDA Singen.
1995 *Architektur und Städtebau,* Hornerkreis Horn.
1996 *Unbekannte Architekten,* Ingenieurschule Burgdorf.
1996 *Alt und Neu,* ETH Zürich, Lehrstuhl für Denkmalpflege, E. Mörsch.
1996 *Eingriffe im Raum,* HTL Winterthur.

Werkverzeichnis

1980
Wohnhaus Not Carl Scuol.
Überbauung im Quartier Brunnen, Uster, Studienauftrag.

1981
Kunsthauserweiterung Chur, Wettbewerb.

1982
Olma St. Gallen, Wettbewerb.

1983
Umbau Einfamilienhaus Schnüriger, Arbon.
Überbauung Bächlistrasse Kreuzlingen, Studienauftrag.
Kantonspolizei Frauenfeld, Wettbewerb, erster Ankauf.

1984
Center Chasa Augustin, Scuol.
Im Center Augustin: Metzgerei Hatecke, Café Benderer, Schweizerische Kreditanstalt, Kur- und Verkehrsverein, 1984/85.

1986
Mehrzweckhalle Bondo, Wettbewerb, zweiter Preis.
Alterswohnungen Fürstenau, Wettbewerb.

1987
Expertise für das Bezirksgericht Maloya.
Mehrzweckhalle Feuerwehrdepot Bauamt, Rorschacherberg, Wettbewerb, zweiter Ankauf.
Wohnbebauung Rosenegg, Rorschacherberg, Wettbewerb, zweiter Ankauf.
Wohnbebauung Rütenen Frauenfeld, Wettbewerb.

1988
Rampeneinbau im Center Augustin Scuol.
Bahnhof St. Gallen, Ideenwettbewerb.
Wohnbebauung Altstätten, Wettbewerb.
Alterswohnungen Widnau, Wettbewerb, erster Ankauf.

1989
Werkstattverkleidung Schlosserei Sonderegger, Frasnacht.
Wohnhaus Sonderegger, Frasnacht, ausgeführt 1989-94.
Mehrzweckhalle Tschlin, Wettbewerb.

1990
Bahnhofstraße, Horn, Umbau und Renovation.
Gallaria d'Art im Center Augustin Scuol, ausgeführt 1992.
Umnutzung Kornhaus Rorschach, Wettbewerb.
Zentrum Buchs, Ideenwettbewerb, dritter Preis.
Handels- und Wirtschaftsschule Chur, Wettbewerb, vierter Preis.
Gemeindehaus, PTT und Kantonalbank Sent, Wettbewerb, vierter Ankauf.
Alterswohnungen Schützenwiese Arbon, Wettbewerb, vierter Preis.

1991
Restaurationsbetrieb im Seepark Ost, Rorschach, Studienauftrag.
Steinbildhauerschule St. Gallen, Wettbewerb, dritter Preis.
Quartierplan Curtin Tarasp, Wettbewerb, Ankauf.
Schloßbergareal Romanshorn, Wettbewerb, vierter Preis.
Mehrzweckhalle Buchen, Wettbewerb, erster Ankauf.
Zentrumsplanung Heerbrugg, Ideenwettbewerb, fünfter Preis.
Kirchgemeindehaus Rorschach, Wettbewerb, erster Ankauf.

1992
Regierungsplatz Chur, Wettbewerb, erster Preis.
Erweiterung Spital Scuol, Wettbewerb, vierter Preis.

1993
Dependenza Hatecke, Scuol.
Überbauung Engadinerhof, Scuol, Studienauftrag.
Dependenza und Restaurant Hatecke, St. Moritz, ausgeführt 1993/94.
Sanierung Wohnhaus Gnädinger, St. Gallen.

1994
Einkaufszentrum Berg, Studienauftrag.
Wohnhaus an der Seestraße Horn, ausgeführt 1994/95.
Zentrumserweiterung Goldach, Ideenwettbewerb, vierter Preis.

1995
Verwaltungsgebäude GVA/FAK Chur, Wettbewerb, fünfter Preis.
Raiffeisenbank Goßau 1995, Wettbewerb, zweiter Preis.
Gemeinschaftszentrum Rütihof Baden, Wettbewerb.

1996
Wohnhaus Egloff, Bottighofen.
Umbau Wohnhaus Koblauch, Ardez, in Planung.
Stellwerk Weinfelden, in Planung.
Haltestelle SBB in Rorschach, Studienauftrag, zur Ausführung empfohlen.
Altersheim und Alterswohnungen, Uznach, Wettbewerb, zweiter Preis.

Bibliografie

Gute Bauten in Graubünden, in: Terra Grischuna Graubünden, 5/1988.
Ursula Riederer, *Ästhetikvorschriften fördern eher schlechte als gute Architektur,* in: DOCU-Bulletin, 1/1988.
So können Fachleute Bauten vergleichen, in: Bündner Zeitung, 17. Februar 1989.
K. R. Lischer, *Für gute Architektur braucht es: Mut, Nerven, Durchhaltewillen,* in: SIA 46/1990.
Chasa Center Augustin Scuol, in: Schweizer Architekturführer 1920-1990, Verlag Werk AG 1992.
Rita Cathomas, *Bemerkenswerte neue Architektur in Graubünden,* in: Revue Schweiz, 7/1994.
Peter Simmen, *Eine Vision auf neun neue Bäume reduziert,* in: Bündner Zeitung, 19. August 1994.
Lore Kelly, *Perfektion der Proportion,* in: Neue Zürcher Zeitung, 4. November 1994.
Andreas Valda, *Betonhaus am Bodensee,* in: Hochparterre, 3/1995.
Martin Tschanz, *Starke Körper,* in: Neue Zürcher Zeitung, 5. Mai 1995.
Lore Kelly, *Perfektion der Proportion,* in: Raum und Wohnen, 7/1995.
Hedy Züger, *Ungewöhnliches Haus – Magnet für Architekten,* in: Bodenseezeitung, 26. Juli 1995.
Wolfgang Jean Stock, *Wohnhaus in Frasnacht,* in: Baumeister, 8/1995.
Ursula Suter, *Beat Consoni – der Marathon Man,* in: Deutsche Bauzeitung, 9/1995
Wohnhaus in Frasnacht und Horn TG, in: Werk, Bauen + Wohnen, 1/2, 1996.
Wohnhaus Gnädinger St. Gallen, in: Werk, Bauen + Wohnen, 3/4, 1996.

Biography

Beat Consoni

1950 Born in Horn.
1966-69 Apprenticeship as architectural drafter.
1969-71 Worked at Lienhard und Strasser, Bern.
1971-74 Studied architecture at HTL Burgdorf.
1974/75 Worked for Hans Jörg Affolter, Romanshorn.
1975 Sommerakademie Salzburg.
1975/76 Graduate study in Regional Planning, Brugg-Windisch.
1977/78 Worked for Hans Peter Menn, Chur.
Since 1980 own office in Rorschach.
Member of the Federation of Swiss Architects and the Schweizer Werkbund.

Awards, Lectures

1987 *Gute Bauten in Graubünden 1987,* Chasa Center Augustin, Scuol.

1994 *Zwischen Engadin und Bodensee,* SIA Section Thurgau and BDA Constance Work and Experience Report, Lake Constance Regional Group.
1994 At the Liechtenstein Engineering School, Vaduz.
1995 *Das Ungebaute, das Gebaute,* Central Swiss Technical School, Lucerne.
1995 *Starke Körper,* Architektur Forum Zurich.
1995 At the ETH Zurich, Professor Peter Quarella.
1995 At the BDA, Singen.
1995 *Architektur und Städtebau,* Hornerkreis, Horn.
1996 *Unbekannte Architekten,* Engineering School, Burgdorf.
1996 *Alt und Neu,* ETH Zürich, Professorial Chair for the Preservation of Historic Monuments, E. Mörsch.
1996 *Eingriffe im Raum,* HTL Winterthur.

List of Works

1980
Residence Not Carl, Schuls.
Brunnen district Uster, superstructure, commissioned study.

1981
Expansion of Art Museum, Chur, competition.

1982
Olma, St. Gallen, competition.

1983
Conversion Schnüriger Family Residence, Arbon.
Bächlistrasse Superstructure, Kreuzlingen, commissioned study.
Canton Police Station, Frauenfeld, competition, first purchase.

1984
Center Chasa Augustin, Scuol.
In Center Augustin, Scuol: Hatecke Butcher Shop, Café Benderer, Swiss Credit Bank, Spa and Tourist Office, 1984/85.

1986
Bondo Multipurpose Hall, Competition, second prize.
Senior Apartment House, Fürstenau, competition.

1987
Expertise for the Maloya local court building.
Mulitpurpose Hall / Fire Station / Department of Building, Rorschacherberg, competition, second purchase.
Rosenegg Housing Development, Rorschacherberg, competition, second purchase.
Rütenen Housing Development, Frauenfeld, competition.

1988
Ramp installation at Center Augustin, Scuol.
St. Gallen Railway Station, concept competition.
Altstätten Housing Development, competition.
Senior Apartment House, Widnau, competition, first purchase.

1989
Workshop covering for Sonderegger Locksmith, Frasnacht.
Sonderegger Residence Home, Frasnacht, executed 1989-94.
Multipurpose Hall, Tschlin, competition.

1990
Bahnhofstrasse, Horn, conversion and renovation.
Gallaria d'Art in Center Augustin, Scuol, executed 1992.
Converted use of grain storage facility, Rorschach, competition.
Buchs Town Center, concept competition, third prize.
School of Business and Economics, Chur, competition, fourth prize.
Community Center, Post Office and Cantonal Bank, Sent, competition, fourth purchase.
Schützenwiese Senior Apartment House, Arbon, competition, fourth prize.

1991
Restaurant operations in Seepark Ost, Rorschach, commissioned study.
Sculpture school, St. Gallen, competition, third prize.
Curtin district plan, Tarasp, competition, purchase.
Schlossberg site Romanshorn, competition, fourth prize.
Buchen Multipurpose Hall, competition, first purchase.
Heerbrugg Center Planning, concept competition fifth prize.

Church Community Center, Rorschach, competition, first purchase.

1992
Regierungsplatz, Chur, competition, first prize.
Expansion of hospital, Scuol, competition, fourth prize.

1993
Dependenza Hatecke, Scuol.
Engadinerhof Superstructure, Scuol, commissioned study.
Dependenza und Restaurant Hatecke, St. Moritz, executed 1993/94.
Renewal and upgrade of Gnädinger Residence, St. Gallen.

1994
Shopping center, Berg, commissioned study.
Residence on Seestrasse, Horn, executed 1994/95.
Expansion of center, Goldach, concept competition, fourth prize.

1995
GVA/FAK Administration Building, Chur, competition, fifth prize.
Raiffeisen Bank, Gossau, 1995, competition, second prize.
Rütihof Community Center, Baden, competition.

1996
Egloff Residence, Bottighofen.
Conversion Knoblauch Residence, Ardenz, in planning.
Switch-tower Weinfelden, in planning.
Rorschach SBB train station, commissioned study, recommended to be carried out.
Senior residence home and senior appartments, Uznach, competition, second price.

Bibliography

Gute Bauten in Graubünden, in: Terra Grischuna Graubünden, 5/1988.
Ursula Riederer, *Ästhetikvorschriften fördern eher schlechte als gute Architektur,* in: DOCU-Bulletin, 1/1988.
So können Fachleute Bauten vergleichen, in: Bündner Zeitung, February 17 1989.
K. R. Lischer, *Für gute Architektur braucht es: Mut, Nerven, Durchhaltewillen,* in: SIA 46/1990.
Chasa Center Augustin Scuol, in: Schweizer Architekturführer 1920-1990, Verlag Werk AG 1992.
Rita Cathomas, *Bemerkenswerte neue Architektur in Graubünden,* in: Revue Schweiz, 7/1994.
Peter Simmen, *Eine Vision auf neun neue Bäume reduziert,* in: Bündner Zeitung, August 19 1994.
Lore Kelly, *Perfektion der Proportion,* in: Neue Zürcher Zeitung, November 4 1994.
Andreas Valda, *Betonhaus am Bodensee,* in: Hochparterre, 3/1995.
Martin Tschanz, *Starke Körper,* in: Neue Zürcher Zeitung, May 5 1995.
Lore Kelly, *Perfektion der Proportion,* in: Raum und Wohnen, 7/1995.
Hedy Züger, *Ungewöhnliches Haus – Magnet für Architekten,* in: Bodenseezeitung, July 26 1995.
Wolfgang Jean Stock, *Wohnhaus in Frasnacht,* in: Baumeister, 8/1995.
Ursula Suter, *Beat Consoni – der Marathon Man,* in: Deutsche Bauzeitung, 9/1996.
Wohnhaus in Frasnacht und Horn TG, in: Werk, Bauen + Wohnen, 1/2, 1996.
Wohnhaus Gnädinger St. Gallen, in: Werk, Bauen + Wohnen, 3/4, 1996.

Herbert Ehrenbold
Barbara Schudel
Bern

Personalrestaurant Polex | Polex Personnel Restaurant | Bern, 1992–94

Verandaausbau | Veranda Extension | Bern-Bümpliz, 1995/96

Hauptgebäude City West | Principle Building City West | Bern, 1994

Wettbewerb Neuer Werkhof | New Work and Storage Grounds, Competition | Köniz, 1996

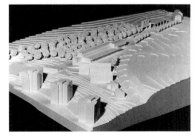

Mitarbeiterinnen und Mitarbeiter
Collaborators
- Jürg Bart
- Urs Bögli
- Thomas Dimov
- Fritz Egli
- Marcel Favre
- Marcel Gyger
- Roger Hartl
- Cyril Haymoz
- Beat Mathys
- Kurt Müller
- Roni Ott
- Mika Probst
- Marion Salm
- Roland Schneider
- Philip Stein
- Raphael Vonlanthen
- Marianne Weber
- Patrik Zurkirchen

Herbert Ehrenbold, Barbara Schudel

Integration, Identität und Irritation.

Der Werdegang von Barbara Schudel und Herbert Ehrenbold ist typisch für viele jüngere Architektinnen und Architekten in der Schweiz. Nach dem Diplom an der ETH in Zürich sammelten sie zunächst in verschiedenen Büros im In- und Ausland Erfahrungen – Barbara Schudel, wie viele ihrer Generation, unter anderem in Spanien. 1988 eröffneten sie in Bern gemeinsam ein Architekturbüro. Hier entstanden einerseits großmaßstäbliche Wettbewerbsbeiträge und Projektstudien. Ermöglicht wurde der Schritt in die Selbständigkeit aber erst durch eine gleichzeitige Assistententätigkeit an den technischen Hochschulen in Zürich und Lausanne und die Arbeit an kleineren Umbauten.

Ehrenbold & Schudel treffen dabei auf die unterschiedlichsten Situationen, auf die sie mit entsprechend differenzierter Architektur reagieren. Im Umbau eines Wohnhauses, das der Architekt des Bundesplatzes, Eduard Joos, 1914 für sich selbst errichtet hat, nehmen sie die behäbige Solidität des Baus auf und lassen ihre Eingriffe zu Nischen in den Wänden werden. Der neu ausgebaute Dachstock wird so gleichsam zu einer Schmucktruhe, die mit einem kostbaren Futteral aus Einbauelementen gefaßt wird. Die sorgfältige Detaillierung unter raffinierter Nutzung des knappen Raumes entspricht dabei dem gehobenen Standard bürgerlichen Wohnens.

Ganz anders ist die Situation beim Umbau der Polizeikantine in Bern-Wankdorf, die sich in einem mediokren Bürobau der Hochkonjunktur befindet. Indem Ehrenbold & Schudel den bestehenden Mittelkorridor sich verengend zulaufen lassen, gewinnen sie Raum, um den Eingang mit einer eigenen Vorzone vor den gewöhnlichen Bürotüren auszuzeichnen und den Großraum der Kantine durch einen intimeren Bereich zu ergänzen. Der speziellen Stimmung des Ortes werden sie mit einem braunen Marmoleum-Boden und dunklen Holzwerkstoffen an Wänden und Decke gerecht. Auch eine Vitrine für Preise und Trophäen fehlt nicht. Das Hirschgeweih hingegen, das vor dem Umbau einen prominenten Platz eingenommen hat, wird auf Wunsch der Wirtin nicht mehr aufgehängt. Es hätte auch nicht gepaßt: Die warmen Brauntöne der industriellen Materialien erzeugen zwar eine gewisse Gemütlichkeit, jedoch ohne Sentimentalität und ohne einen Bruch mit der Bausubstanz der sechziger Jahre zu erzeugen.

In den städtebaulichen Arbeiten teilen Ehrenbold & Schudel die Vorliebe vieler Architekten ihrer Generation für kompakte, freigestellte Baukörper. Mit komplexen Volumen wird auf die städtebauliche Situation eingegangen, ohne die Autonomie der Gebäude aufzugeben. Besondere Aufmerksamkeit gilt dabei der Ausbildung von differenzierten Außenräumen und Wegen, die oft öffentlich oder halböffentlich durch die Gebäude hindurchgeführt werden und so direkt Innen- und Außenräume verknüpfen.

Ein gelegentliches Unbehagen, ausgelöst durch die Voraussetzungen bei verschiedenen Wettbewerben, begründet ein verstärktes Engagement in Planungsfragen, mit dem Ziel, möglichst früh in die Entscheidungsprozesse eingreifen zu können. Hier fließen auch die Erkenntnisse feministischer Stadtkritik mit ihrer erhöhten Sensibilität für Fragen der Alltagstauglichkeit und Sicherheit des öffentlichen Raumes ein. Wie diese Aspekte in städtebaulichen Projekten, die von kompakten, isolierten Körpern ausgehen, thematisiert werden können, ist mit ein Gegenstand der neueren Entwürfe.

Ehrenbold & Schudel hatten bisher noch kaum Gelegenheit, ihre Vorstellungen in der Synthese eines selbständigen Gebäudes zu präsentieren. Wie eine solche aussehen könnte, zeigt das Projekt für einen Supermarkt in dörflicher Umgebung. Das Volumen über fast quadratischem Grundriß wird von einer Ebene überdeckt, welche über die Diagonale leicht geneigt ist. Das Gebäude reagiert so auf das Terrain, indem es – wenigstens an einer Seite – dessen Gefälle mitmacht: eine Herausforderung an den Gleichgewichtssinn. Das Volumen wird durch diese Maßnahme zudem niedriger, wo es an kleinmaßstäbliche Häuser grenzt, höher dagegen gegenüber den großen öffentlichen Gebäuden des Dorfzentrums. Die Fassaden bestehen im wesentlichen aus breiten Bändern, die parallel zur Dachneigung laufen und so den Bau wie eine Verpackung umwickeln. Der Eingang liegt dabei in einem tiefen Einschnitt, was verunklärende Vorbauten unnötig macht. Das Projekt thematisiert so wesentliche Aspekte der aktuellen Architekturdiskussion: Integration in den städtebaulichen Kontext und Identität des Baukörpers, zeichenhafte Bedeutung und wirkungsvolle Irritation der Wahrnehmung. M. T.

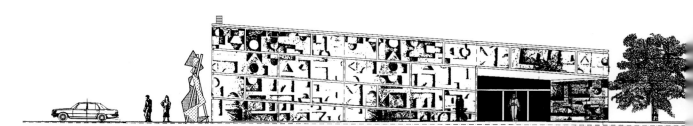

Neubauprojekt Supermarkt, Roggwil, 1995
New building for supermarket project, Roggwil, 1995

Integration, Identity and Irritation.

The professional development of Barbara Schudel and Herbert Ehrenbold is typical of many younger architects in Switzerland. After graduating from the ETH in Zurich, they first of all acquired experience at various offices at home and abroad. Like many of her generation, Barbara Schudel went to Spain, among other locations. In 1988, they opened a joint architecture office in Bern from which, on the one hand, large-scale competition submissions and project studies have emerged; made possible, too, was the step to independence – but only through a simultaneous assistantship at the technical universities in Zurich and Lausanne, plus additional work on smaller conversion projects.

Ehrenbold & Schudel thus meet with a variety of situations to which they respond with correspondingly differentiated architecture. For the conversion of a residence that Eduard Joos, architect of the Bundesplatz, erected for himself in 1914, they incorporate the sedate quality of the building and let their conversion work extend to the niches in the walls. The newly built attic floor thus resembles a jewelry chest enclosed in a precious case of built-in elements. Careful detailing among the sophisticated utilization of the tight space corresponds at the same time to the elevated standard of middle-class living.

A totally different situation presented itself in Bern-Wankdorf with the conversion of a police canteen located in a mediocre office building that was erected during economic boom years. Ehrenbold and Schudel have gained space by allowing the existing middle corridor to narrow towards one end in order to distinguish the entrance with its own foyer in front of the normal office door and to supplement the larger room of the canteen with a more intimate area. Justice is done to the special atmosphere of the place by the use of a brown Marmoleum floor and dark wood material on the walls and ceiling. A showcase for prizes and trophies has not been forgotten, although the stag antlers that used to occupy a prominent place before the conversion will not be returned to the wall – at the express wish of the proprietress. In any case, it would no longer fit in its surroundings: the warm brown tones of the industrial materials in fact provide a coziness without sentimentality and without breaking with the building substance of the 1960s.

In urban development work, Ehrenbold & Schudel share the preference of many architects of their generation for compact, freestanding building elements. Complex volumes respond to the urban situation without giving up the autonomy of the building. Special attention is paid to the development of differentiated exterior areas and paths that lead publicly or semi-publicly through the buildings, connecting interior and exterior spaces.

An occasional unease with the requirements of various competitions has laid the foundation for an intensified engagement with planning issues. The goal has become to step into the decision-making process as early as possible, a goal influenced by the perception of feminist-oriented criticism with its higher sensibility for questions of the everyday suitability and security of public spaces. The way these aspects can be taken up as themes in urban development projects that proceed on the basis of compact, isolated buildings is also a subject of the new designs.

Ehrenbold & Schudel have not yet had the opportunity to present their vision in the synthesis of an autonomous building. How that would look can be seen from a project for a supermarket set in a village environment. The volume over an almost square floor plan is spanned overhead by a flat plane, slightly inclined on the diagonal. The building responds to the terrain in that it goes along with the slope at least on one side: a challenge to one's sense of balance. The volume thereby becomes lower where it borders on houses of smaller dimensions; higher, however, against the tall public buildings of the village center. The façades are built essentially in bands that run parallel to the slope of the roof and wrap around the building like a package. The entrance sits in a deep cut that makes unnecessary any porch that would create a visually confusing effect. The project takes up the theme of such essential aspects of the current architecture discussion as: integration into the urban development context, identity of the building, symbolic significance, and effective irritation of perception. M. T.

Herbert Ehrenbold, Barbara Schudel

Personalrestaurant Polex, Bern, 1992–94.

In einem mediokren zweibündigen Bürogebäude der sechziger Jahre mit geringen Raumhöhen mußte eine bestehende Kantine saniert und vergrößert werden. Die Verkleidung der neuen Lüftung an der Decke im Korridorbereich verschmolzen wir mit einer von der Tragkonstruktion unabhängigen, neuen Wand. Die Schrägstellung der Wand gibt im Saal neu die Blickrichtung ins ferne Grün frei. Durch die plastische Veränderung der Wände und Decken entstanden zusätzliche räumliche Qualitäten.

Polex Personnel Restaurant, Bern, 1992–94.

In a mediocre 1960's two-level office building with low ceilings, an existing canteen was to be upgraded and enlarged. We merged the covering over the new ventilator system in the corridor ceiling with one of the new walls detached from the girder construction. The splaying of the wall opens up a view from the large room into the distant greenery where none existed before. With the formal alteration of the walls and ceiling, additional spatial qualities emerged.

Eingangsbereich mit Blick in den Eßsaal
 Entrance area with view into dining room
Der Eßsaal mit einem niedrigeren Bereich für Bistrotische
 Dining room with low-built area for bistro tables
Grundriß
 Floor plan

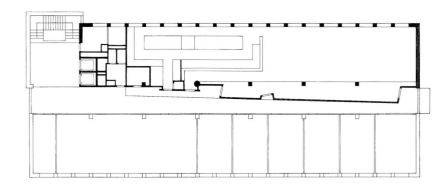

Verandaausbau, Bern-Bümpliz, 1995/96.

Der bestehende Rohbau der vorgelagerten Veranda erhielt eine neue, wärmegedämmte Hülle. Die Lärchenholzverkleidung drückt durch ihre Materialisierung die räumliche Kontinuität des erweiterten Wohnraums aus. Der Übergang von Innen nach Außen kann durch die Tiefe der Konstruktion, den mäandrierenden Verlauf der großformatigen Schiebetüren, als Raumschicht artikuliert werden. Die Auftraggeber haben eine große Vorliebe für das Würfelspiel. Das Konzept nimmt die Idee der Würfel auf und formiert diese zu zwei Quadern um, welche durch Weglassen von Teilen ihre Form und Funktion erhalten. Der eine ist mit großen Öffnungen versehen, der andere dient mit eingeschnittenen Tritten als Terrasse.

Veranda Extension, Bern-Bümpliz, 1995/96.

The existing shell of the front veranda was given a new heat insulated casing. The materialization of the larch wood covering expresses the spatial continuity of the expanded livingroom. The transition from interior to exterior can be actualized as a spatial layer by means of the depth of the construction, the key pattern formed by the sliding of the large-scale doors. The client is very fond of the game of dice. The concept takes the idea of the dice and transforms it into two square blocks that get their form and function through the omission of parts. One is equipped with large openings, the other serves as a terrace with cut-in steps.

Gartenansichten
Garden views
Schnitt und Grundriß Veranda
Cross section and floor plan of veranda

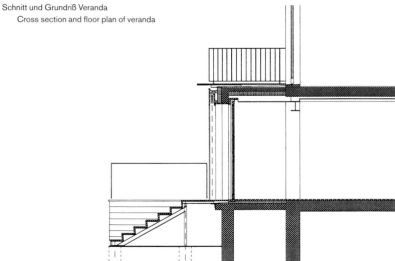
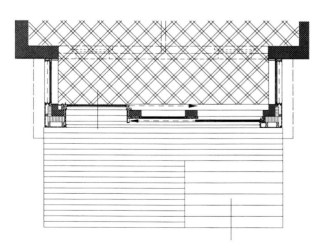

Herbert Ehrenbold, Barbara Schudel

Studienauftrag Hauptgebäude City West, Bern, 1994.

Dieser Studienauftrag bestand aus der Zielvorgabe, den Energieverbrauch, die Umweltbelastung, den Unterhaltsaufwand sowie die Betriebskosten des Gebäudes um mindestens die Hälfte zu reduzieren, und nicht primär einem größeren Raumbedarf zu entsprechen. Mit Hilfe eines interdisziplinären Teams wurde ein Projektvorschlag mit Kostenerfassung und technischem Bericht ausgearbeitet. Dieser umfaßte folgende Variantenabklärung: Fassadenersatz, Fassadensanierung oder Glashülle, ferner enthielt er Berechnungen und Überlegungen zu Haustechnik, Elektronik (Lichttechnik und Lichtlenkung), Photovoltaik, Bauphysik, Akustik, Verkehr, Begrünung, zur Sicherheit im öffentlichen Raum und zum Stoff- und Energiefluß. Daraus entstand unser Vorschlag einer zweiten Hülle mit «hängenden Gärten» als Attraktion für Mensch und Umgebung.

Commissioned Study for Principle Building, City West, Bern, 1994.

This study is the result of the goal to reduce the use of energy, the environmental pollution, the maintenance expenditure and the operation costs of the building by at least one half, a decision not based primarily on the need to alter the space of the structure. With the help of an interdisciplinary team, a suggested project with expense itemization and technical report was drawn up. This included an evaluation of the following possibilities: façade replacement, façade upgrade, or glass casing; further included were calculations and reflections on the building engineering, electronics (light technology and direction), photovoltaics, construction physics, acoustics, traffic, plants and greenery, security in public areas, and material and energy flow. Out of this emerged our suggestion for a double-casing with "hanging garden" as an attraction for both the people and the environment.

Hülle mit dahinterliegenden verzahnten Außenräumen, Modell
  Casing with interlocking exterior spaces in rear, model
Neue Hülle vor der bestehenden Fassade, Modell
  New casing in front of the existing façade, model
Grundriß 18. Stockwerk
  Floor plan 18th floor
Gebäudekomplex City West, rechts das Turmgebäude des Amtes für Bundesbauten
  City West building complex, tower building of the Department of Federal Construction, right

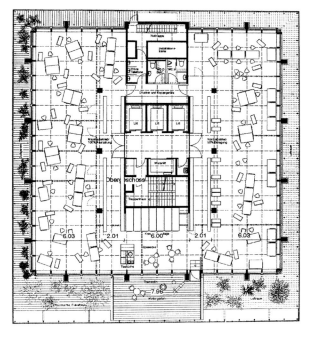

Fassadenausschnitt mit Lüftungslamellen
 Detail of façade with ventilation gills
Konstruktionsschnitt
 Section of construction

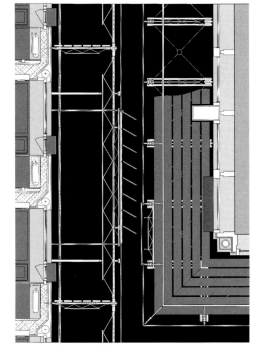

Herbert Ehrenbold, Barbara Schudel

Wettbewerb Neuer Werkhof, Köniz, 1996.

Die Lage außerhalb des Ortszentrums bestimmt die von der Straßengeometrie losgelöste Stellung der Körper. Der eine Körper, quer zu den Höhenlinien im Terrain, steht als fester Block (Hallen, Werkstätten, Büros, Wohnräume) auf der untern Ebene des schmalen, abfallenden Grundstücks. Die Verschiebung innerhalb der Fassade verstärkt seine Verankerung ins Terrain. Die doppelgeschossigen Fassadenteile übernehmen die Höhe der Halle und schaffen so eine Einheitlichkeit der verschiedenen nutzungsbedingten Raumhöhen. Der andere Körper erscheint als klar definierte, aber flexible Gruppe von Dächern (Außenlager, Silos) auf der oberen, flachen Ebene. Obwohl formal als Einheit ausgebildet, können diese Lager, im Gegensatz zum unteren Baukörper, im Selbstbau durch das Werkhofpersonal entsprechend den logistischen Bedürfnissen angepaßt werden oder bei einer späteren Umnutzung beispielsweise einer Wohnsiedlung Platz schaffen. Durch dieselbe Horizonthöhe und gleiche Proportionen können die Körper als zusammenhängende Einheit gelesen werden.

Competition, New Work and Storage Grounds, Köniz, 1996.

The situation outside the town center defines the buildings with their detached positioning in relation to the street geometry. The one building, diagonal to the contour line of the terrain, stands as a fixed block (halls, workshops, offices, living spaces) on the lower plane of the narrow sloping plot. The shift within the façade strengthens its anchoring to the terrain. The two-story façade segments accommodate the height of the hall and create a unity from the variety of room heights dictated by use requirements. The other building appears as a clearly defined but flexible group of roofs (exterior storage, silos) on the upper, flat plane. Although developed as a formal unity, these storage facilities can, in contrast to the lower building, be arranged to suit the various logistical needs in a do-it-yourself fashion by the grounds personnel or, for future use conversions, for example, a housing development court can be created. By means of the same horizontal height and the same proportions, the buildings can be read as a connected unit.

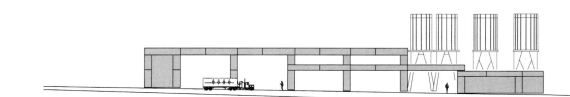

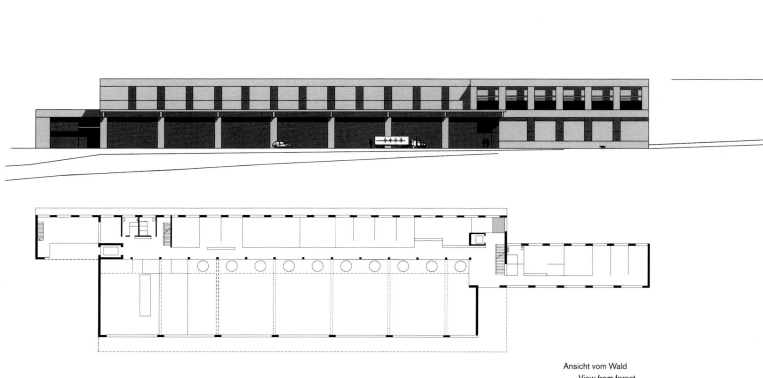

Ansicht vom Wald
View from forest
Ansicht von der Straße
View from street
Eingangsgrundriß mit Bürotrakt und Halle
Entrance floor plan with office tract and hall
Querschnitt durch Bürotrakt und Halle
Cross section of office tract and hall
Situation
Situation

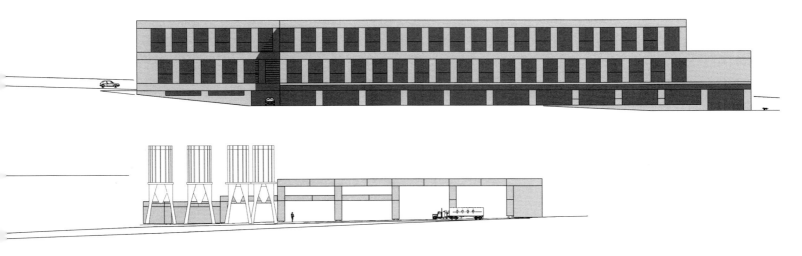
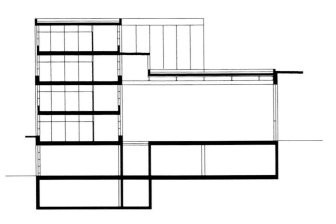
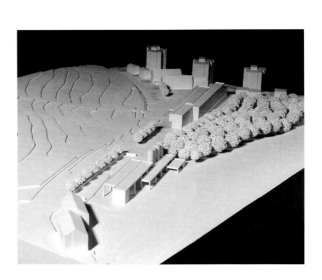

Herbert Ehrenbold, Barbara Schudel

Biografien

Barbara Schudel
1961 geboren in Bern.
1976-80 Literaturgymnasium.
1980-87 Studium an der ETH Zürich.
1987 Diplom bei Prof. D. Schnebli.
1982 Auslandpraktikum in Spanien bei Cruz & Ortiz, Sevilla.
1984-87 Tätigkeit in Architekturbüros in Basel und Zürich.
Ab 1993 verschiedene Architekturjury- und Kommissionstätigkeiten, Engagement in Fachvereinen.
1993 Schlußkritik SCI ARC, Vico Morcote, Tessin, Externe Diplomexpertin EPF Lausanne.
1994 Assistenz an der ETH Zürich bei Dozent P. Devanthéry, Genève.

Herbert Ehrenbold
1960 geboren in Luzern.
1976-80 Wirtschaftsgymnasium.
1981-87 Studium an der ETH Zürich.
1987 Diplom bei Prof. M. Campi.
1981 Auslandaufenthalt in Rom.
1984-87 Tätigkeit in Architekturbüros in Luzern und Basel.
1989-91 Assistenz an der ETH Zürich bei Prof. K. J. Schattner, Eichstätt.
1994-96 Assistenz an EPF Lausanne bei Prof. I. Lamunière, Genève.

Seit 1988 gemeinsames Büro Ehrenbold & Schudel in Bern.

Vorträge, Ausstellung
1995 *Junge Schweizer Architektinnen und Architekten*, Architektur Forum Zürich.
1996 *Frau und Architektin*, organisiert durch ABAP, Arbeitsgruppe Berner Architektinnen und Planerinnen, Kornhaus Bern.

1995 Beitrag in *Neue Bären*, Architektur Forum Zürich.

Werkverzeichnis

Bis 1988
Erweiterung Kantonsschule Gemeinde Reußbühl LU, mit T. Lussi, Projektwettbewerb, Ankauf.
Dreifamilienhaus Witschi-Wyssmann, Neuenegg BE.
Kulturinsel Geßnerallee, Stadt Zürich, Projektwettbewerb, mit E. Offermann, Ankauf.

1989
Feuerwehr-/Werkhof-/Schulgebäude Sägematte, Gemeinde Köniz, Projektwettbewerb, zweiter Preis.
Holzdoppel- und Einzelwohnhaus Rueyres-les-Prés FR, Weiterentwicklung als Holzbau-Prototypen.
Erweiterung Wohn-/Geschäftshaus, Bern, Studienauftrag, Vorprojekt.

1990
Wohn-/Geschäftshausüberbauung Areal Knecht, Lyss BE, Projektwettbewerb, erster Preis.
Umbau Einfamilienhaus Perrin, Bern-Liebefeld.
Anbau Glashaus Cimber, Köniz BE.
Überbauung Baumgarten Ost, Bern, Projektwettbewerb, vierter Preis.

1991
Büroeinbau und Außenraumgestaltung Einfamilienhaus Heilinger, Wabern BE.
Umbau Zweifamilienhaus Meier-Wechsler, Bern.
Gewerbe- und Technopark Heitersheim, Deutschland, Vorprojekt.
Tribschen LU, Städtebaulicher Ideenwettbewerb, sechster Preis.
Wohnsiedlung Altes Schulhausareal Rubigen BE, Projektwettbewerb, fünfter Preis.
Krankenheim Gemeinde Täuffelen BE, Projektwettbewerb, sechster Preis.
Nördliches Bahnhofgebiet Stadt Aarau, Projektwettbewerb, sechster Preis.
Südliches Bahnhofgebiet Stadt Aarau, Ideenwettbewerb, erster Preis.
Verwaltungsgebäude Spar- und Leihkasse Bern, Fischermätteli Bern, Projektwettbewerb.
Seniorenresidenz Überbauung Gemeinde Erlach BE, Projektwettbewerb, dritter Preis.

1992
Wohnungsumbau und Dachausbau Haus Frey-Ryf, Bern.
Umbau Gewässer- und Bodenschutzlabor, Bern, HBA Kanton Bern.
Wohnsiedlung in Gerzensee BE, Projektwettbewerb, Ankauf.

1993
Hintere Bahnhofstraße West, Stadtbauamt Aarau, Städtebauliche Studie.
Erweiterung ETH Lausanne, Ecublens, Projektwettbewerb, Einladung auf Präqualifikation.
Kücheneinbau Mehrfamilienhaus Escher, Bern.
Sanierung Einfamilienhaus Jolles, Jegenstorf BE.

1994
Einbau Personalrestaurant Polex, Bern, Hochbauamt Kanton Bern.
Sanierung Primarschulhaus Bern-Kirchenfeld, HBA Stadt Bern.
Sanierung Hauptgebäude City West, Bern, Studienauftrag mit A. Wenger und P. Bölsterli.
Gangloff-Areal Bern, Grundlagen für eine ZPP, SPA Stadt Bern, ExpertInnenverfahren, mit A. Tschumi und K. Aellen.

Bibliografie

1995
Sanierung Verandaausbau Haus Hirsbrunner, Bern.
Luxuriöser Badeinbau Terrassenhaus Bauer, Konolfingen BE.
Cafeteria Interieur Bürohaus, Bern.
Supermarkt, Roggwil BE, Neubauprojekt und Sanierungsprojektierung.
Wohnsiedlung Meiefeld Burgdorf, Studienauftrag, erster Preis.

1996
Verandaausbau Haus Schaufelberger, Bern.
Erweiterung Halle Tannwald (Projekt: SBB Baukreis II Luzern; Gesamtplanung: B&S Ingenieure, Bern; Ausführung durch Generalunternehmer), Ausführungsplanung.
Verbesserung der Abgänge BLS/GBS, Bahnstation Außerholligen, Bern, Projekt.
Studie im Siedlungsgebiet, Schutzgebiet Gartenstadt, Gemeinde Köniz BE.
Stellungnahme Richtplan Burgdorf BE, frauenspezifische Fragen, Burgdorf.
Umbau EG Wohnung, Haus Frey-Ryf, Bern.
Sanierung Mehrfamilienhaus, Bern, in Ausführung.
Werkhof Schliern, Gemeinde Köniz BE, Projektwettbewerb, zweiter Rang.

Wettbewerb Areal Knecht Lyss, Publikation in: SIA 27/28, 1990.
Bahnhof Aarau, Publikation in: Aktuelle Wettbewerbs Scene 1991.
Benedikt Loderer, *Halt in Aarau,* in: Hochparterre, September 1991.
Wettbewerb Baumgarten Bern, Publikation in: SIA 12/1991.
Krankenheim Täuffelen, Publikation in: Aktuelle Wettbewerbs Scene 3/1992.
Christoph Allenspach, *Neue Bären,* in: Hochparterre, Oktober 1994.
Christoph Allenspach, *Weiterhin auf den Spuren der Moderne,* in: NZZ, 15. November 1994.
Christoph Allenspach, *Zweites Leben für das City West,* in: Berner Zeitung, 4. Oktober 1994.
Martin Tschanz, *Integration, Identität und Irritation,* NZZ, 6. Oktober 1995.

Eigene Veröffentlichung
Ehrenbold/Schudel, *Vorstöße/Dépassements,* in: archithese 2/1991.

Biographies

Barbara Schudel
1961 Born in Bern.
1976-80 Classical secondary school.
1980-87 Studied at the ETH Zurich.
1987 Graduated under Prof. D. Schnebli.
1982 Practicum in Spain with Cruz & Ortiz, Seville.
1984-87 Activitie in architecture offices in Basle and Zurich.
From 1993 various architecture jury and commission activities, involvement with professional associations.
1993 End critique SCI ARC, Vico Morcote Ticino External Expert EPF Lausanne.
1994 Assistant to Docent P. Devanthéry, Geneva, at the ETH Zurich.

Herbert Ehrenbold
1960 Born in Lucerne.
1976-80 Graduation from business secondary school.
1981-87 Studied at the ETH Zurich.
1987 Graduated under Prof. M. Campi.
1981 Stay in Rome.
1984-87 Activity in architecture offices in Lucerne and Basle.
1989-91 Assistant to Prof. K. J. Schattner, Eichstätt, at the ETH Zurich.
1994-96 Assistant to Prof. I. Lamunière, Geneva, at the EPF Lausanne.

Since 1988 joint office Ehrenbold & Schudel in Bern.

Lectures, Exhibitions
1995 *Junge Schweizer Architektinnen und Architekten,* Architektur Forum Zurich.
1996 *Frau und Architektin,* organized through ABAP, Bern Women's Work Group of Architects and Planners, Kornhaus Bern.

1995 Contribution to *Neue Bären,* Architektur Forum Zurich.

List of Works

Until 1988
Expansion of Canton School, Municipality of Reussbühl, with T. Lussi, project competition, purchase.
Three-family House Witschi-Wyssmann, Neuenegg.
Kulturinsel Gessnerallee, City of Zurich, project competition, with E. Offermann, purchase.

1989
Building for fire department Sägematte, work grounds, school, Municipality of Köniz, project competition, second prize.
Double and single wooden house, Rueyres-les-Prés, further development as wooden prototypes.
Expansion of residence and business building, Bern, commissioned study, preliminary project.

1990
Areal Knecht residence and business superstructure, Lyss, project competition, first prize.
Conversion of Perrin One-family House, Bern-Liebefeld.
Annex to Cimber Glass House, Köniz.
Baumgarten East Superstructure, Bern, project competition, fourth prize.

1991
Office installation and grounds design of Heilinger One-Family House, Wabern.
Conversion of Meier-Wechsler Two-family House, Bern.
Gewerbe- und Technopark Heitersheim, Germany, preliminary project.
Urban development concept competition, Tribschen, sixth prize.
Altes Schulhausareal Housing Community, Rubigen, project competition, fifth prize.
Convalescent Home Municipality of Täuffelen, project competition, sixth prize.
Northern Railway Station Grounds, City of Aarau, project competition, sixth prize.
Southern Railway Station Grounds, City of Aarau, concept competition, first prize.
Administration Building, Spar- und Leihkasse Bern, Fischermätteli, Bern, project competition.
Municipality of Erlach Senior Residence, project competition, third prize.

1992
Frey-Ryf Residence, conversion of house and expansion of roof construction, Bern.
Conversion of Water and Land Protection Laboratory, Bern, HBA Canton Bern.
Housing community in Gerzensee, project competition, purchase.

1993
Hintere Bahnhofstrasse West, Aarau City Building Department, town development study.
Expansion of ETH Lausanne, Ecublens, project competition, invitation to pre-qualification.
Kitchen installation in Escher Multi-family House, Bern.
Jolles One-family House, renewal, Jegenstorf.

Bibliography

1994
Polex Personnel Restaurant Installation, Bern, Department of Architecture, Canton Bern.
Renewal of schoolhouse, Primary School, Bern-Kirchenfeld, HBA City of Bern.
Renewal of Principle Buildings, City West, Bern, commissioned study, with A. Wenger and P. Bölsterli.
Gangloff-Areal Bern, Basis for a ZPP, SPA City of Bern, advisory process, with A. Tschumi and K. Aellen.

1995
Hirsbrunner House, renewal of veranda extension, Bern.
Bauer Terrace House, luxurious bath installation, Konolfingen.
Office building cafeteria interior, Bern.
Supermarket, Roggwil, new building project and project development for renewal.
Meiefeld Housing Community, Burgdorf, commissioned project, first prize.

1996
Schaufelberger House, veranda extension, Bern.
Tannwald Hall expansion (project: SBB Building District II Lucerne; overall planning: B & S Ingenieure, Bern; execution through general contractor), final planning.
Improvement of exits, BLS/GBS, Ausserholligen Train Station, Bern, project.
Study of housing community grounds, Schutzgebiet Gartenstadt, Municipality of Köniz.
Opinion to town development plan of Burgdorf, women-specific issues, Burgdorf.
Frey-Ryf House, conversion of ground floor, Bern.
Renewal of multi-family house, Bern, in process.
Schliern work and storage grounds, Municipality of Köniz, project competition, second ranking.

Wettbewerb Areal Knecht Lyss, publication in: SIA 27/28, 1990.
Bahnhof Aarau, publication in: Aktuelle Wettbewerbs Scene 1991.
Benedikt Loderer, *Halt in Aarau,* in: Hochparterre, September 1991.
Wettbewerb Baumgarten Bern, publication in: SIA 12/1991.
Krankenheim Täuffelen, publication in: Aktuelle Wettbewerbs Scene 3/1992.
Christoph Allenspach, *Neue Bären,* in: Hochparterre, October 1994.
Christoph Allenspach, *Weiterhin auf den Spuren der Moderne,* in: NZZ, November 15 1994.
Christoph Allenspach, *Zweites Leben für das City West,* in: Berner Zeitung, October 4 1994.
Martin Tschanz, *Integration, Identität und Irritation,* NZZ, October 6 1995.

Publications by the Architects
Ehrenbold/Schudel, *Vorstösse/Dépassements,* in: archithese 2/1991.

Jasmin Grego
Joseph Smolenicky
Zürich

Mitarbeiterinnen und Mitarbeiter
Collaborators
    Mark Geissmann
    Mark van Kleef
    Stefanie Kühnle
    Roberto Lüder

Schweizer Pavillon Weltausstellung | Swiss Pavilion, 1992 World's Fair | Sevilla, 1992

Jockey/Vollmoeller AG, Anbau Bürogebäude | Jockey/Vollmoeller AG, Office Building Annex | Uster, 1994

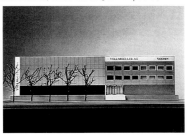

Holzhäuser im Misox, Graubünden | Wooden Houses in the Misox Valley, Grisons | 1995

Unterirdischer Ballettsaal, Opernhaus | Underground Ballet Hall, Opera House | Zürich, 1995

Das Filtern paralleler Realitäten.

Erste Aufmerksamkeit erlangten Jasmin Grego und Joseph Smolenicky mit dem farbenfrohen Coiffeursalon Sfax in Zürich-Seefeld (1992), in dem alles zugunsten der elementaren Farbgestaltung reduziert wurde. Der Salon sollte nicht auf den ersten Blick als Coiffeurgeschäft erkennbar sein, sondern wie eine Bühne auf seine eigene Inszenierung hinweisen. Besonders abends wirken die drei Fenster wie große Plakate, die die unterschiedlichen Realitäten oder die mehrfachen Codierungen sinnfällig werden lassen. Das «Filtern der parallelen Realitäten» regt die beiden Architekten an, unterschiedliche Entwurfsansätze miteinander zu verbinden, so daß sich verschiedene Bilder überschneiden und zu einer Art visueller Collage verbinden. Das scheint kompliziert, läßt sich aber gerade bei dem Coiffeursalon ganz einfach nachvollziehen, da bei den Arbeiten von Grego und Smolenicky die Bezugssysteme immer streng aus der jeweiligen Aufgabe heraus entwickelt werden. Deshalb wollten sie auch keine weiteren Läden in derselben Weise entwerfen, obwohl Angebote dafür vorgelegen hätten.

Eine weitere Arbeit, die auf der Installation einer stark veränderten Visualisierung des Raumes basierte, war ein Projekt für den unterirdischen Ballettsaal des Opernhauses in Zürich. Dieser Übungssaal liegt im dritten Untergeschoß des Opernhaus-Neubaus und ist vom natürlichen Licht und jeglichem Bezug zur Außenwelt abgeschlossen. Mit einer Lichtinstallation, die lineare, flächige, punktuelle und diagonale Lichtkonstellationen ermöglicht, soll der Kelleratmosphäre entgegengewirkt und per Computersteuerung das künstliche Licht in einem 24-Stunden-Rhythmus dem biologischen Tagesverlauf nachempfunden werden. Dadurch ist zum einen eine eigene räumliche Choreographie möglich, zum anderen kann der triste Übungsraum durch die alleinige Bestimmung des Lichtes und die raumsetzenden farbigen Lichtwandlungen neu definiert und erfahrbar werden.

Sowohl der Coiffeursalon Sfax als auch das Ballettsaal-Projekt waren rein installative Arbeiten, das Architektonische trat dabei nur wenig in Erscheinung. Das war bei dem ersten Achtungserfolg der Architekten ganz anders: 1990 waren sie unter den Preisträgern bei dem Wettbewerb für den Schweizer Pavillon der Weltausstellung in Sevilla 1992. Ihr Entwurf sah einen geschlossenen, spitz zulaufenden, kristallinen Körper vor, der Assoziationen an einen Berg oder einen Bergkristall hervorrief. Aber auch hier wieder die «Zusammenfügung von unterschiedlichen Bildmotiven»: Bei dem Pavillon war eine Materialisierung aus einfachen horizontalen Holzbrettern vorgesehen, die der massiven Bergwelt das Ephemere und Flüchtige eines Ausstellungsbaus gegenüberstellt.

Während für Jasmin Grego und Joseph Smolenicky die Arbeit für den Schweizer Pavillon noch ganz einen damaligen Hochschuldiskurs widerspiegelte – beide haben an der ETH Zürich studiert und diplomiert –, bot sich mit der Projektierung einiger Ferienhäuser im Misox, Graubünden, eine ganz andere Aufgabe. Neben die traditionellen giebelständigen Häuser der Umgebung stellten Grego und Smolenicky kubische Bauformen, die ganz bewußt den Zustand des temporären Aufenthaltes thematisieren wollen. Die minimale Wohnform des Ein-Raum-Hauses und dessen zeitlich begrenzter Gebrauch stehen dabei in einem direkten Verhältnis. Sind die Häuser bewohnt, erhalten sie mit den tiefen Öffnungen der Terrasse und der Garage eine betont plastische Gestalt. Sind die Tore der Terrasse und der Garage geschlossen, scheinen alle Öffnungen verschwunden zu sein. So wird das unbewohnte Ferienhaus in seinem geschlossenen Zustand zu einem Schmuckkasten in der Landschaft, zu einem «intarsienbestückten Holzmöbel», wie es die Architekten benennen, und nicht zu einem die meiste Zeit des Jahres leerstehenden Haus. Dadurch findet auch das nicht bewohnte Ferienhaus einen eigenständigen ästhetischen Ausdruck.

Für die Firma Jockey/Vollmoeller AG galt es, die bestehende Lagerhalle mit einem neuen Gebäudekörper für Büros und Administration zu verbinden. Das Firmengelände liegt in einem Quartier in Uster, das durch das Nebeneinander kleinteiliger, individualistischer Wohn- und Gewerbebauten geprägt ist. Das neue Firmengebäude sollte sich von der Provinzialität des Quartiers absetzen und zugleich mit der vorhandenen Struktur verschmelzen. Hier strebten die Architekten keinen additiven Baukomplex an, vielmehr wurden die verschiedenen Funktionsbereiche in einen Gesamtbau integriert. Sinnfällig verfolgten sie dabei die «Strategie des Quilts»: Gemeint ist damit, aus alten und neuen Teilen ein neues Ganzes entstehen zu lassen. Ein «Fassadenquilt» macht die innere funktionale Struktur des Gebäudes sichtbar, und die Großform des Gebäudekörpers gibt sich so als eine aus einer Vielzahl äußerst unterschiedlicher Nutzungen bestehende Einheit zu erkennen. Die Oberflächen der Fassaden fügen sich in einer Vielfalt von Materialien und Fassadenöffnungen zu einem ausgewogenen Bild, alle Fassadenelemente werden grundlegende Bestandteile dieses Bildes. Je nach Wahl und Komposition der Materialien ändert sich der Ausdruck des Gebäudes.

Dieses Projekt verdeutlicht den bildhaften Entwurfsansatz von Jasmin Grego und Joseph Smolenicky. Sie vertreten kein spezielles Dogma. Natürlich werden die Bezugssysteme aus der Aufgabe heraus entwickelt, zudem wird aber die «Einschränkung der Realität über unsere Wahrnehmung» thematisiert oder, anders ausgedrückt, das Filtern der parallelen Realitäten. Die Vielschichtigkeit ihrer bisherigen Projekte und Arbeiten zeigt überzeugend, daß es ihnen nicht um die Ausschließlichkeit des architektonischen Ansatzes geht, sondern vielmehr um die Einschließlichkeit verschiedener Strategien. J. C. B.

The filtering of Parallel Realities.

Jasmin Grego and Joseph Smolenicky attracted their first attention with the gayly colored hairdressing salon, Coiffeursalon Sfax, in Zürich-Seefeld (1992), in which everything was reduced in favor of the elementary color design. The salon was not meant to be recognizable at first glance as a hairdressing business, but rather as a stage hinting at the salon's own show. The three windows, especially in the evenings, act as huge placards where the various realities or multiple encodings are perceivable. The "filters of parallel realities" stimulate the two architects to connect different design approaches to one another so that various images overlap and join to form a kind of visual collage. This appears complicated, but exactly here, with the salon, it is easily assimilated and understood, because the reference system in Gregor and Smolenicky's work always rigorously develops out of the problem at hand. It is for this reason that they have not been willing to design further shops along the same idea, although opportunities would have been available.

Another work based on the installation of a strongly altered visualization of the space was a project for the underground ballet hall at the Opera House in Zurich. This practice hall lies in the third floor below the new building of the Opera House and is closed off from natural light and from any relation to the outside world. With a light installation that allows for linear, flat, pointed and diagonal light constellations, the cellar atmosphere is counteracted and the daily biological flow interpreted in a computer-controlled 24-hour rhythm. Through this, on the one hand, a spatial choreography specific to the hall is possible; on the other, the dreary practice space can be newly defined and made possible to experience solely through the regulation and colorful space-defining changing of the light.

Both the Coiffeursalon Sfax and the ballet hall project were pure installation work, with the architectonic aspect not much in evidence. With architects' first *succès d'estime,* the situation was quite different. In 1990 they were among the prize winners of the competition for the Swiss Pavilion at the 1992 World's Fair in Seville. Their design presented a closed, peaked, crystalline body evoking associations with a mountain or a rock crystal. But here again, the "assembly of various image motifs": in the pavilion, a materialization of simple, horizontal wooden boards was intended to contrast the solid mountain-ness with the ephemera and transitoriness of an exhibition building.

For Jasmin Grego and Joseph Smolenicky, the work for the Swiss Pavilion still wholly reflected a university discourse of that time – both studied at and graduated from the ETH Zurich. The project work for a group of vacation houses in Misox, Grisons, however, presented a completely different problem. Next to the traditional consistently gabled houses in the area, Grego and Smolenicky placed cubic forms that intentionally took up the theme of the condition of temporary residences. The minimal housing form of a studio unit is in direct relationship to its temporally limited use. When the houses are occupied, the buildings acquire a markedly sculptural appearance with the deep openings of the terrace and garage. When the doors to the terrace and garage are closed, all the openings seem to disappear. The unoccupied vacation house in its closed state thus becomes a jewelry box in the landscape, "a piece of intarsia furniture", as the architects call it, and not a house that sits empty most of the year. In this way, the unoccupied vacation house also finds an independent aesthetic expression.

For the firm Jockey/Vollmoeller AG, it was necessary to connect the existing warehouse to a new building unit for offices and administration. The firm's property lies in a district of Uster typified by a checkerboard of individualistic living and business industrial structures. The new company building was to set itself apart from the provinciality of the district and at the same time to merge with the structure that was already there. Here, the architects did not aim at an additive building complex; they wanted rather to integrate the different functional areas into one overall structure. They obviously pursued this according to the "quilt strategy", meaning that from the old and new parts a new whole was allowed to emerge. A "façade quilt" renders the functional interior structure of the building visible, and the larger form of the building's body declares itself as being one unit formed from a multitude of very different uses. The surfaces of the façade surrender themselves in the multiplicity of materials and façade openings to a well-balanced picture, where all façade elements become basic components of the image. The expression of the building alters according to choice and composition of the materials.

This project makes clear the pictorial design approach of Jasmin Grego and Joseph Smolenicky. They represent no special dogma. The reference systems are developed naturally from the task, and the theme of the "limitation of reality through our perception" is moreover taken up – or, said another way, the filtering of parallel realities. The intricacy of their projects and work to date demonstrates convincingly that the point is not the exclusiveness of architectural methods, but rather the inclusiveness of various strategies. J.C.B.

Jasmin Grego, Joseph Smolenicky

Schweizer Pavillon Weltausstellung Sevilla, 1992.

Der zehngeschossige, pyramidiale Pavillon ist außen mit Holzbrettern verkleidet. Die Holzverkleidung ist in einem dunklen Silbergrau lasierend gestrichen und mit einem Seidenglanz lackiert. Dies verleiht dem Gebäude eine zurückhaltende und gebrochene Eleganz. In der starken Sonne des Südens werden die lichtzugewandten Seiten des Pavillons sehr hell reflektieren und die lichtabgewandten dunkel schimmernd erscheinen. Das Gebäude kann somit sehr hell oder auch sehr dunkel wirken. Um bei den mit visuellen Reizen überfluteten Besuchern der Weltausstellung das Interesse zu wecken, ist ein durch seine ausgeprägt klare, monolithische Form starkes und von weitem sichtbares Zeichen nötig. Das Potential des Klischees als allgemein verständliche Sprache wird genutzt. Die Gefahr der Banalität des Klischees wird durch zwei Maßnahmen verhindert. Als erstes ist die Erscheinung des Projektes mehrdeutig assoziierbar als Berg, Pyramide, Bauernhaus oder Zelt. Zweitens entsteht von weitem die körperliche Wirkung einer monumentalen, schweren Masse. Aus der Nähe erfahren, verändert sich die Massivität in eine hautähnliche, dünne Bretterarchitektur aus Holz. Von nahem ist es auch nicht mehr möglich, die Form als Ganzes nachzuvollziehen. Seinem Zweck entsprechend will das Projekt gleichzeitig Attraktion und würdevolle Selbstdarstellung sein.

Swiss Pavilion, 1992 World's Fair, Seville.

The exterior of the ten-story pyramidic pavilion is covered with wooden boards glazed a dark silver-gray and lacquered to a satin finish. This lends the building a reserved and understated elegance. In the strong sun of the south, the sides of the pavilion facing the light become brightly reflective while the sides facing away from the light seem to shimmer darkly. The building can therefore appear either very light or very dark. In order to catch the interest of the visitors to the Fair, barraged to overflowing with visual stimulation, a strong symbol distinguished by its distinctly clear monolithic form and visible from afar is necessary. The potential of the cliché as generally understandable language has been utilized, while the danger of the banality of the cliché has been diminished in two ways. Firstly, the appearance of the project is ambiguously associable as mountain, pyramid, farmhouse or tent. Secondly, the physical effect of the structure from a distance is that of a heavy, monumental mass. At close range, the massiveness changes into an architecture of fine, skin-like wooden shuttering, and it is no longer possible to take in the form as a whole. Correspondingly, its purpose is to be an attraction and, at the same time, a dignified representation of Switzerland.

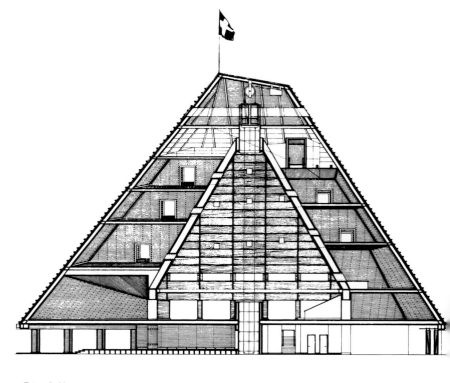

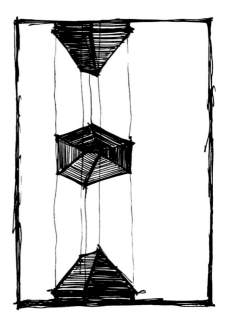

Entwurfsskizze
  Design sketch
Schnitt
  Section

Grundriß Aussichtsplattform
   Floor plan of viewing platform
Ansicht
   View

Jasmin Grego, Joseph Smolenicky

Jockey/Vollmoeller AG, Erweiterung einer Lagerhalle mit einem Bürogebäude, Uster, 1994.

Auf dem Grundstück mit einer bestehenden Lagerhalle aus den sechziger Jahren sollte ein neues, repräsentatives Verwaltungsgebäude projektiert werden. Ein bestehender, eingeschossiger Anlieferungsanbau wird abgerissen. Dadurch entsteht ein klarer Gebäudekubus und eine flache Fassade gegen die Straße. In dieser Ebene werden die neuen Nutzungen an die bestehende Halle angebaut. Insgesamt entsteht so eine neue Großform. Diese Großform aus heterogenen Teilen wird über die Proportionen der verschiedenen Fassadenflächen zusammengehalten. Die äußere Fassadeneinteilung entspricht zum großen Teil dem inneren Aufbau. Einige Flächen, wie etwa die Firmenbeschriftung, haben den Charakter von Intarsien.

Die innere Halle mit den hierarchischen Öffnungen ist sowohl Zentrum der Firma, wie auch Guckkasten in die verschiedenen Abteilungen. Sie erzeugt die Kommunikation zwischen Betriebsbereichen und ein konkretes Verständnis der inneren Abläufe.

Jockey/Vollmoeller AG, Expansion of a Warehouse with Office Building, Uster, 1994.

A new, representative administration building is to be developed on the site of an existing warehouse from the 1960s. A one-story delivery and supply annex already on the property is torn down. A clear cube of a building with a flat façade facing the street remains. On this level, the new utilities are built onto the existing hall. Altogether they emerge as a large new form. This larger form, composed of heterogeneous parts, is held together by the proportions of the different façade surfaces. The exterior subdivision of the façade corresponds in large measure to the interior construction. Some surfaces, such as the inscription of the firm's name, have the character of intarsia.

The interior hall with hierarchical openings is the center of the firm as well as a peep-show box of the various departments. The hall generates communication between operational groups and a concrete understanding of the course of events occurring on the interior.

Hauptfassade und Fassade Anlieferung
Main façade and delivery façade

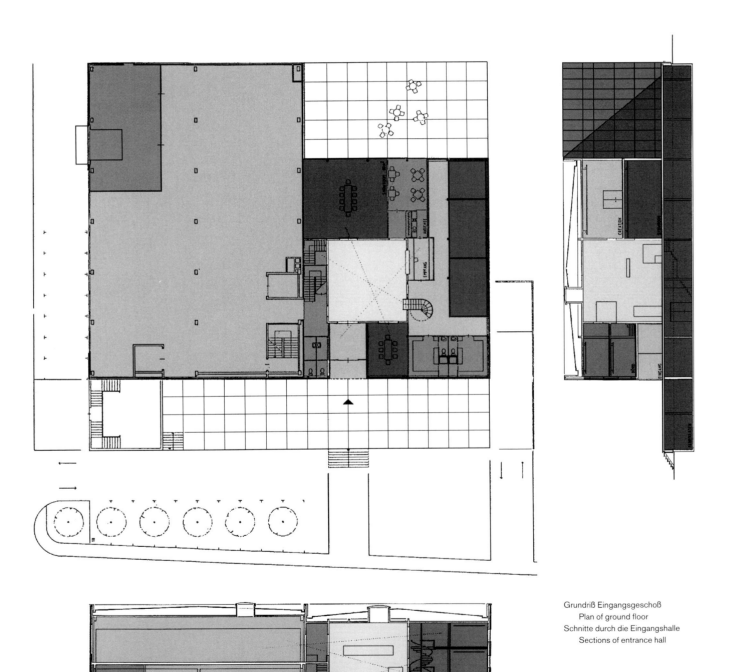

Grundriß Eingangsgeschoß
Plan of ground floor
Schnitte durch die Eingangshalle
Sections of entrance hall

Jasmin Grego, Joseph Smolenicky

Holzhäuser im Misox, Graubünden, 1995.

Die Idee basiert auf einer additiven Reihung dreier verschieden breiter Haussegmente. Das System funktioniert wie eine Bergsteiger-Ausrüstung, die mit verschiedenen Rucksäcken erweitert werden kann. Es erlaubt eine große Anzahl Kombinationen, die verschiedene Wohnarten und dadurch auch Lebensweisen generieren. Die entstehenden Wohnformen könnte man folgendermaßen benennen: Ein-Raum-Haus, Loft, Einfamilienhaus, minimales Ferienhaus oder einfaches Haus für die ältere Generation.

Die Dramaturgie des Innenraums wird durch die Steigung des Geländes erzeugt. Im gleichen Raum entfalten sich so verschiedene räumliche Qualitäten. Im hinteren Teil gegen den Hang entsteht eine intime Kleinräumlichkeit mit einem direkten Bezug zum Boden. Gegen vorne weitet sich der Raum loftartig in die gedeckte Terrasse zur Aussicht hin aus.

Wooden Houses in the Misox Valley, Grisons, 1995.

The idea is based on an additive series of house segments of three varying widths. The system functions like a mountaineering outfit that can be expanded with various backpacks. It allows a large number of combinations that generate differing lifestyles and thereby ways of life as well. One could call the resulting housing forms in the following way: studio, loft, one-family house, minimal vacation house, or simple house for the older generation.

The dramaturgy of the interior space is exhibited in the gradient of the countryside. In the same space, very different spatial qualities unfold. In the back against the slope, a small, intimate space is formed with an exact relationship to the ground. In the front, the space extends loft-like into the covered terrace and out towards the view.

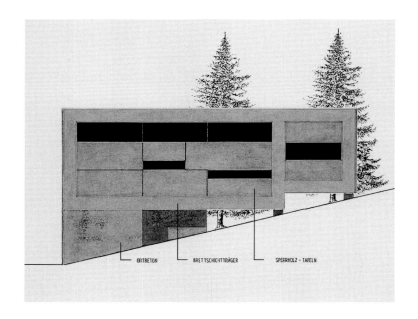

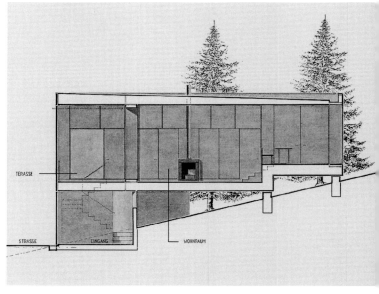

Längsfassade
  Elevation of façade
Längsschnitt durch den Wohnraum
  Elevation section of living room
Situation
  Situation

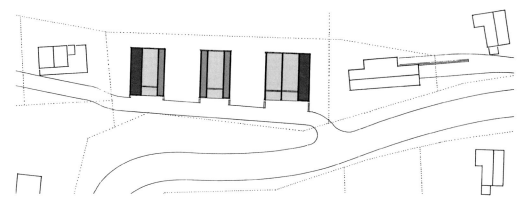

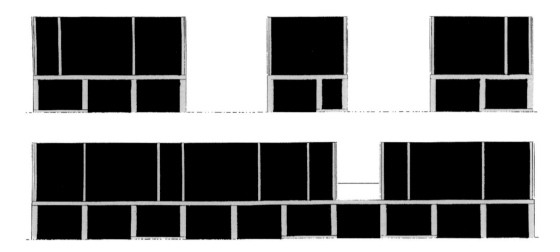

Einzelhäuser und Reihenhäuser
Detached houses and attached housing unit

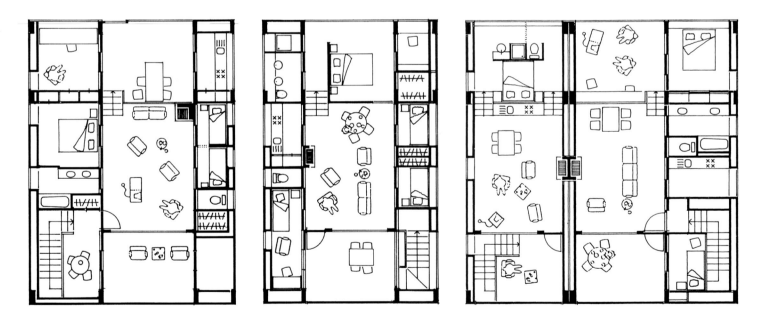

Einfamilienhaus, großes Ferienhaus, Studio und größeres Ferienhaus
One-family house, large vacation house, studio and larger vacation house

Jasmin Grego, Joseph Smolenicky

Unterirdischer Ballettsaal, Opernhaus Zürich, 1995.

Der Übungsraum des Zürcher Ballettensembles befindet sich, abgeschlossen von jeglichem Bezug zur Außenwelt, im dritten Untergeschoß des Opernhaus-Neubaus. In diesem Raum werden Choreographien entwickelt, und Tänzer absolvieren hier täglich ein sechs- bis achtstündiges Training. Die unterirdische Lage des Ballettsaals als Ort intensiver körperlicher Arbeit ist an sich problematisch, kann aber aus vielfältigen Gründen nicht vermieden werden.

Das Projekt basiert auf zwei Eingriffen: Erstens wird der Raum «aufgeräumt», das heißt von vielfältigen nachträglichen Zusätzen wie Vorhängen, Vorhangschienen und überzähligen Spiegeln und so weiter befreit. Der zweite Eingriff betrifft das Licht, die elementare Voraussetzung, um einen unterirdischen Raum zum «Leben zu erwecken». In der künstlichen Beleuchtung verbinden sich hier absolute Notwendigkeit und Ausdruck.

Zunächst wird das weiße Deckenlicht in fünf mal fünf separat schaltbare Felder aufgeteilt, so daß lineare, flächige, punktuelle und diagonale Lichtkonstellationen als Ausdruck einer räumlichen Choreographie möglich werden. Die Intensität der weißen Fluoreszenzröhren wird von einem Computer gesteuert. Die Software moduliert das Licht in einem 24-Stunden-Rhythmus, entsprechend dem natürlichen Rhythmus des Tageslichts und des menschlichen Körpers.

Die zweite Ebene der Arbeit mit dem Licht betrifft die Wände. Unsichtbar an der Deckenkante werden entlang den drei nichtverspiegelten Wänden je drei Reihen farbiger Fluoreszenzröhren in den drei Grundfarben Rot, Gelb und Blau angebracht. Jede dieser drei indirekten Wandbeleuchtungen wird unabhängig von den andern über einen Zufallsgenerator gesteuert. Es entstehen farbige Lichtspiele an den Wänden, deren Kombinatorik fast unendlich ist. Der Lichtwechsel, der sich in einem sehr langsamen, fast unbewußten Rhythmus vollzieht, findet jedoch ausschließlich auf den Wänden statt – die Tänzer befinden sich immer im weißen Licht.

Mit künstlichen Mitteln wird so eine analoge Wirkung zu dem sich ständig verändernden Tageslicht erzeugt. Die Mittel – Fluoreszenzröhren und schlichte Software – sind ganz bewußt einfach gewählt und damit kompatibel mit der Nutzung des Saales als Übungsraum und der kellerhaften Atmosphäre der angrenzenden Räume. In diesem Sinn haben wir versucht, den Übungsraum nicht als Bühne mit ihrer hochentwickelten, preziösen Technik zu sehen, sondern als ein grobes Instrument, das erlaubt, fast skizzenhaft die Grundkonstellation einer Choreographie zu setzen. Ein solcher Raum ist nicht mehr der klassische Raum, der durch Wände definiert wird. Es ist ein Zustand ohne präzise Form. Die indirekten Lichtwandlungen lösen die Körperlichkeit der Wände völlig auf. Der Raum existiert gleichsam nur als Lichterscheinung. Wird das Licht gelöscht, verschwindet er.

Underground Ballet Hall, Opera House, Zurich, 1995.

The practice room of the Zurich Ballet is located in the third underground floor of the Opera House's new building, closed off from any contact with the outside world. In this room, choreography is developed and dancers complete six to eight hours of training a day. The underground location of the ballet hall as a place for intensive physical work is problematic in itself, but cannot be avoided for a multitude of reasons.

The project is based on two operations: First, the room is "tidied up". This means that the many superfluous additions, such as curtains, curtain rods, surplus mirrors and so on, are removed. The second stage concerns the light, the elementary prerequisite for "awakening" the room "to life". Here, the artificial light joins together expression and absolute necessity.

First, the white ceiling light is split up into five times five separately controlled fields, so that linear, flat, pointed and diagonal constellations of light as the expression of a spatial choreography become possible. The intensity of the white fluorescent bulbs is controlled by computer, and the software modulates the light in a 24-hour rhythm, corresponding to the natural rhythm of daylight and the human body.

The second level of work with the light concerns the walls. Three series of colored fluorescent bulbs in the three primary colors – red, yellow, blue – are affixed out of sight to the edge of the ceiling along each of the three non-reflective walls. Each of these three indirect wall lighting systems is controlled independently of the others by a random generator. The combinational possibilities of lightplay on the walls is almost endless. The variation of light is carried out in a very slow, almost unconscious rhythm, but it always takes place exclusively on the walls. The dancers themselves are always in white light.

Thus, by artificial means, an effect analogous to the constantly changing light of the day is produced. The means – fluorescent bulbs and uncomplicated software – have been consciously chosen for their simplicity and are thus compatible with the function of the hall as a practice room and with the cellar-like atmosphere of the adjacent spaces. In this sense, we have tried to see the practice room not as a stage with its highly-developed, refined technology, but rather as a roughhewn instrument that allows us to set, almost sketchily, the basic constellation of a choreography. Such a space is no longer a classical room, defined by walls. It is a situation without precise form. The indirect shifts of light completely dissolve the substantiality of the walls. The room exists virtually only as an apparition of the light. When the light is turned off, it disappears.

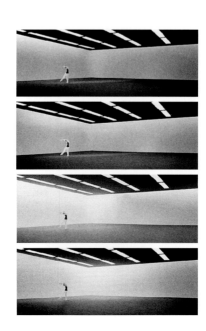

Lichtsequenzen
Light sequences

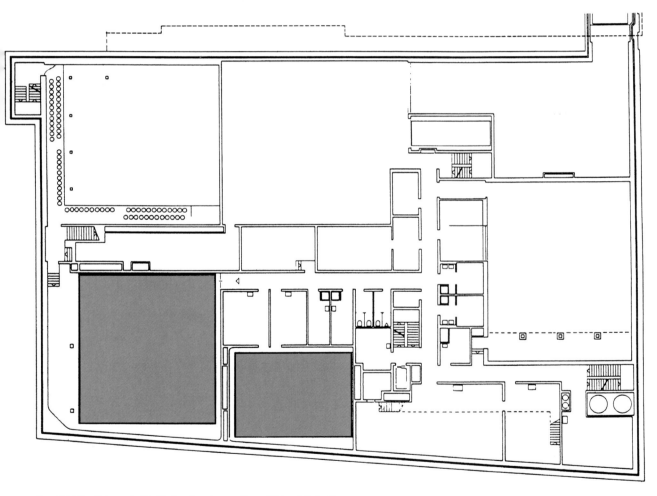

Grundriß drittes Untergeschoß im Zürcher Opernhaus, großer und kleiner Ballettsaal
Floor plan of third basement floor of the Zurich Opera House, large and small ballet halls

Jasmin Grego, Joseph Smolenicky

| **Biografien** | **Werkverzeichnis** | **Bibliografie** |

Jasmin Grego
1964 geboren in Zürich.
Zwei Jahre Studium der Kunstgeschichte an der Universität in Zürich.
Architekturstudium an der ETH Zürich.
Diplom bei Prof. Wolfgang Schett.

Joseph Smolenicky
1960 geboren in der ČSSR.
Architekturstudium an der ETH Zürich.
Diplom bei Prof. Fabio Reinhart, ETH Zürich.
Assistent bei Miroslav Šik, ETH Zürich.
Seit 1992 Assistent bei Prof. Hans Kollhoff, ETH Zürich.

Seit 1992 gemeinsames Büro in Zürich.

Auszeichnung
Ikarus-Preis 1995, Sfax in Zürich wird zum schönsten Coiffeursalon Europas gewählt.

1992
Schweizer Pavillon für die Weltausstellung Sevilla, Preisträger.
Paris Kulturhauptstadt Europas, Wohnungsbau, Wettbewerbseinladung.
Umbau Coiffeursalon Sfax (heute Zelo), Zürich-Seefeld.

1993
Berlin Kulturhauptstadt Europas, Wohnungsbau, Wettbewerbseinladung.
Umbau Villa am Niederhofenrain in Zürich.

1994
Jockey/Vollmoeller AG, Verwaltungsgebäude in Uster, Wettbewerbseinladung, zweiter Preis.

1995
Neugestaltung Theaterplatz in Baden, Wettbewerbseinladung.
Umbau Kommunikationsagentur Viva AG, Zürich.
Coiffeursalon Sfax, Zürich.
Umbau Kleiderladen Fidelio, Münzplatz Zürich, in Zusammenarbeit mit Konrad Hürlimann, dipl. Arch. ETH.
Holzhäuser im Misox, Graubünden, Projekt.
Unterirdischer Ballettsaal, Opernhaus Zürich, Projekt.

Jos Bosmann, *New neofunctional architecture,* in: Quaderns 202/1994.
Ulla Rogalski, *Farbe pur und satt,* MD 11/92, Deutschland.
Verena Huber, Alfred Hablützel, *Coiffeursalon Sfax,* in: Innenarchitektur in der Schweiz 1942-1992, VSI Verlag.
Color, in: Wind, World Interior Design, Japan, Spring 96.

Veröffentlichungen von Grego & Smolenicky
Nur Fassade, in: archithese, 3/92.
Farbige Räume, in: archithese 6/94.
Bauen in Holz, in: archithese 5/95.
Farbe, in: Baumeister, 3/94, Deutschland.

Biographies

Jasmin Grego
1964 Born in Zurich.
Two year study of art history at the University in Zurich.
Studied architecture at the ETH Zurich.
Graduated under Prof. Wolfgang Schett.

Joseph Smolenicky
1960 Born in the ČSSR.
Studied architecture at the ETH Zurich.
Graduated under Prof. Fabio Reinhart, ETH Zurich.
Assistant to Miroslav Šik, ETH Zurich.
Since 1992 assistant to Prof. Hans Kollhoff, ETH Zurich.

Since 1992 joint office in Zurich.

Award
Ikarus Price 1995, Sfax in Zurich is chosen most beautiful hairdressing salon in Europe.

List of Works

1992
Swiss Pavilion for the World's Fair, Seville, prize-winner.
Paris Culture Capital of Europe, apartment building, competition invitation.
Conversion Coiffeursalon Sfax (today Zelo), Zurich-Seefeld.

1993
Berlin Culture Capital of Europe, apartment building, competition invitation.
Conversion Villa on Niederhofenrain, Zurich.

1994
Jockey/Vollmoeller AG, administration building in Uster, competition invitation, second prize.

1995
Theaterplatz in Baden, new design, competition invitation.
Conversion Viva AG communication agency, Zurich.
Coiffeursalon Sfax, Zurich.
Conversion Fidelio clothes store, Münzplatz Zurich, in collaboration with Konrad Hürlimann, dipl. Arch. ETH.
Wooden Houses in the Misox Valley, Grisons, project.
Underground Ballet Hall, Opera House, Zurich, project.

Bibliography

Jos Bosmann, *New neofunctional architecture,* in: Quaderns 202/1994.
Ulla Rogalski, *Farbe pur und satt,* MD 11/92, Germany.
Verena Huber, Albert Hablützel, *Coiffeursalon Sfax,* in: Innenarchitektur in der Schweiz 1942-1992, VSI Verlag.
Color, in: Wind, World Interior Design, Japan, Spring 96.

Publications by Grego & Smolenicky
Nur Fassade, in: archithese, 3/92.
Farbige Räume, in: archithese 6/94.
Bauen in Holz, in: archithese 5/95.
Farbe, in: Baumeister, 3/94, Germany.

Kaschka Knapkiewicz
Axel Fickert
Zürich

Mitarbeiterinnen und Mitarbeiter
Collaborators
  Fritz Brügger
  Regula Klöti
  Hanspeter Odermatt
  Anita Widmann

Wettbewerbe Wohnungsbau | Apartment Building Competitions | 1986–92

Landhaus mit Pferdestallungen | Country House with Horse Stalls | Hütten, 1992–94

Gewerbebau für ein Musikhaus | Commercial Building for a Music Store | Effretikon, 1994

Perrondächer Hauptbahnhof | Platform Roofs for Main Station | Zürich, 1995

Räumliche Komplexität.

Einer breiten Öffentlichkeit sind die Arbeiten von Kaschka Knapkiewicz und Axel Fickert noch kaum bekannt. Das wird sich mit der Fertigstellung der neuen seitlichen Perrondächer des Zürcher Hauptbahnhofs ändern, die sie zusammen mit Marcel Meili und Markus Peter geplant haben und die der Stadt mit ihrer Leichtigkeit und Monumentalität zu einer ungewohnt eleganten und offenen Verbindung zu den Geleisen verhelfen. Unter Architekten hingegen finden ihre Projekte schon lange große Beachtung. Sie stellen als Ergebnis einer geduldigen und kontinuierlichen Forschung oft exemplarische Lösungen in den zentralen Bereichen Büro- und Wohnungsbau dar. So ist etwa der sogenannte «Schnabelschnitt» schon etliche Male von anderen Architekten als Typ übernommen worden und damit zu einem Teil des allgemeinen architektonischen Repertoires geworden. Es handelt sich um einen besonderen Anschluß der Fassade an die Geschoßdecken, bei dem in einer Betonskelettkonstruktion die als Träger wirkenden Brüstungen mit einem nach außen schnabelartig auskragenden, horizontalen Element ergänzt werden, an dem die Fassade aufgehängt wird. Damit lassen sich die räumlichen und statischen Vorteile einer massiven Brüstung mit den Vorteilen einer vollständig verglasten Fassade kombinieren. Es entstehen so helle Räume mit viel direktem Himmelslicht, die gleichzeitig durch die niedrige Brüstung klar gefaßt sind. Im Bereich des «Schnabels» wird längs der Fassade eine eigene Raumschicht geschaffen, in der sich einige technische und konstruktive Probleme elegant lösen lassen, die zudem als Ablagefläche oder Sitzbank dienen kann, vor allem aber den Raum gliedert und ihm eine spezifische Qualität verleiht.

Komplexe und differenzierte Räume sind auch das Thema der «recherche patiente» im Wohnungsbau. Für den Wettbewerb zur Überbauung des ehemaligen Bahhofareals Selnau in Zürich entwickelten Kaschka Knapkiewicz und Axel Fickert 1986/87 eine Gebäudetypologie, bei der sich vier große und eine kleine Wohnung über drei Geschosse ineinander verschränken. In den großen Einheiten werden dabei verhältnismäßig bescheidene, niedrige Zimmer mit einem großzügigen, anderthalbgeschossigen Wohnraum kombiniert. Durch die Inszenierung von Blickbeziehungen über die Diagonale entsteht so eine Weiträumigkeit und Offenheit, wie man sie aus dem Wohnungsbau sonst kaum kennt. Die plastische Durchbildung von Elementen wie den Brüstungen und der Fassadenschicht vermehrt den räumlichen Reichtum und sorgt dafür, daß bei aller Größe des Raums der Bezug zum menschlichen Maß stets erhalten bleibt. Dies gilt auch für die äußere Erscheinung der Baukörper, wobei hier zusätzlich mit der Irritation gespielt wird, die durch die ungewohnten Geschoßhöhen und die damit verbundenen Maßstabsverschiebungen entsteht.

Kaschka Knapkiewicz und Axel Fickert knüpfen mit ihren Wohnungen an eine Entwicklung an, die unter anderem auf Le Corbusiers «Unité d'Habitation» zurückgeht und vor allem in den sechziger Jahren zu Wohnhäusern mit komplexen Schnittlösungen geführt hat. Meist wurde dabei jedoch das Potential von differenzierten, der Raumgröße und -nutzung angepaßten Raumhöhen nicht genutzt, die gerade die wesentliche Qualität des Selnau-Projektes ausmachen. Die hier erarbeiteten Typen werden in der Folge im Hinblick auf eine noch stärkere Mischung von unterschiedlich großen Wohnungen und verschiedenen konkreten Situationen weiterentwickelt. Im Wettbewerb für eine Wohnüberbauung in Wettswil gelang es, die Hanglage des Grundstückes mit einem parallel zum Terrain verlaufenden Dach in raffinierter Weise für die ineinander verschachtelten Wohnungen zu nutzen und dabei den ökonomischen Nachteil des relativ großen Raumvolumens zu minimieren. In der Bebauungsstruktur entstanden durch eine Aneinanderreihung der Wohnungsgruppen lange Zeilen, die durch ihre konstante Höhe, mit dem großen, zusammenfassenden Dach und einer besonderen Ausbildung der Kopfteile als einheitliche Baukörper mit beinahe zoomorphen Zügen in Erscheinung treten. Die Siedlung erhielt so eine prägnante Gestalt, die präzise auf die Topographie reagiert.

Trotz eines ersten Preises im Wettbewerb wird auch dieses Projekt, wie die vorhergehenden, nicht gebaut werden. Immerhin können Kaschka Knapkiewicz und Axel Fickert ihre räumlichen Vorstellungen mittlerweile auch in einigen eigenen Bauten realisiert sehen. Die in den Projekten gemachten Versprechen werden dabei eingelöst. Räumliche Vielfalt und plastische Gestaltung im Innenausbau finden eine adäquate Umsetzung in Materialisierung, Detaillierung und farblicher Gestaltung. M. T.

Perrondach Hauptbahnhof Zürich, 1995
Roof over platform, main train station, Zurich, 1995

Spatial Complexity.

The works of Kaschka Knapkiewicz and Axel Fickert are not yet known to a wider public. This will change with the completion of the new side platform roofs at Zurich's main train station, Hauptbahnhof, which were planned in conjunction with Marcel Meili and Markus Peter and which display a lightness and monumentality that helps the city make an unusually elegant and open connection with the tracks. Yet among architects, their projects have long since attracted great attention. They represent often exemplary solutions in the central field of office and residence construction that is the result of patient and continuous research. Their so-called "beak section" has already more than once been taken up by other architects as a type and thereby become part of the general architectonic repertoire. The beak is created in the special union of the façade with the story floors in which, in a concrete skeletal construction, the parapets, acting as supports, are supplemented towards the outside with a beak-like, cantilevered horizontal element on which the façade hangs. In this way, the spatial and constructive advantages of a massive parapet are combined with the advantages of a fully glazed façade. The result is rooms bright with plenty of direct sunlight and yet distinctly held, at the same time, by the low parapets. In the area of the "beak", along the façade, a separate level of space is created in which several technical and constructive problems are solved, which moreover can be used as storage or sitting space, but which above all structures the room and lends it a specific quality.

Complex and differentiated spaces is the theme of the *recherche patiente* in residence building. For the competition for the superstructure of the former Selnau train station grounds in Zurich, Kaschka Knapkiewicz and Axel Fickert developed a building typology in 1986/87 in which one small and four large apartments are staggered into one another over the space of three floors. Proportionally modest and unpretentious rooms are simultaneously combined in the larger unit with a generous one-and-a-half floor living space. Through the staging, over the diagonals, of relationships between various outward views, a spaciousness and openness emerges that one seldom encounters in the construction of apartments. The plastic structural design of elements such as parapets and the façade layer augment the spatial richness and in this way ensure that, in all room sizes, the relationship to the human scale is kept constant throughout. This goes as well for the exterior appearance of the building, which further irritates senses with unusual floor heights and the shifts in scale arising from them.

With their apartments, Kaschka Knapkiewicz and Axel Fickert tie into a development that refers back to Le Corbusier's *Unité d'Habitation*, among others, and that led above all in the 1960s to houses with complex sectional solutions. These, for the most part, though, did not utilize the potential of differentiated room heights that matched the size and use of the rooms. Exactly this, however, is what comprises the essential quality of the Selnau project. The types elaborated on here are developed with regard to an even stronger mixture of differently sized apartments and various concrete situations. In the competition for a residence superstructure in Wettswil, they succeeded in using the incline of the land in a sophisticated way for the interlocking of the apartments, with a roof running parallel to the terrain, and through this, they minimized the economic disadvantage of a relatively large spatial volume. Because of the arrangement of the apartment groups in strings, long rows emerged in the development structure which, with their constant height, large combined roof and a special development of head pieces, came to look like a unified building unit with almost zoomorphic features. The settlement thus retains a poignant appearance which responds precisely to the topography.

Despite a first prize in the competition, this project too, like the others before it, will not be built. For all that, Kaschka Knapkiewicz and Axel Fickert were able, in the meantime, to see their spatial ideas realized in several of their own buildings. Thus, the promises made in their projects are redeemed. Spatial multiplicity and plastic design in interior construction work are appropriately realized in materialization, detailling and color design. M.T.

Kaschka Knapkiewicz, Axel Fickert

Wettbewerbe Wohnungsbau, 1986-92.

Am Anfang einer Reihe von Wohnbauentwürfen mit ähnlicher Thematik steht das im Architekturbüro Steigerpartner, Zürich, entworfene Wettbewerbsprojekt auf dem Areal des ehemaligen Bahnhofs Selnau in Zürich. Hier wurden zwei Wohntypen entwickelt, deren räumliche Charaktere in Projekten wie für Barcelona und Effretikon fortlaufend weiterentwickelt werden. Sie sind geprägt vom Spiel unterschiedlicher Geschoßhöhen innerhalb der Wohneinheit.

Um den inneren Erschließungsgang gruppieren sich drei Wohneinheiten, deren Zimmerbereiche normale Raumhöhe aufweisen, während Wohnbereiche, Küche und Loggien einen halbgeschossigen Versatz nach unten oder nach oben mit entsprechend größerer Raumhöhe haben. Dieser Wohntyp steht in der Tradition von Le Corbusiers «Immeuble Villa» und «Unité d'Habitation» bis zu Ginzburgs «Narkomfin».

Der andere Wohntyp weist im Längsschnitt den Geschoßversatz in Verbindung mit einem durch die ganze Bautiefe gehenden Wohnbereich und einer L-förmig angeschlossenen Küche auf. So entsteht eine Gruppe von vier Wohneinheiten mit dreieinhalb Zimmern und einer Zweizimmerwohnung, die um ein inneres Treppen-

Apartment Building Competitions, 1986-92.

At the beginning of a series of housing construction designs with a similar range of themes was the competition project for the site of the former Selnau Train Station in Zurich. In this project, two housing types were developed whose spatial characters are continuously being elaborated further in such projects as those for Barcelona and Effretikon. They are characterized by a play of various floor heights within the living unit.

Three such units are grouped around the inner access way. Within the rooms, the floor heights remain normal, while the living and loggia areas and the kitchen have a half-story displacement either upwards or downwards, with correspondingly larger story heights. This housing type is in the tradition of Le Corbusier's *Immeuble Villa* and *Unité d'Habitation*, and on to Ginsburg's *Narkomfin*.

The other housing type features floor displacement in the elevation, in connection with a living area running the entire depth of the building and an adjoining L-shaped kitchen. A group of four three-and-a-half room housing units plus a two-room apartment were developed in this way, all laid out around an inner stairway. In the Barcelona project, this type is being expanded around a room

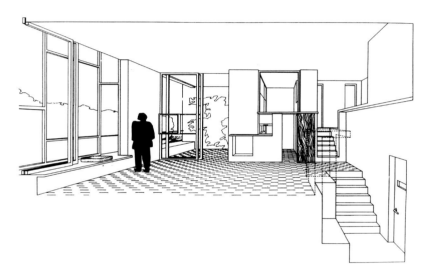

Wettbewerbsmodell
    Competition model
Gruppe von fünf Wohnungen, Modell
    Group of five apartments, model
Innenraumansicht einer Wohnung
    View of apartment interior
Erschließung, Schnitt
    Access system, section

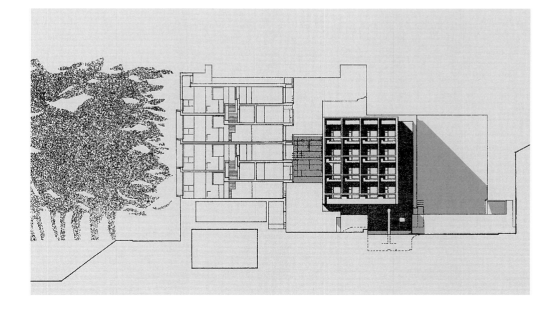

Projekt Selnau, 1986/87

haus angeordnet sind. Im Projekt Barcelona wird dieser Typ um eine normalhohe Zimmertranche erweitert. Durch die Schaltmöglichkeit von Zimmern entstehen somit Wohnungen von beliebiger Größe, deren räumliche Komplexität durch Bewegungsabläufe in der Längsrichtung erst richtig inszeniert werden kann. Der durchgehende hohe Wohnraum ist nicht mehr Endstation einer Raumfolge, sondern wird zum Zentrum der gegenüberliegenden Zimmertrakte. Ein Zimmer wird durch Weglassen einer Wand zur seitlichen Galerie; es entsteht somit eine zur L-förmig anschließenden Küche punktsymmetrische Raumerweiterung. Die räumlichen Ereignisse entlang der Niveausprünge spielen sich nie im inneren, dunklen Bereich der Wohnung ab (wie dies bei Galerietypen wie «Citrohan» der Fall ist), sondern immer im wechselnden Seitenlicht. Die seitwärts zur Richtung der klaren Schotenstruktur des Grundrisses ausbuchtenden Raumbereiche (Küche, Galerie) schaffen in ihrer räumlichen Zuordnung mehrdeutige Zonen, die den fließenden Charakter dieses Raumgebildes erst ausmachen. Dabei wird das Verhältnis von Wänden zu den durch sie definierten Räumen im Sinne von Positiv-/Negativ-Phänomenen ambivalent. Die durch Wände abgeschlossenen Zimmergruppen können als Körper in fließenden Leerräumen gelesen werden.

segment of normal height. The possibility of switching rooms around in this way results in apartments of any desired size, whose spatial complexity can only truly be staged through the flow of movement in the longitudinal direction. The high continuous living space is no longer the last stop in a succession of rooms, but rather becomes the center of the room tracts facing it. Through the omission of a wall, a room turns into a side gallery and expands the space symmetrically to an adjacent L-shaped kitchen. The spatial results along the jumps in levels never take place in a dark inner area of the apartment (as is the case with the *Citrohan* gallery type), rather always in shifting side light. The convex room areas sideways to the direction of the clear pod-structure of the floor plan (kitchen, gallery) create, in their spatial ordering, ambiguous zones that only then begin to define the fluid character of this room form. At the same time, the relationship of the walls to the rooms they define is, in the sense of positive-negative phenomena, ambivalent. The groups of rooms closed off by the walls could be read as bodies in empty flowing space.

We have worked on the principle of the half-story displacement in three further projects and with other requirements. If the contrast of room heights was in the foreground in the competitions

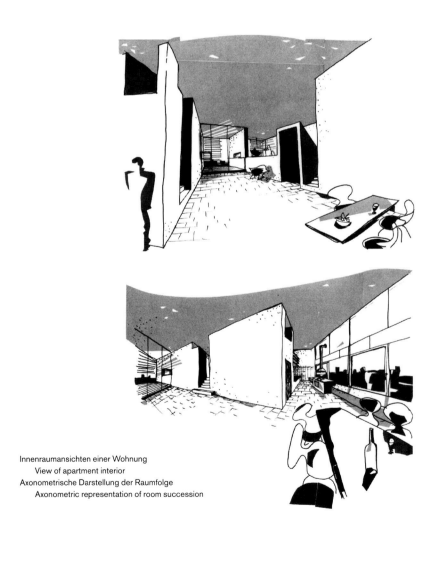
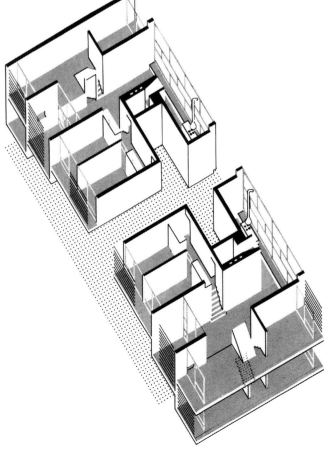

Innenraumansichten einer Wohnung
View of apartment interior
Axonometrische Darstellung der Raumfolge
Axonometric representation of room succession

Projekt Barcelona, 1989

Kaschka Knapkiewicz, Axel Fickert

Das Prinzip des halben Geschoßversatzes haben wir in drei weiteren Projekten und unter anderen Voraussetzungen weiter bearbeitet. Stand in den Wettbewerben für Selnau und Barcelona der Kontrast der Raumhöhen im Vordergrund, stellt nun der Geschoßversatz die Topographie des vorgefundenen Geländes dar. Bei leichter Hangneigung werden die Wohnbereiche von Winkelhäusern im Schnitt S-förmig übereinandergeschoben, so daß alternierend hang- und talseitige Höfe entstehen. Dieses Prinzip wird beim Projekt für Wettswil in den Innenräumen der Wohnungen wirksam. Durch die S-förmige Verschränkung der Wohnräume werden die Dimensionen der Hauseinheit seitlich erweitert, ganz im Gegensatz zum traditionellen Reihenhaus mit seiner starren Ausrichtung innerhalb der Schoten. Beim Übereinanderschieben der Häuser zeichnet sich das Volumen der jeweils oberen Wohnräume im Luftraum der unteren als Einbuchtung ab und schafft räumlich kontrastierende Zonen zwischen Hoch und Niedrig. Die Topographie des Geländes wird dabei zum bestimmenden Teil des inneren Raumgefüges.

for Selnau and Barcelona, it is now the topography of the land found at the site that delineates the displacement of the floors. With a slight decline, the living areas of angular houses are, on the average, thrust over one another in an S-shape, so that alternating uphill and downhill courtyards are formed. This principle is effective in the interior spaces of the apartments in the Wettswil project. The S-form staggering of the living spaces widens the dimensions of the housing unit, in total contrast to traditional attached houses with their rigid organization within the pod. With houses shifted on top of one another, the volume of each of the upper living areas shows up as an indentation in the air space of the one below it and creates a spatially contrasting zone between high and low. The topography of the land therefore becomes a defining part of the interior spatial structure.

Dachaufbau, Innenraum
Development of roof, interior

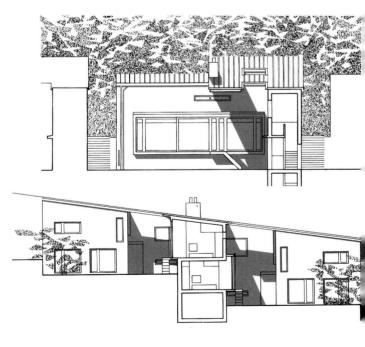

Wettbewerbsmodell
Competition model
Hofhäuser, Schnitte
Houses with courtyards, sections

Effretikon, 1988

Projekt Binz, 1989

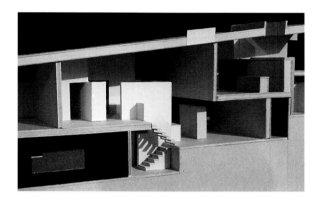 

Wettbewerbsmodell
    Competition model
Verschränkung der Innenräume, Modell
    Staggering of interior spaces, model
Ostfassade, Modell
    East façade, model
Innenraumansicht einer Wohnung
    View of apartment interior
Raumfolgen, Längsschnitt
    Succession of rooms, elevation section

Projekt Wettswil, 1992

Landhaus mit Pferdestallungen in Hütten, 1992–94.

Für ein Landhaus mit Pferdestallungen in Hütten ZH waren mit der schon bestehenden Scheune die Randbedingungen zum Anbau eines Wohnhauses gegeben. Dieses Wohnhaus ist, ähnlich einem Flarzhaus, als schmale Tranche angebaut. Wohnhaus und Stall sind durch einen durchgehenden Wirtschaftsgang in Talachse getrennt. Bergseitig ist das Haus in eine Art Wanne gestellt, die durch Oberlichter beleuchtete Raumnischen sowie eine doppelte Kaminanlage, als seitliche Ausweitung im schlanken Grundriß ausscheidet. Angeregt durch die topographische Situation (eine leicht ansteigende Talstufe), arbeiteten wir auch hier im Querschnitt mit einem Halbgeschoßversatz. Aufgrund der durch die erlaubte Ausnützung sowie des gegebenen Hausumrisses bedingten massiven Einschränkungen entstanden Räume von ungewohnter Höhe und Schlankheit, die Kontraste verschiedener Raumgrößen zulassen, so etwa im Übergang von gepreßtem zu hohem Wohnraum. Wir konnten eine Raumbewegung herstellen, die, auf der untersten Ebene beginnend, durch das ganze Haus führt und der aufsteigenden Bewegung der weiteren landschaftlichen Topographie entspricht. So entstand eine durchgehende Raumfolge vom Eßraum über den Wohnraum und das Schlafzimmer bis zum Studio unter dem Dach.

Country House with Horse Stalls in Hütten, 1992–94.

For a country house with horse stalls in Hütten there were, because of the existing barn, already clear preconditions concerning the expansion that could take place around the edges of the house. The house itself is built up of smaller segments, in a way similar to a *Flarzhaus*. Residence and stall are separated by a farming and work roadway running the length of the valley. The house is placed on the mountain side of the road in a kind of tub. This, combined with sky-lit niches and double fireplace, rules out sideways expansion of the narrow floor plan. Inspired by the topographical site (a slightly climbing valley grade), we worked here too with half-story displacement in the cross section. Because of massive limitations concerning the permitted use factor and in the given contour of the house, the rooms developed in unusual heights and narrow widths that allowed the contrasts of various room formats, as in the transition from compressed to high living space. In this way, we were able to display a spatial movement that leads from the lowest levels throughout the whole house, and that corresponds to the rising movement of the topography of the wider countryside; we thus produced a continuous succession of rooms from the dining room, through the living area, into the bedroom and up into the studio in the attic.

Wohnteil, Ostfassade
Segment of house, east façade

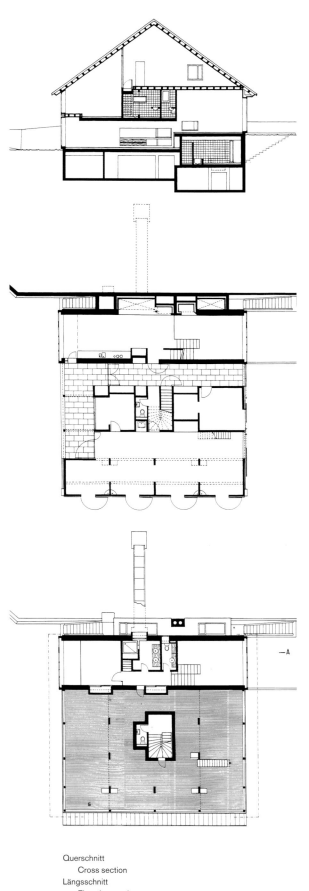
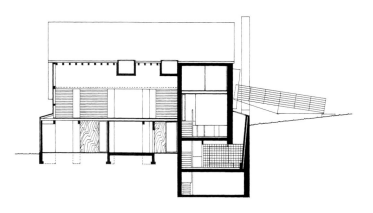

Querschnitt
  Cross section
Längsschnitt
  Elevation section
Erdgeschoß
  Ground floor
Obergeschoß
  Upper floor

Raumfolge zwischen Eß- und Wohnraum
Spatial flow between dining and living rooms

Kaschka Knapkiewicz, Axel Fickert

Gewerbebau für ein Musikhaus in Effretikon, 1994.

Aufgabe war die Projektierung eines umfangreichen Baukörpers an einer beliebigen Stelle unmittelbar an der Autobahn. Die Schlankheit und Ausrichtung des Gebäudes erreichten wir durch geometrische Deformation des Volumens. Fast beiläufig wurde dabei auch die außenräumliche Situation im Bereich des Zugangs als Raumbildung von Zufahrt, ausgeklapptem Eingang und schräggestellter Fassade präzisiert. In den geplanten weiteren Etappen wird die rhomboide Form zur Blitzform erweitert. Der Grundriß ist Ausdruck des Raumprogramms: Es sind große Flächen mit Handlagern vorgesehen, denen einige wenige Arbeitsplätze zugeordnet sind. Die Nutzung besteht ferner vor allem aus Großräumen, etwa Schauräumen für Pianos.

Ein Problem war, in der Gleichförmigkeit der Geschoßstapel Raumhierarchien zu schaffen. Eine entsprechende Interpretation des Raumprogramms ergab die Möglichkeit, maisonetteähnliche Situationen für die zusammenhängenden Räume im Erdgeschoß und in den beiden obersten Geschossen, den Pianoschauräumen, zu schaffen. Vom Eingangskörper ausgehend, verbindet als Aussparung an der Gebäudeecke eine durchgehende Erschließungshalle sämtliche Geschosse miteinander. Der Eingang wird durch einfache Ausdrehung aus der Fassadenflucht betont. Gleichzeitig entsteht mit der durchgehend verglasten Fassade eine beschriftbare geschlossene Wand.

Die Firmenbeschriftung auf den beiden schräg zur Autobahn stehenden Glasfassaden war ein wichtiges Anliegen der Bauherrschaft. Zusammen mit dem Atelier WBG Weiersmüller Bosshard Grüninger wurde ein Konzept erarbeitet. An der aus Gründen der Lärmdämmung zweischichtigen Fassade wird die Beschriftung in Siebdruck auf die äußere Glasschicht aufgedruckt. Die geschoßhohen Buchstaben, die durch Lüftungsflügel teilweise abgedeckt werden, ergeben trotz der Störung ein lesbares Gesamtbild.

Commercial Building for a Music Store in Effretikon, 1994.

The problem was to develop the project for an extensive building unit on a desirable location directly on the highway. We arrived at the narrowness and orientation of the building through geometric deformation of the volume. Almost incidentally, the exterior arrangement of space was clarified in the process where, in the area of entry to the building, the driveway, the extruding entrance and the angular façade form a spatial image. In further planned stages, the rhomboid form will be expanded to a lightning form. The floor plan is an expression of the spatial program. Large surfaces with handy storage facilities are foreseen, several of which are assigned a few work places. Moreover, the utility is composed primarily of large rooms, for example, piano showrooms.

One problem was to create hierarchical space in the uniformity of the stack of stories. One corresponding interpretation of the spatial program resulted in the possibility to create a maisonette-like situation for the connected rooms on the ground floor and the piano showrooms on the two upper floors. Starting from the entrance area as a recess in the corner of the building, a continuous open access hall connects all the stories with one another. The entrance is emphasized by the simple rotation of a piece of the flush façade. At the same time, a self-contained wall that can be written on is created from the continuous glass façade.

The firm's inscription on the two angular façades facing the highway was an important request of the clients. The concept was developed in conjunction with the Atelier WBG Weiersmüller Bosshard Grüninger. To act as a barrier to the noise, the façade was made two layers thick; the inscription was then silk-screened onto the outer layer of glass. The one-story-high lettering, despite the partial concealing by window vents, presents a wholly readable image.

Wettbewerbsmodell mit Bauetappen
Competition model with construction stages

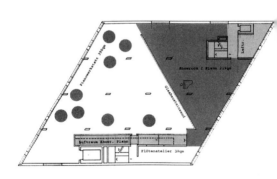

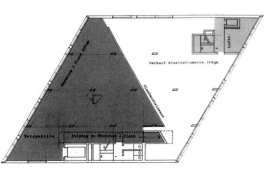

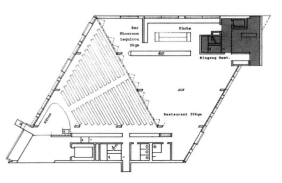

Viertes Obergeschoß
Fourth floor
Drittes Obergeschoß
Third floor
Erdgeschoß
Ground floor

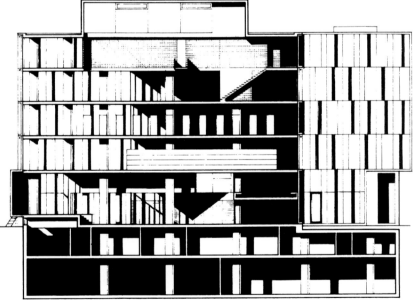

Arbeitsmodell, Eingangsfassade
 Working model, entrance façade
Raumfolge, Längsschnitt
 Succession of rooms, elevation section

Innenraumansicht, Galerie in den Pianoschauräumen
 View of interior, gallery with piano showrooms
Werbekonzept auf der Glasfassade
 Advertising concept on the glass façade

Perrondächer und Querhalle, Hauptbahnhof Zürich, 1995.

In Arbeitsgemeinschaft mit den Architekten Marcel Meili und Markus Peter bearbeiteten wir den Studienauftrag für die Perrondächer des Bahnhofs Zürich. Es galt einen Vorschlag zu machen für die äußersten Perrondächer, die heute die eigentlichen Fassaden des Bahnhofs zur Stadt hin bilden. Die heutige Situation ist auf den äußersten Perrons durch diverse Straßenverbreiterungen extrem eng geworden, zumal Perron, Trottoir und ein Drahtzaun als pemanenter Nachtabschluß den knappen Raum zerteilen. Wir schlugen vor, einen großzügigen Bereich zu schaffen, bei dem Trottoir und Perron fließend ineinander übergehen. Eine solche diffundierende Zone entspricht weitgehend den heutigen Bedürfnissen in diesem hochfrequentierten Bahnhof. Die Geste der aufgeklappten, weit vorkragenden Dächer formt (darin Mies van der Rohes Nationalgalerie in Berlin ähnlich) den introvertierten Charakter des bestehenden Hallenfeldes in einen Bestandteil des Stadtraums um.

Wichtig für die Formulierung eines solchen offenen Bereichs waren extrem weite Stützabstände (etwa 40 Meter) der massiven Betonpfeiler, deren Schrägstellung die räumliche Geste des Daches zusätzlich unterstützt. Der Aufbau des Daches besteht aus einer einfachen, leichten Fachwerkkonstruktion, die allseitig beplankt ist. Die großen Spannweiten werden mit doppelten Längsträgern überspannt, die gleichzeitig den Dachversatz definieren. Die Konstruktion wirkt raum- und lichthaltig durch die stehenden Oberlichter, die über die Reflexion an den Dachflächen vor allem den inneren Bereich des Perrons aufhellen. Das Licht wird diffundiert durch großflächige, durchscheinende Holzroste als Dachuntersicht. Die im Hohlraum vorgesehene, künstliche Beleuchtung schafft nachts eine ähnliche Lichtsituation wie am Tag.

Der Bahnhof wird nachts geschlossen. Um die räumliche Situation beibehalten zu können, ordneten wir den Nachtabschluß auf dem nächstinneren Perron in Form von Falttoren im Bereich der alten Perronstützen an. Die geschlossenen Tore setzen die halbtransparente Haut der Dachuntersicht fort und bilden eine große, zur Stadt hin offene Fuge des Bahnhofskörpers. Die beiden äußeren Gleise verbleiben so im Stadtraum, und späte Züge können in einen bereits geschlossenen Bahnhof einfahren. In der Ausführung wird jedoch eine andere Lösung des Nachtabschlusses realisiert.

Der Neubau der Querhalle war Teil des Studienauftrages, wird aber erst später realisiert werden. Wir schlugen eine in der äußeren Erscheinung flache Halle vor, die die Silhouette der Haupthalle im Gegensatz zu heute freispielt. Die neue Querhalle würde einen größeren Bereich als heute überspannen, eine Stützenreihe auf dem Querperron würde entfallen, und damit auch ihre eindeutige Ausrichtung. Sie würde in Richtung der Gleise durch einen hohen, raumhaltigen Glaskasten mit Abfahrtsanzeigern und weiteren Informationen abgeschlossen, der in Bezug zur Halle als Front wie als seitliche Flanke wirkt. Mehrere Richtungen sind hier gleichzeitig präsent, vor allem im Bereich der Aus- und Eingänge der Querhalle, die aufgrund der großen Stützabstände weitgehend unverstellt sind.

Platform Roofs and Transept Hall, Hauptbahnhof Zurich, 1995.

In association with architects Marcel Meili and Markus Peter, we created a commissioned study for the platform roofs of the Hauptbahnhof, the main train station in Zurich. The task was to make a proposal regarding the outermost platform roofs, which currently form the actual façade the train station displays to the city. The situation at the outer platforms has become extremely narrow with time as a result of various street-widening activity. Particularly tight is the division of space into platform, sidewalk, and wire fence for the nightly lock-up. We proposed to create a generous area in which the sidewalk and platform merge fluidly. Such a diffused zone largely corresponds to the current requirements of this highly-frequented train station. The gesture of the unfolding, widely jutting roofs transforms (and here they are similar to Mies van der Rohe's Nationalgalerie in Berlin) the introverted character of the existing field of the hall into a component of the city space.

An important factor for the formulation of such an open area was the extremely wide intervals (around 40 meters) between the massive concrete pillars, which additionally support the spatial gesture of the roof. The roofs are constructed in a simple, light framework planked on all sides. The wide spacing is spanned by double longitudinal girders that define at the same time the displacement of the roof. The construction contains space and light with its standing skylights, which especially brighten the inner area of the platform by reflecting on the surfaces of the roof. The light is diffused through large, flat, translucent wooden grids on the underside of the roof. In the large, hollow central room, artificial light is planned which will simulate daylight in the dark.

The train station is closed up at night. In order to be able to maintain the spatial situation, we have arranged the night lock-up on the second platform from the end, by the old platform supports, in the form of folding doors. The closed doors continue the translucent skin of the roof underside and form a large open seam on the train station building towards the city. Both outer platforms thus remain in the city space, and late trains can pull into an already closed train station. In the execution, however, another solution to the nightly lock-up will be created.

The new building's transept hall was part of the study, but will be realized only at a later date. We have proposed a hall, flat in its outward appearance, which clarifies the current silhouette of the main hall. The new transept hall would span a larger area than it does today, a row of supports on the cross platform would fall away, and thereby also the platform's unmistakable orientation. It would be closed off in the direction of the platforms by a tall, roomy glass case displaying departure and other information, which would work as a front as well as side flank in relation to the hall. Several directions are simultaneously present here, above all in the area of the transept hall's exits and entrances, largely undisguised due to the wide intervals between the supports.

Fassade, Schnitt
Façade, section

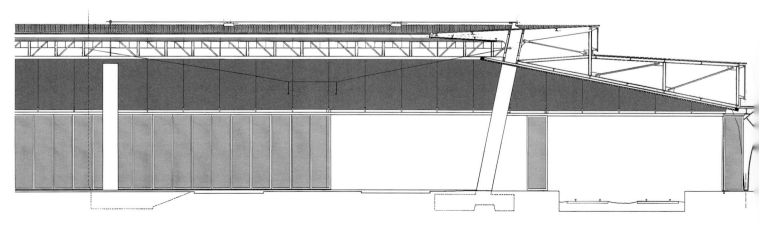

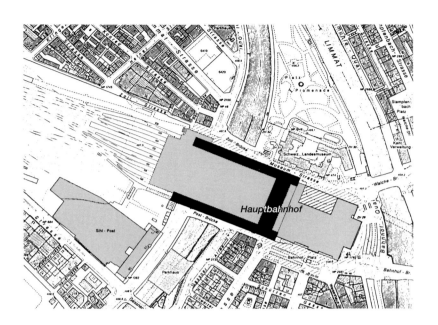

Situation
Situation

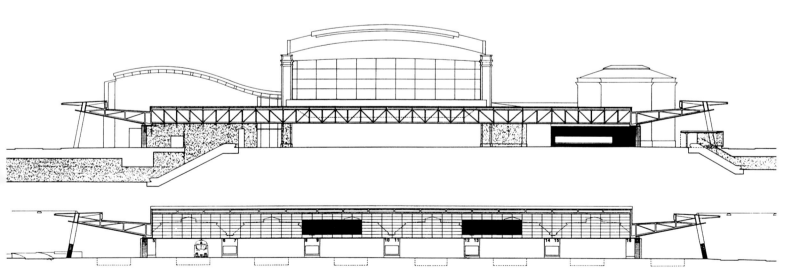

Querhalle, Längsschnitte
Transept hall, elevation section

Blick vom Perron in Richtung Stadt, Modell
View from platform towards city, model
Querhalle, Blick vom Landesmuseum her
Transept hall, view from Landesmuseum
Querhalle, Ausgang Landesmuseum
Transept hall, exit to Landesmuseum

Biografien

Kaschka Knapkiewicz
1950 geboren in Winterthur.
1971 Matura Typus A.
1978 Diplom an der Architekturabteilung der ETH Zürich.
1978-81 Aufenthalt in London, Mitarbeit in verschiedenen Architekturbüros, Pentagramm, Douglas Stephens & Partners.
1980/81 Mitarbeit im Architekturbüro von Zaha Hadid, London.
1981-83 Assistentin bei Prof. Ernst Studer an der ETH Zürich.
1983 Aufenthalt in Berlin, Arbeiten im Büro von Stefan Schroth, dipl. Ing. BDA, eigenes Architekturbüro in Zürich, verschiedene Ausstellungen von Bildern in der Galerie Wiedenkeller in Zürich.
Seit 1995 Lehrbeauftragte am Technikum Winterthur.

Axel Fickert
1952 geboren in Hof Oberfranken.
1971 Abitur in Eßlingen BRD.
1972-78 Architekturstudium an der ETH Zürich.
1979 Diplomarbeit bei Prof. Dolf Schnebli an der Architekturabteilung der ETH Zürich.
1979-82 Diplomassistent bei Prof. Dolf Schnebli an der ETH Zürich.
1983-85 Mitarbeit im Architekturbüro Theo Hotz Zürich.
1985-87 Mitarbeit im Architekturbüro Steigerpartner Zürich.
1986/87 Assistent bei Gastprofessor Heinz Tesar, Wien, an der ETH Zürich.
1987-91 Mitarbeit im Architekturbüro Burckhardt & Partner Zürich.

Seit 1992 gemeinsames Architekturbüro in Zürich.

Werkverzeichnis

1981
Erweiterung Universität Zürich, Wettbewerb, erster Preis, Axel Fickert mit Marcel Meili.

1983
Buchbinderei Burkhard in Mönchaltorf ZH, Axel Fickert mit Markus Schaefle in Büro Theo Hotz.

1986
Wohnüberbauung Bahnhof Selnau, Wettbewerb, fünfter Preis, Axel Fickert im Büro Steigerpartner.

1988
Dachaufbau Effretikon ZH, Kaschka Knapkiewicz.
Bürohaus Hatt-Haller in Dietlikon ZH, Axel Fickert im Büro Burckhardt & Partner.

1989
Gartenpavillon Gockhausen, Kaschka Knapkiewicz.
Wettbewerb Barcelona, Fickert und Knapkiewicz.
Wohnüberbauung Binz, Wettbewerb, Projektstudie.
Wohnüberbauung, Luzernerring Basel, Wettbewerb, dritter Preis, Axel Fickert mit Erich Offermann im Büro Burckhardt & Partner.
Umbau Haus Dubach Bassersdorf ZH, Kaschka Knapkiewicz.

1990
Bürohaus Firma Halter Zürich, Studienauftrag, Axel Fickert im Büro Burckhardt & Partner.
Technikum Rapperswil SG, Wettbewerb, dritter Preis, Fickert und Knapkiewicz.
Polizei- und Feuerwehrgebäude, Winterthur, Wettbewerb, Ankauf, Fickert und Knapkiewicz.

1991
Wandbilder für Gebrüder Sulzer AG in Halle 180, Architekturabteilung Technikum Winterthur, Kaschka Knapkiewicz.

1992
Wohnüberbauung Moosburg, Illnau-Effretikon ZH, Wettbewerb, dritter Preis.
Wohnüberbauung Wannweid, Wettswil ZH, Wettbewerb, erster Preis.
Wandbild für Gebrüder Sulzer AG in CIM-Halle, Technikum Winterthur, Kaschka Knapkiewicz.
Einfamilienhaus mit Ökonomiegebäude in Hütten ZH, ausgeführt 1994.

1993
Zentrumsüberbauung, Zollikerberg ZH, Wettbewerb, zweiter Preis.
Ecole professionelle de Bulle FR, Wettbewerb, zweiter Preis.
Umfeld S-Bahnhof Tiergarten/Königliche Porzellanmanufaktur KPM Berlin, Städtebaulicher Wettbewerb, mit Walter Nägeli.

1994
Wohnhaus mit zehn Wohnungen in Winterthur, Vorprojekt.
Musikhaus Hug, Effretikon ZH, Studienauftrag, erster Preis.
Längi-Hanselmaa, Egg, Wettbewerb.

1995
Umbau Akademie für Erwachsenenbildung, Stampfenbachstraße 48, Zürich.
Arbeitsheim Wangen, Wettbewerb, zweiter Preis.
Perronhallen SBB, HB Zürich, Studienauftrag, erster Preis, mit Meili & Peter Architekten, Zürich.
Modell eines Hotelzimmers M 1/1 als Messestand an der Igeho '95 in Basel, mit Meili & Peter Architekten, Zürich.

Bibliografie

Wettbewerb Erweiterung Universität Zürich, in: archithese 1/82.
Buchbinderei Burkhard in Mönchaltorf ZH, in: archithese 4, 1985/86.
Buchbinderei Burkhard in Mönchaltorf ZH, in: Werk Bauen + Wohnen, Beilage 11/1987.
Peter Disch, *Buchbinderei Burkhard in Mönchaltorf ZH,* in: Architektur in der deutschen Schweiz 1980-1990.
Wettbewerb Wohnüberbauung Bahnhof Selnau, in: Werk, Bauen + Wohnen 9/1986.
Dachaufbau Effretikon, in: Werk, Bauen + Wohnen 6/1989.
Habitatge i Ciutat, Wettbewerb Barcelona, in: Quaderns 1990.
Peter Disch, *Bürohaus Hatt-Haller in Dietlikon,* in: Architektur in der deutschen Schweiz, 1991.
Wettbewerb Wohnüberbauung Luzernerring Basel, in: Werk, Bauen + Wohnen 1/1990.
Umbau Haus Dubach Bassersdorf, in: Faces 23/1992.
Umbau Haus Dubach Bassersdorf, in: Abitare 4/1994.
Wettbewerb Wohnüberbauung Moosburg Illnau-Effretikon, in: Aktuelle Wettbewerbsszene 4/5, 1992.
Wettbewerb Wohnüberbauung Wannweid, Wettswil, in: Werk, Bauen + Wohnen 1/1993.
Studienauftrag Musikhaus Hug Effretikon ZH, in: Hochparterre, Mai 95.
Studienauftrag Perronhallen SBB Zürich, in: Werk, Bauen + Wohnen 11/1995.
Modell eines Hotelzimmers M 1/1 als Messestand an der Igeho '95 Basel, in: Werk, Bauen + Wohnen 3/1996.

Eigene Veröffentlichung
Axel Fickert und Kaschka Knapkiewicz, *Reichtum im Schnitt,* in: archithese 4/1996.

Biographies

Kaschka Knapkiewicz
1950 Born in Winterthur.
1971 University entrance qualifying exam, Type A.
1978 Graduated from the Architecture Department of the ETH Zurich.
1978-81 Stay in London, worked at various architecture offices, Pentagramm, Douglas Stephens & Partners.
1980/81 Worked in architecture office of Zaha Hadid, London.
1981-83 Assistant to Prof. Ernst Studer at the ETH Zurich.
1983 Stay in Berlin, worked at office of Stefan Schroth, dipl. Ing. BDA, own architecture office in Zurich, various exhibitions of pictures at the Galerie Wiedenkeller in Zurich.
Since 1995 Post as teacher at the Technikum Winterthur.

Axel Fickert
1952 Born in Hof Oberfranken.
1971 University entrance qualifying exam in Esslingen, BDR.
1972-78 Studied architecture at the ETH Zurich.
1979 Graduate work with Prof. Dolf Schnebli at the Architecture Department of the ETH Zurich.
1979-82 Graduate assistant to Prof. Dolf Schnebli at the ETH Zurich.
1983-85 Worked at architecture office Theo Hotz, Zurich.
1985-87 Worked at architecture office Steigerpartner, Zurich.
1986/87 Assistant to Visiting Professor Heinz Tesar, Vienna, at the ETH Zurich.
1987-91 Worked at architecture office Burckhardt & Partner, Zurich.

Since 1992 joint architecture office in Zurich.

List of Works

1981
Expansion of the University of Zurich, competition, first prize, Axel Fickert with Marcel Meili.

1983
Buchbinderei Burckhardt in Mönchaltorf, Axel Fickert with Markus Schaefle in office of Theo Hotz.

1986
Housing superstructure Selnau Train Station, competition, fifth prize, Axel Fickert in office of Steigerpartner.

1988
Roofing system in Effretikon, Kaschka Knapkiewicz.
Hatt-Haller office building in Dietlikon, Axel Fickert in office of Burckhardt & Partner.

1989
Gockhausen garden pavilion, Kaschka Knapkiewicz.
Barcelona competition, Fickert and Knapkiewicz.
Binz housing superstructure, competition, project study.
Housing superstructure, Luzernerring Basle, competition, third prize, Axel Fickert with Erich Offermann in office of Burckhardt & Partner.
Dubach house conversion, Bassersdorf, Kaschka Knapkiewicz.

1990
Firma Halter office building, Zurich, commissioned study, Axel Fickert in office of Burckhardt & Partner.
Technikum Rapperswil, competition, third prize, Fickert and Knapkiewicz.
Police and Fire Department building, Winterthur, competition, purchase, Fickert and Knapkiewicz.

1991
Wall pictures for Gebrüder Sulzer AG in Hall 180, Architecture Department of Technikum Winterthur, Kaschka Knapkiewicz.

1992
Moosburg housing superstructure, Illnau-Effretikon, competition, third prize.
Wannweid housing superstructure, Wettswil, competition, first prize.
Wall picture for Gebrüder Sulzer AG in CIM Hall, Technikum, Winterthur, Kaschka Knapkiewicz.
Family residence with agriculture building in Hütten, executed 1994.

1993
Center superstructure, Zollikerberg, competition, second prize.
Ecole professionelle de Bulle, competition, second prize.
Immediate surroundings of S-Bahnhof Tiergarten/ Königliche Porzellanmanufaktur KPM Berlin, town planning competition, with Walter Nägeli.

1994
Housing block with ten apartments in Winterthur, preliminary project.
Musikhaus Hug, Effretikon, commissioned study, first prize.
Längi-Hanselmaa, Egg, competition.

1995
Conversion Akademie für Erwachsenenbildung, Stampfenbachstrasse 48, Zurich.
Arbeitsheim Wangen, competition, second prize.
Platform halls, SBB, Hauptbahnhof Zurich, commissioned study, first prize, with Meili & Peter, Architects, Zurich.
Model of a hotel room M 1/1 as fair booth at the Igeho '95 in Basle, with Meili & Peter, Architects, Zurich.

Bibliography

Wettbewerb Erweiterung Universität Zürich, in: archithese 1/1982.
Buchbinderei Burkhardt in Mönchaltorf ZH, in: archithese 4, 1985/86.
Buchbinderei Burkhardt in Mönchaltorf ZH, in: Werk, Bauen + Wohnen, supplement 11/1987.
Peter Disch, *Buchbinderei Burkhardt in Mönchaltorf ZH,* in: Architektur in der deutschen Schweiz 1980-90.
Wettbewerb Wohnüberbauung Bahnhof Selnau, in: Werk, Bauen + Wohnen 9/1986.
Dachaufbau Effretikon, in: Werk, Bauen + Wohnen 6/1989.
Habitatge i Ciutat, Wettbewerb Barcelona, in: Quaderns 1990.
Peter Disch, *Bürohaus Hatt-Haller in Dietlikon,* in: Architektur in der deutschen Schweiz, 1991.
Wettbewerb Wohnüberbauung Luzernerring Basel, in: Werk, Bauen + Wohnen 1/1990.
Umbau Haus Dubach Bassersdorf, in: Faces 23/1992.
Umbau Haus Dubach Bassersdorf, in: Abitare 4/1994.
Wettbewerb Wohnüberbauung Moosburg Illnau-Effretikon, in: Aktuelle Wettbewerbsszene 4/5, 1992.
Wettbewerb Wohnüberbauung Wannweid, Wettswil, in: Werk, Bauen + Wohnen 1/1993.
Studienauftrag Musikhaus Hug Effretikon ZH, in: Hochparterre, May 1995.
Studienauftrag Perronhallen SBB Zürich, in: Werk, Bauen + Wohnen 11/1995.
Modell eines Hotelzimmers M 1/1 als Messestand an der Igeho '95 Basel, in: Werk, Bauen + Wohnen 3/1996.

Publications by the Architects
Axel Fickert and Kaschka Knapkiewicz, Reichtum im Schnitt, in: archithese 4/1996.

Quintus Miller
Paola Maranta
Basel und Chur

Markthalle Färberplatz | Färberplatz Market Hall | Aarau, 1996

Bündner Lehrerseminar | Grisons Teachers' Training College | Chur, 1994–98

Restaurant Stadtkeller | Stadtkeller Restaurant | Aarau, 1993/94

Fußgängerpasserelle Werdenberg | Werdenberg Pedestrian Overpass | Sevelen, 1989/90

Mitarbeiterinnen und Mitarbeiter
Collaborators
- Peter Baumberger
- Dominik Buxtorf
- Andreas Bründler
- Leopold Dostal
- Aja Huber
- Michele Lardieri
- Reto Pederocchi
- Michel Pfister
- Xenia Riva
- Ursula Spitz
- Jean-Phillippe Stähelin
- Marina Zimmermann

Analogien des Ortes.

Bereits mit ihrem ersten Projekt, einer 1990 bei der Autobahnraststätte Werdenberg im St. Galler Rheintal errichteten Fußgängerüberführung, erlangte das Architektenteam Paola Maranta und Quintus Miller überregionale Beachtung. Diese Passerelle über die Autobahn, die eine markante Zäsur setzt, ist mittlerweile zu einem Markenzeichen für die Raststätte Werdenberg geworden. Erreicht wurde dies nicht zuletzt mit einer einheitlichen und feingliedrigen Holzstruktur, die an Ausstellungsbauten oder Aussichtstürme erinnert, mit dem Versuch also, an bekannte Typologien anzuknüpfen und durch das bewußte Formulieren des Alltäglichen, des Bekannten eine zugleich signifikante architektonische Aussage zu erzeugen. Das geschieht jedoch anders als beispielsweise bei Bruno Reichlins und Fabio Reinharts ungewöhnlichem Mövenpick-Hotel, das an der Autobahnausfahrt Bellinzona-Süd mit der Aufnahme zahlreicher örtlicher Zitate die Aufmerksamkeit der Autofahrer auf sich lenkt. Zwar findet man dort Formen des Kastells, Quadersteine und Wehrturm, sie werden aber, einer Kulisse gleich, als Doppelcodierung und bloße Aneignung von Zitaten aus längst vergangener Zeit auch kenntlich gemacht.

Dennoch sind Maranta und Miller, die am Lehrstuhl Reinhart an der ETH Zürich diplomierten, von dessen «analoger Architektur» nachhaltig geprägt. Die bewußte Auseinandersetzung mit dem jeweiligen Ort und die Verwendung formaler Vorbilder sind zwar keine Erfindungen der Analogen, aber die Eindringlichkeit, mit der die Widersprüche und die prägenden Eigenschaften einer spezifischen örtlichen Umgebung als wichtigster Bestandteil des Entwurfsprozesses zugelassen wurden, haben zu Ergebnissen geführt, die heute aus der neueren Architektur in der Schweiz nicht mehr wegzudenken sind. Das zeigen die Arbeiten von Maranta und Miller ebenso überzeugend wie die jüngsten Arbeiten von Dieter Jüngling und Andreas Hagmann, Valentin Bearth und Andrea Deplazes und anderer. Die Metamorphose von der geschlossenen akademischen Theoriebildung zur «Architekturfähigkeit» erlangte die «analoge Architektur» jedoch erst, als sie von der allzu dogmatischen Nachahmung formaler Vorbilder mehr auf einen integrativen Entwurfsprozeß setzte, der auch Momente der Verfremdung und die Verwendung zeitgemäßer, konnotativ nicht eindeutig festgelegter Typologien zuließ.

Eine größere Umsetzung ihrer Arbeit sollte für Maranta und Miller aus dem ersten Preis in dem Wettbewerb für die Erweiterung des Restaurants Stadtkeller in Aarau mit der Gestaltung des Kasinoparks entstehen. Ihr Projekt sah als überzeugend einfache Lösung die Abgrenzung des Parkareals durch einen schlichten Längsbau vor, der die Erhaltung des klassizistischen Hübscherhauses determinierte und zugleich, durch die Aufnahme des Gartenrestaurants, die Integration des eigenständigen Parkbezirkes mit der bis anhin anonymen Durchgangszone bewirken sollte. Nach einer langen Projektierungsphase wurde das Bauvorhaben schließlich wegen fehlender Mittel aufgegeben.

Seit 1994 beschäftigten sich Maranta und Miller nun mit einem Projekt für die Erweiterung des Bündner Lehrerseminars in Chur, das in den sechziger Jahren dem Zeitgeist und der Aufgabe entsprechend als rechtwinkliger Solitär geplant worden war. Aufgrund ihrer Arbeitsweise, so Maranta und Miller, ist der Entwurfsprozeß immer gleich: «Am Anfang steht die intensive Suche nach dem für den Ort und die Aufgabe adäquaten Thema. Das ist die Grundlage für die entwerferischen Entscheidungen bis ins kleinste Detail.» Da der Altbau bereits einen Campus umschreibt, fiel die Entscheidung, das bestehende Gebäude zu ergänzen, jedoch ohne ihm eine kontrastierende Architektur entgegenzusetzen und ohne direkt an den Baukörper anzubauen. Zugleich wurde an die Typologie der vorhandenen Schulbauten der näheren Umgebung angeknüpft. So sieht der Entwurf zwei einfache Quader vor, die den bereits existierenden Bereich komplettieren, einen Grünraum eingrenzen und mit dem bestehenden Gebäude ein sinnfälliges Ensemble bilden. Der Vorschlag ist in zwei Etappen zu realisieren: In der ersten Etappe wird der Hauptbau an der Nordseite mit einem Laborgebäude ergänzt, in der zweiten Phase schließt der westliche Trakt das Gelände ab und bildet so mit dem Altbau eine festgefügte Baugruppe. Mit dem Vorteil, daß das vorhandene Gebäude in seiner urbanen Gestalt erhalten und außerdem in jeder Phase der Erweiterung bestehen bleibt. Die Architekten versuchten, die dominierende Stellung der nördlich am Hang gelegenen Kathedrale sowohl in der Raumwirkung des zunächst zu erstellenden naturwissenschaftlichen Traktes an der Nordseite des Gebäudes als auch in der Konstruktion wirksam werden zu lassen. Um den Blick nach oben zu lenken und das Bild des Laborgebäudes umzusetzen, sind die Nord- und Südfassaden vollständig in Glas aufgelöst und zu den Geschoßebenen versetzt angeordnet, wodurch sich für die Schulräume zusätzlich eine optimale Belichtung ergibt. Der Versprung der Fassaden wird mit durchgehenden Bänken auf den Fluren genutzt, die an altes Schulmobiliar erinnern, in den Schulzimmern dient er als Nebenarbeitsplatz. Diese Raumwirkung ist somit aus der mit Jürg Conzett entwickelten Konstruktion entstanden: Die an den versetzten Stockwerken sichtbaren Brüstungen sind zugleich die durchlaufenden Träger, an denen die Geschoßdecken aufgehängt werden. Diese Brüstungsträger sind vorgespannt und ermöglichen dadurch weitgehend flexible Raumeinteilungen. Durch die Entwurfselemente der städtebaulichen Integration, der räumlichen Bezugnahme zur Umgebung und der konstruktiven Einheit wird die Qualität des Ensembles für die Nutzer erlebbar und nachvollziehbar. Der Charakter der bestehenden Bebauung wird aufgenommen und zugleich eine neue, prägende Wirklichkeit formuliert. J. C. B.

Lehrerseminar Chur, Erweiterungsbauten, Studienmodell, 1994
Teachers' Training College, Chur, additions, study model, 1994

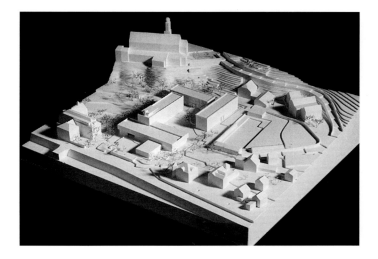

Analogies of the Site.

Already with their first project, a pedestrian overpass erected in 1990 close to the Werdenberg freeway rest stop in St. Gallen's Rhine Valley, the architect team of Paola Maranta and Quintus Miller attracted supra-regional attention. This bridge over the freeway, which creates a distinctive caesura, has in the meantime become a trademark of the Werdenberg rest stop. This was achieved not least by a uniform and finely built wooden structure reminiscent of exhibition buildings or lookout towers, in an attempt, then, to tie into familiar typologies and, through the conscious formulation of the everyday, the known, to make at the same time a significant architectural statement. This occurs, however, in a different way than with the unusual Mövenpick Hotel by Bruno Reichlin and Fabio Reinhart at the Bellinzona-South freeway exit, for example, which attracts the attention of drivers with its integration of numerous local references. In fact, one can see there forms of citadel, ashlar stones and defense tower, but, like stage scenery, they also become immediately recognizable as double-coding and merely the appropriation of references from a distant past.

The *analoge Architektur* ("analogy architecture") of Professor Reinhart, under whom they both studied and graduated at the ETH Zurich, nevertheless has left a lasting impression on Maranta and Miller. The conscious dialogue with each location and the employment of formal models are, in fact, not an invention of those engaged in *analoge Architektur*. But the urgency with which the contradictions and marked characteristics of a specific location's environment have been admitted as the most important components of the design process has led to results that today are an essential characteristic of the new architecture of Switzerland. The works of Maranta and Miller demonstrate this just as convincingly as the most recent works by Dieter Jüngling and Andreas Hagmann, Valentin Bearth and Andrea Deplazes, and others. *Analoge Architektur,* however, did not succeed in the metamorphosis from the closed, academic formulation of theories to "architectural competence", until it committed itself less to a far too dogmatic imitation of formal models and more to an integrated design process that also tolerates moments of alienation and the use of current, connotative, not clearly fixed typologies.

A greater realization of Maranta and Miller's work was to develop from the first prize in the competition for the expansion of the Stadtkeller restaurant in Aarau, with the designing of the Kasinopark. Their project came up with a compellingly simple solution: the demarcation of the park grounds with a long plain building that determined the preservation of the classic Hübscher House and, by way of the absorption of the garden restaurant, the integration of the independent park district with its until then anonymous thoroughfare zone. After a long phase of project development, the building plan was finally abandoned due to insufficient funds.

Maranta and Miller have been occupied since 1994 with a project for the expansion of the Bündner Lehrseminar (Grisons Teachers' Training College) in Chur, planned in the 1960s as a solitary rectangular unit that corresponded to the *Zeitgeist* and the problem. Because of their working method, say Maranta and Miller, the design process is always the same: "At the beginning, we search intensively for the theme appropriate to the site and the task. This is the foundation for the design decisions, down to the smallest detail." Because the old building already circumscribed a campus, the decision was made to complement the already existing building, but without confronting it with a contrasting architecture and without adding on directly to the body of the building. At the same time, they tied into the typology of the existing school buildings in the region. Thus two simple cubes were planned that complete the existing area, enclose a green area, and form a striking ensemble with the existing buildings. The proposal is to be realized in two steps: In the first stage, a laboratory building will be added on to the north side of the main unit; during the second phase, the western tract will close up the plot and form a firmly structured grouping with the old building. This has the advantage that the existing building will retain its urban appearance and, next to that, that it will remain standing throughout each phase of the expansion. The architects have tried to let the dominating position of the cathedral on the incline to the north have an impact on the construction as well as on the spatial effect of the natural sciences wing on the north side of the building, which is to be erected first. In order to direct the eye upward and realize the idea of the laboratory building, the north and south façades are dissolved completely in glass and displaced at each floor level, which results additionally in optimal lighting for the schoolrooms. The jog created by the displacement of the façades is utilized with benches running along the corridor, reminiscent of old school furniture; inside the schoolrooms, these spaces serve as extra work places. This spatial effect thus arose from a construction developed with Jürg Conzett: the parapets visible on the staggered floors are at the same time a continuous girder upon which the floors are hung. These parapet supports are pre-stressed and make possible thereby the largely flexible division of space. Through the design elements of the urban development integration, the spatial references to the environment and the constructive unity, it becomes possible for the user to experience and assimilate the quality of the ensemble. The character of the existing development is integrated, and at the same time a new, distinctive reality is formulated. J. C. B.

Quintus Miller, Paola Maranta

Markthalle Färberplatz, Aarau (Bauingenieur: Jürg Conzett), 1996.

Die aus vier Häuserblöcken bestehende Altstadt Aaraus wird von zwei Mauerringen aus Wohn- und Geschäftshäusern gefaßt. Zwischen diesen Ringen hatten sich in der östlichen Hälfte ursprünglich Gewerbetreibende mit ihren Werkstätten angesiedelt. Anfang der achtziger Jahre wurde eine Zeile dieser Gewerbebauten niedergerissen und vorerst nicht ersetzt. Um diese städtebauliche Lücke zu schließen, war im Rahmen eines Wettbewerbes ein Vorschlag für eine offene Markthalle gesucht, die verschiedensten Nutzungen gerecht werden kann.

Die vorgeschlagene Halle fügt sich an einer wichtigen Nahtstelle in den Stadtraum ein. Sie schließt die Gasse «Zwischen den Toren» ab und bildet mit ihrer Frontfassade den Färberplatz. Dieser gewährleistet die enge Verbindung der Innenstadt mit der vor der äußeren Mauer liegenden Grabenallee. Seitlich definiert das Volumen zwei kleine Nebengassen. Hinter der Markthalle entsteht der intimere Färberhof, der den umliegenden Häusern zugedacht ist.

Die Haupttragelemente der Konstruktion sind zwei Rahmen, die im Grundriß kreuzförmig angeordnet sind. Sie schneiden sich in der Mitte der Halle auf einer stark dimensionierten Stütze. An den Längsrippen dieses Rahmenkreuzes sind in engem Abstand Sparren befestigt, die einzeln auf den außenliegenden, flachrechteckigen Stützen aufgelagert sind. Die Dacheindeckung aus Dreischichtplatten wird mit beschieferter Dachpappe abgedichtet. Die Raumbegrenzung wird durch bewegliche Wandelemente entlang der Tragstruktur verstärkt, und Tore ermöglichen das Verschließen des Raumes.

Die Markthalle am Färberplatz evoziert mit dem Moiré der dichtgesetzten Stützen und Sparren die Wirkung dünner Stoffe. Neben dieser Anspielung auf die ursprüngliche gewerbliche Nutzung des Ortes, erinnert ihre innere Gestalt an die Lagerräume von Korn- und Zeughäusern.

Färberplatz Market Hall, Aarau (Construction Engineer: Jürg Conzett), 1996.

The existing old city center of Aarau is composed of four housing blocks and is ringed by two city walls, themselves made up of residence and commercial buildings. The original traders in the area with their workshops had settled in the eastern half between the two rings of walls. At the beginning of the 1980s, a row of these trade buildings were torn down and have not yet been replaced. With the intention of filling in these holes in the town's development, a proposal was sought within the framework of a competition for an open market hall that would do justice to the various uses required of it.

The proposed hall fits into an important seam within the city area. It seals off the alley "Zwischen den Toren" and forms the Färberplatz plaza with its front façade. The plaza guarantees a narrow connection between the inner city and the Grabenallee (the walkway by the trench) in front of the outer wall. From the side, the volume defines two small side alleys. Behind the market hall is the more intimate Färberhof, intended for the houses lying around its borders.

The main girder elements of the construction are two frames arranged as a cruciform in the floor plan. They intersect in the middle of the hall at a thickly built pillar. Spars are fixed to the longitudinal ribs of this frame cross at narrow intervals and each stands on the outer, flat rectangular supports. The roofing, made up of three-layered sandwich plates, has been made airtight with slated roofing pasteboard. The boundaries of the room are reinforced with movable wall elements along the girder structure, and huge doorways make lock-up possible.

The market hall on Färberplatz evokes, with the moiré of the close-set supports and spars, the effect of a more delicate material. Next to this allusion to the original commercial function of the location, the hall's interior design recalls storage rooms of grain warehouses and arsenals.

Modellaufnahmen
Photos of model

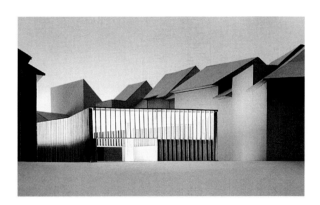
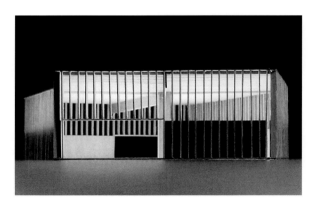

Längsschnitt und Ansichten
Elevation section and views

Wettbewerbsmodell und Situationsplan
Competition model and site plan

Quintus Miller, Paola Maranta

Bündner Lehrerseminar, Naturwissenschaftstrakt, Chur (Bauingenieur: Jürg Conzett), 1994–98.

Das Bündner Lehrerseminar aus den frühen sechziger Jahren liegt am südöstlichen Rand der Churer Altstadt. Der Schulkomplex ist zwischen die Plessur und die auf einem Felsen sitzende Kathedrale eingebettet. Er steht leicht vom Plessurquai zurückversetzt in den Bäumen eines locker bepflanzten Parks und ist wie die meisten öffentlichen Gebäude entlang des Flusses als Solitär definiert.

Die vorgeschlagenen zwei Erweiterungsbauten für die Naturwissenschaften sind analog zum Bestehenden als einfache Volumen in den Park eingepaßt. Ihre rechtwinklige Anordnung nimmt als Variation des Themas auf den Hauptbau Bezug. In der ersten Etappe wird dem Hauptbau ein Annexgebäude als Pavillon hinzugefügt, in der zweiten Etappe bilden die neuen Baukörper mit dem Altbau ein fest gefügtes Ensemble. Letzterer bleibt in seiner urbanen Gestalt und in seinem Charakter erhalten.

Ihrer Nutzung entsprechend ist die erste Erweiterung als einfacher Labortrakt konzipiert. Der Grundriß ist einbündig gegliedert und durch Treppe und Lift vertikal erschlossen. Die südseitigen Gänge mit den langen Sitzbänken entlang den Fenstern sind als Pausenhalle und Aufenthaltsraum gedacht. Gegen die Nordseite sind die Klassenzimmer und Labors angeordnet.

Die Längsfassaden werden vollständig verglast, die Stirnfassaden sind geschlossen. Von außen überbrückt die hohe Transparenz die räumliche Enge. Für das Innere ermöglicht sie eine optimale Belichtung der Schulräume.

Der Brüstungsversatz thematisiert den für den Ort typischen Blick hinauf zur Kathedrale und zu den Bergen. Gleichzeitig kann mit dieser Maßnahme ein maximaler Himmelslichtanteil auf beiden Längsseiten genutzt werden. Im Gang entsteht eine Sitzgelegenheit für die Schüler, im Klassenzimmer ein Bereich für Präparate oder Nebenarbeitsplätze. Statisch ermöglicht der Versatz durch die Ausbildung als vorgespannter Träger einen möglichst stützenfreien Innenraum.

Grisons Teachers' Training College, Natural Sciences Wing, Chur (Construction Engineer: Jürg Conzett), 1994–98.

The Grisons Teacher's Training College was built in the early 1960s and lies on the southeastern edge of Chur's old city center. The school complex is embedded between the Plessur River and the cathedral on a nearby cliff. It is set back slightly from the Plessur quay, in the trees of a loosely planted park, and is defined as a solitary unit, like most of the public buildings along the river.

The two proposed expansions for the natural sciences building are fit into the park as simple volumes analogous to those already existing. Their rectangular arrangement takes as its reference a variation on the theme of the main building. In the first stage, an annex is added to the main building in the form of a pavilion; in the second stage, the new building unit forms a solid construction with the old. The latter retains its urban design and its character.

Corresponding to its use, the first expansion is conceived as a simple laboratory. The floor plan is designed as a single-depth organization and is accessed vertically by means of a stairway and elevator. The passages on the south side are earmarked as break halls and day rooms, with long benches running the length of the windows. On the north side are classrooms and laboratories.

The long façades are fully glazed, the end façades are closed. From the outside, the great amount of transparency bridges the spatial narrowness. For the interior, it allows optimal lighting of the schoolrooms.

Displacement of the parapets makes the view of cathedral and mountains, typical for this location, into a theme. At the same time, this device utilizes the maximal amount of sky on both long sides. Sitting possibilities for the students along the walkway develop, as do a preparation area or extra work spaces inside the classrooms. Constructively, the displacement creates the most support-free interior space possible through its development as a prestressed girder system.

Lehrerseminar Chur mit dem geplanten Naturwissenschaftstrakt
Teachers' Training College, Chur, with planned natural sciences wing

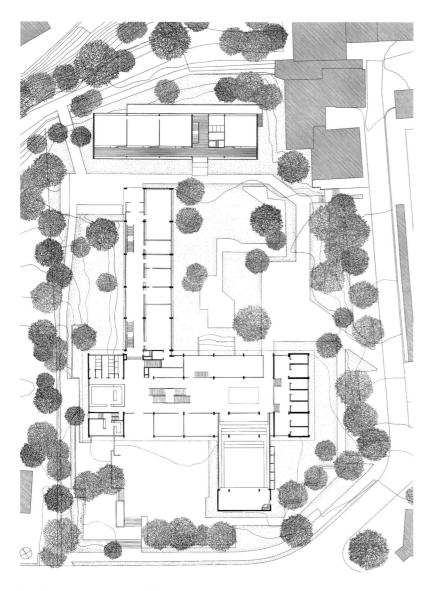

Situationsplan mit Erdgeschoßgrundriß
Site plan with ground floor plan

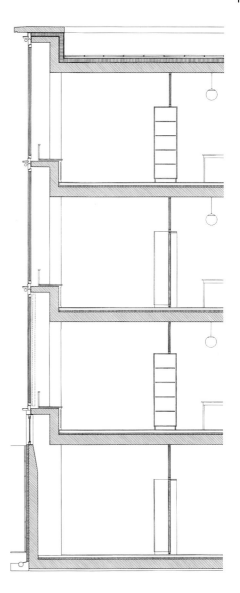

Fassadenschnitt
Façade section

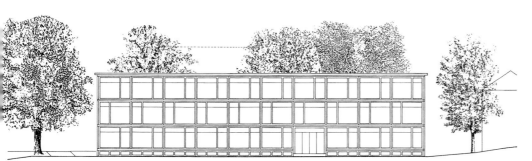
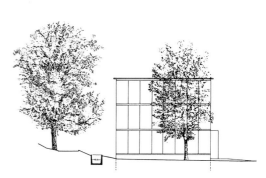

Längsfassade und Stirnfassade
Elevation façade and end façade
Studienmodell
Study model

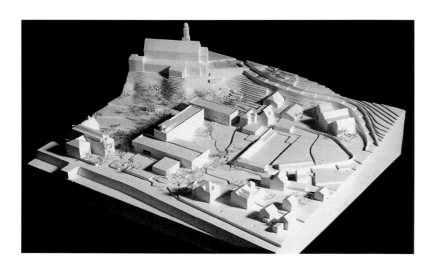

Quintus Miller, Paola Maranta

Restaurant Stadtkeller und Kasinopark, Aarau, 1993/94.

Am Ostrand der Altstadt von Aarau befanden sich ursprünglich mehrere klassizistische Bürgerhäuser, die sich mit ihrer Hauptseite zur Grabenallee orientierten und rückseitig in privaten Gärten standen. In den fünfziger Jahren wurden diese eingefriedeten Grünräume in einen öffentlichen Park umgewandelt. Zusätzlich zur unterirdischen Nutzung des Parks als Tiefgarage, ließen ihn heute zahlreiche öffentliche Einrichtungen wie Toilettenautomaten, Telefonkabinen, Altglassammelcontainer und Veloständer zum städtebaulichen Niemandsland verkommen.

Zur Wiederherstellung der Identität des Ortes wird im Projekt, analog zu den ursprünglichen Gärten, der Park von den zahlreichen Möblierungen befreit und mit einer Begrenzung gefaßt. Diese bindet die übriggebliebenen Bürgerhäuser in die Abwicklung des Grabens ein, welche dadurch wieder eine Vorder- und eine Rückseite erhalten.

Das Bauvolumen des neuen Restaurants wird an den Rand des Parkes gelegt, um einerseits den Park minimal zu beschneiden und andererseits einen Abschluß zum benachbarten Einkaufszentrum zu gewährleisten. Zusammen mit dem Hübscherhaus bildet es den Rahmen für das Gartenrestaurant, das im Sinne eines klassischen Biergartens auf einem feinbekiesten Platz im Schatten der mächtigen Blutbuche liegt. Das Gebäude ist als Leichtbau gedacht. Sein Restaurantraum spannt sich zwischen zwei Servicezonen ein und öffnet seine Hauptseite zum Garten hin.

In der Überarbeitung des Projektes wurde die Einfassung des Parkes durch eine verdichtete Bepflanzung zum Rand hin ersetzt. Das nun freistehende Gebäude wurde zu einem massiven Volumen mit einem großen Innenraum. Die Massivität des Baukörpers wird durch die präzise Plazierung einer einzigen Öffnung pro Fassade verstärkt.

Stadtkeller Restaurant and Kasinopark, Aarau, 1993/94.

On the eastern edge of the old city center of Aarau stand several original classic houses once belonging to wealthier citizens of the past. The houses' main sides are oriented toward the Grabenallee (the walkway by the trench) and their backs towards private gardens. In the 1950s, these enclosed green areas were transformed into a public park. In addition to the park's use as an underground garage, numerous public facilities – such as coin-operated restrooms, telephone booths, recycling containers for glass, and bicycle stands – have today been allowed to decay into a no man's land of urban development.

To restore the identity of the locale, the project frees the park of much of its effects and contains it within a boundary, analogous to the original gardens. This ties the remaining original houses to the trench as it unwinds along its way, and gives them once again a front and back side.

The volume of the new restaurant building is set on the border of the park in order, on the one hand, to restrict the park as little as possible and, on the other, to guarantee a final barrier to the neighboring shopping center. Together with the Hübscher House, it forms a frame for the restaurant garden which, like a traditional beer garden, lies in a courtyard covered with fine gravel under the shade of a mighty copper beech. The restaurant is conceived as a light construction. Its actual restaurant room spans two service zones and opens its main side to the garden.

In the revision of the project, the closure around the park was replaced with a denser border of plants reaching to the edge. The building now stood free and became a massive volume with a large interior. The massiveness of the building is reinforced by the precise positioning of one single opening per façade.

Wettbewerbsmodell
Competition model

Modellaufnahmen des überarbeiteten Projekts
Photos of revised project model

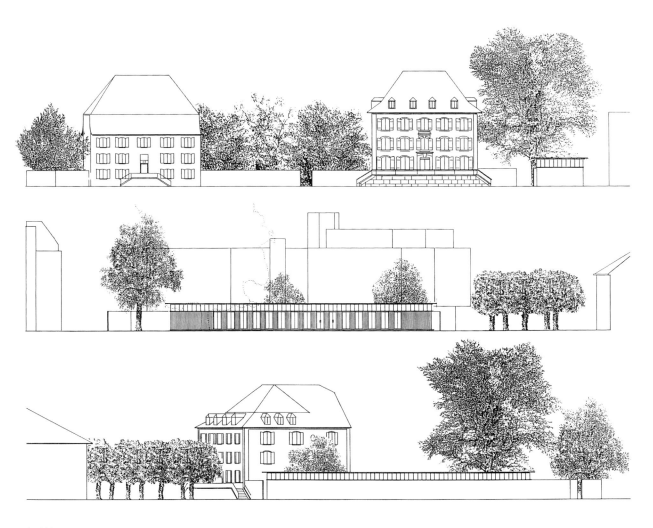

Ansichten
Views

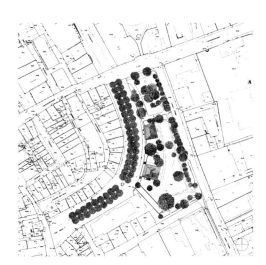
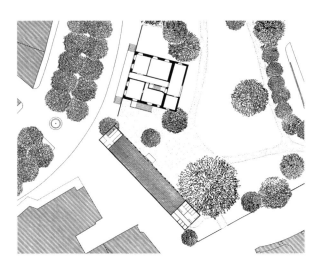

Situationsplan und Erdgeschoßgrundriß
Site plan and ground floor plan

Werdenberg Pedestrian Overpass, in collaboration with Christoph Mathys, Sevelen, 1989/90.

The St. Gallen Rhine Valley is characterized by the surrounding mountain ranges, the course of the Rhine between embankments spanned by numerous bridges, and the freeway. Between the Sevelen and Buchs freeway exits lie the two Werdenberg rest stops. On the eastern side of the freeway, the rest stop is slipped in between the freeway and the Rhine embankment; on the other side, the restaurant opens toward the plain in the west.

The passageway is conceived as a triple-bayed wooden construction with massive access towers on its ends. It should produce, for pedestrians as well as for the needs of the restaurant operations, a dry, wind-protected and level connection between the two rest stops.

One enters the tower-like abutment under the bridge and climbs the steps in the dark. After three light curves, one reaches the wooden superstructure as if ascending a viewing platform. From the western bridgehead, the meadow landscape stretches far into the distance; from the east, the eye falls over the Rhine embankment and off to the castle of Vaduz. The bridge itself leads like a high path over the freeway to the other side and invites lingering, whether for a view of the distant plain, the surrounding mountain massif, or the cars speeding by.

The massive pillars and abutments carry the support structure, which is finished with laminated wood boards and covered on its exposed places with plastic wood sheeting. This gives the structure a modest character and ties the bridge in with the massive supports. The wooden interior opens up to the viewer only when he enters the footbridge. The finely built superstructure, tipped towards the outer edges from the central axis, carries a roof covered with titanium zinc sheeting and accommodates the glazing. From the inside, the high transparency gives the eye free reign over the landscape, while from the outside it underscores the fine work of the building and prevents the bridge from turning into a dam.

Middle bay and visible underside of passageway

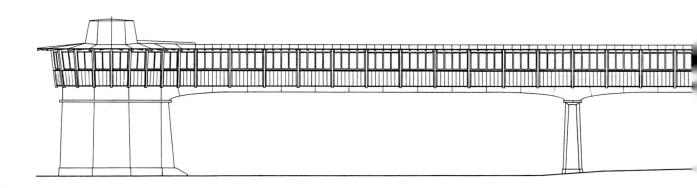

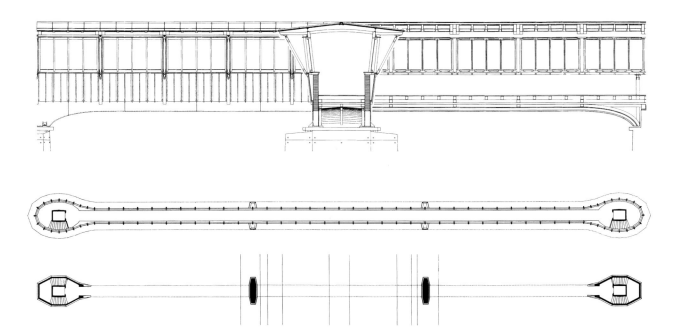

Konstruktionsschnitt
  Section of structural system
Grundrißebene Passerelle
  Floor plan plane of passageway
Grundrißebene Auflager
  Floor plan plane of support system

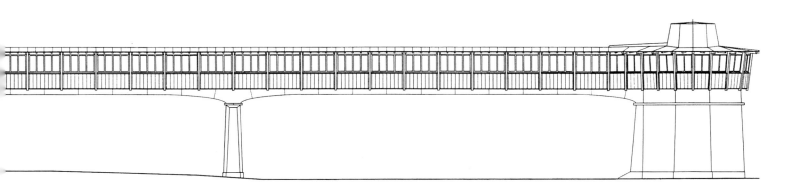

Biografien

Paola Maranta
1959 geboren in Chur.
1980-86 Architekturstudium an der EPF Lausanne und der ETH Zürich.
1986 Diplom bei Prof. Fabio Reinhart an der ETH Zürich.
1987 Mitarbeiterin am Archiv des Institut gta der ETH Zürich.
1988/89 selbständige Tätigkeit als Architektin, teilweise in Zusammenarbeit mit Quintus Miller.
1990 MBA, IMD Lausanne.
1991-94 Unternehmensberaterin bei McKinsey & Co., Zürich.

Quintus Miller
1961 Geboren in Aarau.
1981-87 Architekturstudium an der ETH Zürich.
1986 Mitarbeiter am Archiv des Institut gta der ETH Zürich.
1987 Diplom bei Prof. Fabio Reinhart an der ETH Zürich.
1991 eigenes Büro in Basel.
1990-94 Assistent bei Prof. Inès Lamunière an der EPF Lausanne und der ETH Zürich.

Seit 1994 gemeinsames Büro in Chur und Basel.

Ausstellung
Junge Basler Architekturbüros I, Architekturmuseum Basel, 1996.

Werkverzeichnis

1989
Fußgängerpasserelle Werdenberg in Sevelen. Zusammenarbeit mit Christoph Mathys, Zürich. Holzbauingenieur W. Bieler, Bonaduz.
Mehrzweckgebäude in Tschlin, Wettbewerb, zweiter Rang.

1990
Umbau Talstation Davos–Schatzalp-Bahn in Davos, Projekt.

1991
Informationspavillon, Alpinum Schatzalp in Davos.

1992
Das Sanatorium. Die Entstehung eines Prototyps der modernen Architektur, Ausstellungen an den Architekturabteilungen der EPF Lausanne, der ETH Zürich und an der HTL Chur.

1993
Restaurant Stadtkeller und Kasinopark in Aarau, Wettbewerb, erster Preis.
Restrukturierung eines Verpflegungsbetriebes der Sulzer-Rüti mit Seminarhotel in Zuchwil, Studie.

1994
Stadtkeller Aarau und Kasinopark in Aarau, Überarbeitung Wettbewerbsprojekt, Landschaftsarchitekt Dieter Kienast, Zürich.
Ausstellungsraum im ehemaligen Transformatorenhaus Schatzalp in Davos.
Kassahaus Talstation Davos–Schatzalp-Bahn in Davos.
Erweiterung Naturwissenschaftlicher Trakt, Bündner Lehrerseminar, Chur, Studienauftrag, Ausführung 1997/98. Zusammenarbeit mit Jürg Conzett, Chur.

1995
Umbau und Erweiterung Stadtbibliothek in Aarau. Projekt.
Erweiterung Schulanlage in Bonaduz, Wettbewerb.
Umbau Haus Dr. W. und H. in Riehen.
Umbau Hotel Waldhaus in Sils-Maria.

1996
Umbau Haus Engelapotheke in Basel.
Ingenieurschule HTL in Oensingen, Wettbewerb, zweiter Preis.
Markthalle Färberplatz in Aarau, Wettbewerb, erster Preis. Zusammenarbeit mit Jürg Conzett, Chur.
Forstliches Betriebsgebäude in Aarau, Wettbewerb, dritter Preis.
Alte Landstrasse 85 in Zollikon, Studienauftrag, zweiter Preis.

Bibliografie

Fußgängerpasserelle Werdenberg, in: Hochparterre, 6/1990.
Fußgängerpasserelle Werdenberg, Sevelen, in: Werner Stadelmann: Holzbrücken der Schweiz – ein Inventar, Verlag Bündner Monatsblatt, Chur 1990.
Fußgängerpasserelle Werdenberg in Sevelen SG, in: Werk, Bauen und Wohnen 3/1992.
Fußgängerpasserelle Werdenberg, Sevelen, in: Christa Zeller: Schweizer Architekturführer, Werk Verlag, Zürich 1992.
Fußgängerüberführung Raststätte Werdenberg/Sevelen, in: Holzbulletin 32/1993.
Fußgängerpasserelle Werdenberg, Sevelen, in: Mercedes Daguerre: Guida all'architettura svizzera del Novecento, Electa Elemond, 1995.
Analogien des Ortes, Zur Architektur von Quintus Miller und Paola Maranta, in: Neue Zürcher Zeitung, 5. Januar 1996.
Ingenieurschule HTL Oensingen, in: SI+A 22/1996.
Markthalle Färberplatz, Aarau, in: SI+A 24/1996.
Ingenieurschule HTL, Oensingen, in: archithese 3/1996.
Inversion, in: Werk, Bauen + Wohnen 7/8 1996.
Dinge, die da sind. Martin Steinmann, Basel, 1996.
Der Bauch von Aarau, in: archithese 4/1996.

Eigene Veröffentlichungen
Das Sanatorium Schatzalp in Davos. Ein Beispiel zwischen Klassizismus und englischer Wohnlichkeit, in: archithese 2/1988.
Das Eisbahnhaus Davos von Rudolf Gaberel, in: Schatzette 2/1991.
Die Entstehung und Entwicklung des Kurortes Davos und *Die Entstehung der Tuberkulosesanatorien im Rahmen des Bündner Kurtourismus,* in: Bündner Hotellerie um 1900 in Bildern, Chur 1992.
Le sanatorium. Architecture d'un isolement sublime, in: DA informations 136 / EPF Lausanne.
Die Kolonie Bergheim und die Gartenstadt Kapf in Zürich Hirslanden. Zwei Gartenstadtkolonien im Frühwerk der Gebrüder Pfister, in: archithese 1/1993.
Erweitern ohne zu zerstören! Die chirurgische Klinik Clavadel in Davos von Rudolf Gaberel, 1931/32, in: archithese 1/1994.

Biographies

Paola Maranta
1959 Born in Chur.
1980-86 Studied architecture at the EPF Lausanne and the ETH Zurich.
1986 Graduated from the ETH Zurich under Prof. Fabio Reinhart
1987 Worked in archives at the Institut gta (Institute for the History and Theory of Architecture) at the ETH Zurich.
1988/89 Independent activities as architect, partly in collaboration with Quintus Miller.
1990 MBA, IMD Lausanne.
1991-94 Management consultant at McKinsey & Co., Zurich.

Quintus Miller
1961 Born in Aarau.
1981-87 Studied architecture at the ETH Zurich.
1986 Worked in archives at the Institut gta (Institute for the History and Theory of Architecture) at the ETH Zurich.
1987 Graduated from the ETH Zurich under Prof. Fabio Reinhart
1991 Own office in Basel.
1990-94 Assistant to Prof. Inès Lamunière at the EPF Lausanne and the ETH Zurich.

Since 1994 joint office in Chur and Basle.

Exhibition
Junge Basler Architekturbüros I, Architecture Museum Basle, 1996.

List of Works

1989
Werdenberg pedestrian overpass in Sevelen. In collaboration with Christoph Mathys, Zurich. Wood construction engineer W. Bieler, Bonaduz.
Multipurpose building, Tschlin, competition, second ranking.

1990
Davos–Schatzalp-Bahn valley station, conversion, Davos, project.

1991
Information pavilion, Alpinum Schatzalp in Davos.

1992
Das Sanatorium. Die Entstehung eines Prototyps der modernen Architektur, Exhibitions at the Architecture Department of the EPF Lausanne, the ETH Zurich and the HTL Chur.

1993
Stadtkeller Restaurant and Kasinopark in Aarau, competition, first prize.
Restructuring and expansion of Sulzer-Rüti catering operations, with a hotel in Zuchwil, study.

1994
Stadtkeller Aarau and Kasinopark in Aarau, revision of competition project, landscape architect Dieter Kienast, Zurich.
Exhibition space in the former transformer house Schatzalp in Davos.
Skilift station ticket office, Davos–Schatzalp-Bahn in Davos.
Bündner Lehrseminar (Grisons Teacher's Training College), expansion of natural sciences wing, Chur, execution 1997/98. In collaboration with Jürg Conzett, Chur.

1995
City library, conversion and expansion, Aarau, project.
Expansion of school complex in Bonaduz, competition.
Conversion House of Drs.W. and H. in Riehen.
Hotel Waldhaus, conversion, Sils-Maria.

1996
Engelapotheke building (pharmacy), conversion, Basle.
Ingenieurschule HTL in Oensingen, competition, second prize.
Färberplatz Market Hall in Aarau, competition, first prize. In collaboration with Jürg Conzett, Chur.
Forest management building in Aarau, competition, third prize.
Alte Landstrasse 85 in Zollikon, commissioned study, second prize.

Bibliography

Fussgängerpasserelle Werdenberg, in: Hochparterre, 6/1990.
Fussgängerpasserelle Werdenberg, Sevelen, in: Werner Stadelmann: Holzbrücken der Schweiz – ein Inventar, Verlag Bündner Monatsblatt, Chur 1990.
Fussgängerpasserelle Werdenberg in Sevelen, in: Werk, Bauen + Wohnen 3/1992.
Fussgängerpasserelle Werdenberg, Sevelen, in: Christa Zeller: Schweizer Architekturführer, Werk Verlag, Zurich 1992.
Fussgängerüberführung Raststätte Werdenberg/Sevelen, in: Holzbulletin 32/1993.
Fussgängerpasserelle Werdenberg, Sevelen, in: Mercedes Daguerre: Guida all'architettura svizzera del Novecento, Electa Elemond, 1995.
Analogien des Ortes, Zur Architektur von Quintus Miller und Paola Maranta, in: Neue Zürcher Zeitung, January 5 1996.
Ingenieurschule HTL Oensingen, in: SI+A 22/1996.
Markthalle Färberplatz, Aarau, in: SI+A 24/1996.
Ingenieurschule HTL, Oensingen, in: archithese 3/1996.
Inversion, in: Werk, Bauen + Wohnen 7/8 1996.
Dinge, die da sind. Martin Steinmann, Basle, 1996.
Der Bauch von Aarau, in: archithese 4/1996.

Publications by the Architects
Das Sanatorium Schatzalp in Davos. Ein Beispiel zwischen Klassizismus und englischer Wohnlichkeit, in: archithese 2/1988.
Das Eisbahnhaus Davos von Rudolf Gaberel, in: Schatzette 2/1991.
Die Entstehung und Entwicklung des Kurortes Davos und Die Entstehung der Tuberkulosesanatorien im Rahmen des Bündner Kurtourismus, in: Bündner Hotellerie um 1900 in Bildern, Chur 1992.
Le sanatorium. Architecture d'un isolement sublime, in: DA informations 136 / EPF Lausanne.
Die Kolonie Bergheim und die Gartenstadt Kapf in Zürich Hirsladen. Zwei Gartenstadtkolonien im Frühwerk der Gebrüder Pfister, in: archithese 1/1993.
Erweitern ohne zu zerstören! Die chirurgische Klinik Clavadel in Davos von Rudolf Gaberel, 1931/32, in: archithese 1/1994.

Valerio Olgiati
Zürich

Mitarbeiterinnen und Mitarbeiter
Collaborators
    Markus Graf
    Daniel Mettler
    Gaudenz Zindel

Haus Kucher | Kucher House | Rottenburg am Neckar, 1989–91

Quartierplan Cuncas | Plan for Cuncas Quarter | Sils, Engadin, 1991

Wiederaufbau des Souk von Beirut | Redevelopment of the Souk of Beirut | 1994

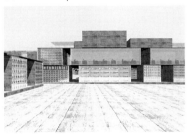

Entwerfen mit polarisierten Widersprüchlichkeiten.

Bereits im Alter von 25 Jahren konnte Valerio Olgiati sein erstes Einfamilienhaus in Chur realisieren. Rückblickend bezeichnet er es heute als «erstes postmodernes Haus im Bündnerland», gemeint sind damit unterschiedliche inhaltliche und formale Bezüge, die das Haus bestimmen. Bereits damals wollte Olgiati Wertesysteme mit sich widersprechenden Definitionen verarbeiten, und ganz ähnlich läßt sich auch das Haus Kucher in Rottenburg am Neckar einordnen, das Olgiati 1989–91 zusammen mit Markus Graf realisierte und für das er gleich zwei Auszeichnungen erhielt: 1993 eine Anerkennung des Deutschen Architekturpreises und 1995 eine der Architektenkammer Baden-Württembergs. Das Haus Kucher lehnt sich an die Typologie eines traditionellen Einfamilienhauses an; durch bewußte Steigerung der Details sowie einiger formaler «Eigenheiten» wird diese Einheit im Sinne einer mehrfachen Kodierung wieder aufgebrochen. So hat das Haus serielle, überhohe Dachgauben mit französischen Fenstern, ein auskragendes Badezimmer, das in seiner kubischen Form fast das Satteldach konterkariert, und auf der Südseite ist die Außenhaut leicht vorgewölbt, so daß das Haus beinahe aus den Nähten platzt, die geschlossene Form aufgebrochen erscheint.

Für Olgiati, der 1986 an der ETH Zürich diplomierte, 1986/87 Assistent am Lehrstuhl von Fabio Reinhard war und 1994/95 an der Fachhochschule in Stuttgart lehrte, sollte es eigentlich keine entwurfsbestimmenden Vorgaben geben, schon gar keine formalen Anleihen. Diese sind bei seinen Entwürfen nicht immer ganz auszuschließen, weil gleichzeitig Analogien zur umgebenden Bebauung gesucht werden. Klar ist jedoch, daß zugrundeliegende Ideen mit unnachgiebiger Konsequenz umgesetzt werden. So ist es nicht verwunderlich, daß für Olgiati die Arbeitsweise und Konsequenz Mies van der Rohes immer wieder gern zitiertes Ziel ist. 1993 projektierte er ein Einfamilienhaus in Malans, das von dieser Maxime getragen zu sein scheint. Das kleine Haus sollte im inneren Geviert des Dorfes liegen, das von einzelnen Häusern in örtlichem Baustil geprägt ist. Zwar lehnt sich Olgiatis Projekt in Kubatur und Dachneigung an die umgebende Bebauung an, zeichnet sich aber räumlich durch ein völlig geschlossenes Sockelgeschoß aus, mit einem darüberliegenden, freitragenden und vierseitig verglasten ersten Wohngeschoß, mit einem wiederum allseitig geschlossenen Dachgeschoß, das lediglich von Oberlichtern erhellt wird. Mit durchdachten und reduzierten Raumbezügen wird das Innere des Hauses im Zusammenhang mit seiner konsequenten Schichtung noch gesteigert. Gleichzeitig wird die körperliche Präsenz durch die geschlossenen Flächen, die zugleich die prismatische Form des Hauses betonen, noch präzisiert. Der Bauherr wäre dem eigenwilligen Konzept gefolgt, die Gemeinde jedoch lehnte den Entwurf ab.

Valerio Olgiati hat zwei Jahre in Amerika gelebt und dort zusammen mit Frank Escher ein Architekturbüro geführt. Erst seit Ende 1994 ist er wieder in der Schweiz und seitdem bemüht, sich mit einem eigenen Architekturbüro – zumeist durch Wettbewerbsbeteiligungen – zu etablieren. Neben den Projekten für den Wiederaufbau des Souk in Beirut und dem Korean Cultural Center (KOMA) in Los Angeles beteiligte er sich an der Quartiersplanung Cuncas in Sils im Engadin, die ihm den dritten Preis einbrachte. Um die Landschaft des idyllisch gelegenen Dorfes im Oberengadin trotz der geplanten Erweiterung so wenig wie möglich zu beeinträchtigen, schlug Olgiati zwei große Wohnhochhäuser vor. Die mit weißem Marmor verkleideten Türme umschreiben eine rechteckige Ebene aus ebenfalls hellem Material. Jene exakte Fläche ist eine Reflexion der ruhigen Seen und Wiesen der umgebenden Landschaft, deren spezifischer Ausdruck in der Polarisierung von Ebene und Berg, von Fläche und kristalliner Form liegt. Die schlanken Türme lassen zwei Ordnungssysteme erkennen: Die geschlossene äußere Form ist gleichsam eine geordnete Figur, und die Anordnung der Öffnungen kann als ungeordnete Figur bezeichnet werden. Dieses «regionale» Prinzip und die relative Größe der Türme soll laut Olgiati eine Besonderheit einer Engadiner Tradition aufnehmen: Die Gegensätzlichkeit und das Miteinander von Bauernhaus und Hotelpalast, von Ländlichkeit und Urbanität und von Regionalität und Internationalität. In den Türmen sollten die vielen Zweitwohnungen untergebracht werden, wie es in der Ausschreibung gefordert ist, ohne die Landschaft weiter zu zersiedeln. Zugleich soll mit der plastischen Qualität der Türme die Verlassenheit des Ortes thematisiert werden, wenn das Quartier Cuncas in der Zwischensaison nahezu unbewohnt sein wird. Die Tatsache der Leere jedoch enthält noch keine Aussage über Qualität, sie ist weder schlecht noch gut. Durch die bewußte Gestaltung dieser Leere will Olgiati einen weiteren qualitativen Aspekt formulieren, das Projekt hat unter anderem die poetische Darstellung der Leere zum Ziel. Die energetisch sinnvollen Fensterläden aus Marmor – bei Abwesenheit geschlossen – sind weiß, schließen bündig mit der Marmorfassade ab und lassen die Türme – eine präzise Detaillierung vorausgesetzt – als stelenartige Landmarken erscheinen. Sie wirken in der Zwischensaison durch ihre Geschlossenheit, verlieren den Maßstab der Geschoßhöhen und erlangen dadurch einen Abstraktionsgrad, der diese Türme nicht mehr als «Häuser» erscheinen läßt. Sie mutieren zu plastischen Körpern einer anderen Realität.

Die Projekte von Olgiati zeichnen sich einerseits durch eine eindringliche Komplexität der durchdachten Aufgabenstellung aus, zum anderen bekennt sich der Architekt zu einer bewußten Unentschlossenheit, die sich jeder Doktrin, jeder Vorgabe zunächst verschließt. In den inhärenten Widersprüchlichkeiten der jeweils gestellten Aufgabe liegt für Olgiati der jeweils erst zu findende Lösungsansatz. Dabei kann das Ziel ruhig so hoch gesteckt werden, daß es nie zu erreichen ist. «Es ist enorm abstumpfend», so Olgiati, «sich mit einem nur funktionierenden oder nur schönen, aber langweiligen Objekt beschäftigen zu müssen ...» J. C. B.

Designing with polar opposites.

Already at 25 years of age, Valerio Olgiati was able to see his first one-family residence in Chur built. Looking back today, he describes it as "the first post-modern house in the Grisons", referring to the various relationships of content and form that define the house. Already at that time, Olgiati intended to work on value systems with contradictory definitions. In a very similar category is the Kucher House in Rottenburg on the Neckar, which Olgiati realized in 1989–91 in conjunction with Markus Graf in 1989–91, and for which he immediately received two distinctions: the *Anerkennung des Deutschen Architekturpreises* in 1993, and one from the *Architekturkammer Baden-Württemberg* in 1995. The Kucher House leans on the typology of a traditional one-family house; through conscious increase in detail, as well as some "idiosyncrasies" of form, this unity is broken apart like a multiple encoding. Thus the house has serial, super-elevated dormer ventilation with French windows, a projecting bathroom whose cubic form almost counters the squared saddleback roof, and a light bulging of the outer skin on the south side, so that the house nearly bursts at the seams and the closed form appears ready to fly apart.

For Olgiati, who graduated from the ETH in 1986, was assistant to Professorial Chair of Fabio Rheinhard in 1986/87 and taught at the Fachhochschule (technical college) in Stuttgart in 1994/95, there actually should be no set of givens inherent in the design, certainly no borrowing of form at all. These are not always totally excluded from his designs, because analogies to the surrounding development are simultaneously sought, but it is clear that fundamental ideas are realized with uncompromising resolution. It is thus no wonder that, for Olgiati, the work method and consistency of Mies van der Rohe is a goal willingly cited time and again. In 1993, he developed the project for a one-family residence in Malans that seems to be carried by this maxim. The little house is to lie within an inner quarter of the village typified by single houses in the local building style. Although Olgiati's project leans towards the regional development in cubature and roof slope, it is distinguished spatially by a fully closed basement, a cantilevered ground floor positioned above with four glazed sides, and an attic story that is once again closed on all sides and lit solely by skylights. With well-thought-out and reduced spatial references, the logical layering of the interior of the house is improved. At the same time, its physical presence is made even more precise by the closed surfaces that emphasize the prismatic form of the house. The concept has its own will and the client would have it built, but the local government has rejected the design.

Valerio Olgiati lived in America for two years and ran an architectural office there together with Frank Escher. Only at the end of 1994 did he return to Switzerland and has been occupied since then with establishing his own architectural office – for the most part with participation in competitions. In addition to the projects for the redevelopment of the Souk in Beirut and the Korean Cultural Center (KOMA) in Los Angeles, he took part in the planning for the Cuncas quarter of Sils in the Engadine, which brought him third prize. In order to detract as little as possible from the idyllic landscape of the village in the Upper Engadine, despite the intended expansion, Olgiati proposed two large high-rise housing blocks. The towers, covered with white marble, define a rectangular plain of a material just as light in color. These exact surfaces are a reflection of the calm lakes and meadows of the surrounding landscape which finds its specific expression in the polarization of plain and mountain, of flat surface and crystalline form. Two ordering systems are recognizable in the towers: the closed outer form is, as it were, an orderly and systematic figure, and the arrangement of openings can be characterized as a disorderly figure. This "regional" principle and the relative largeness of the towers should, according to Olgiati, integrate a special feature of an Engadine tradition: the contrast and togetherness of farmhouse and palace hotel, of rusticity and urbanity, of regionality and internationality. Many second and vacation apartments are to be accommodated in the towers, as required in the client's written specifications, without bringing further urban sprawl into the countryside. At the same time, the sculptural quality of the towers is to take up the forlornness of the site as a theme; the Cuncas quarter is as good as uninhabited during the off-seasons. The fact of the emptiness, however, contains no declaration about the quality. Emptiness is neither good nor bad. Through the conscious designing of this emptiness, Olgiati wants to formulate a further qualitative aspect; the project has, among other things, the goal of the poetic representation of emptiness. The energy sensible marble shutters are white, close flush with the marble façade when no one is there, and let the towers – requiring a precise detailling – appear as stele-like landmarks. In the off-seasons, their impermeability exerts its effect, and they achieve with this a degree of abstraction that keeps them from looking at all like "houses". They mutate into sculptural entities from another reality.

Olgiati's projects on the one hand distinguish themselves by a forceful complexity of the well-thought-out requirements of the commission. On the other, the architect confesses to a conscious irresolution that shuts out every doctrine, every given, from the start. For Olgiati, the approach to the solution of each problem presented is to be found at the outset in the inherent contradictions of that problem. Yet the goal can easily be placed so high that it can never be attained. "It dulls one's senses enormously," says Olgiati, "to always have to work on a purely functional or simply beautiful, but boring, object…" J. C. B.

Haus Dr. Hardt, Malans, 1993
Residence Dr. Hardt, Malans, 1993

Haus Kucher, Rottenburg am Neckar, 1989–91.

Der Standort der Parzelle am Rande eines kleinen Städtchens mit Steildachhäusern sowie der Wunsch der jungen Bauherrschaft nach einem einfachen, kleinen Wohnhaus bildeten die Ausgangslage. Der gewählte Wohnhaustyp entspricht dem Wesen des Quartiers und hat seinen Ursprung zwischen Tradition und Moderne im Deutschland der zwanziger Jahre. In der gewählten Holzbauweise äußert sich die Ästhetik der Geometrie und der Konstruktion. Wie die Bauchung der Fassade oder die überhohen Gauben ist auch sie nur Mittel zum Zweck. Sie akademisiert durch ihre akribische Anwendung den banalen Typ und macht ihn dadurch schön. Die vielen, sich konstruktiv nicht immer entsprechenden architektonischen Anordnungen ließen keine einheitliche Konstruktionsweise zu. Es ergaben sich komplexe maßliche und konstruktive Zusammenhänge, welchen mit einer Ausführung vor Ort nicht entsprochen werden konnte. Deshalb wurde das Haus vorfabriziert, was eine maximale Maßabweichung von nur drei Millimetern über die gesamte Gebäudelänge ermöglichte.

Kucher House, Rottenburg on the Neckar, 1989–91.

The starting point for this project was formed by the location of the parcel on the edge of a small town populated with houses with steep-pitched roofs and by the wish of the young clients for a small, simple house in which to live. The selected residence house type corresponds to the essence of the quarter. Its origins lie in 1920s Germany and somewhere between traditional and modern. The aesthetic of the geometry and the construction is expressed in the chosen wood construction method. Like the bulge of the façade or the super-elevated dormers, the method is only a means to an end. It creates an academic formalism through its meticulous application of the banal type and makes it thoroughly beautiful. The many architectonic patterns, not always equivalent, did not allow for a uniform method of construction. Complex connections of measurement and construction resulted which could not be carried out at the site. The house was therefore prefabricated, which made a maximal measurement discrepancy of only three millimeters possible over the entire house.

Südfassade, Westfassade, Ausschnitt Nordfassade, Korridor Erdgeschoß, Südfassade und Korridor Obergeschoß
South façade, west façade, detail of north façade, first floor corridor, south façade and upper floor corridor

Situation und Querschnitt
Situation and cross section

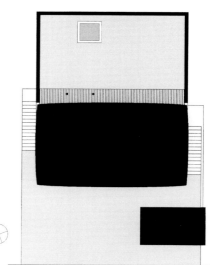

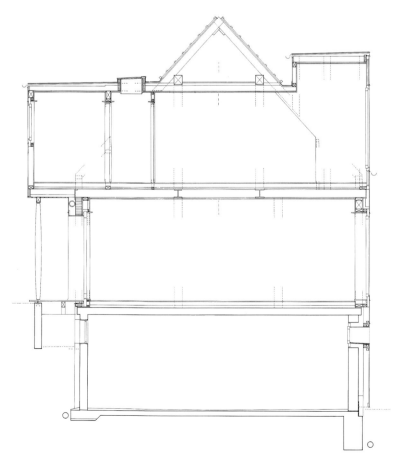

Valerio Olgiati

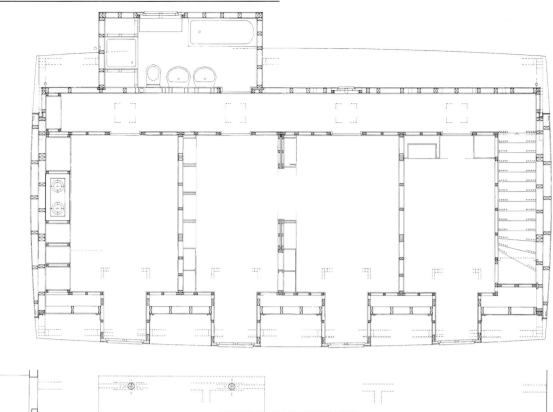

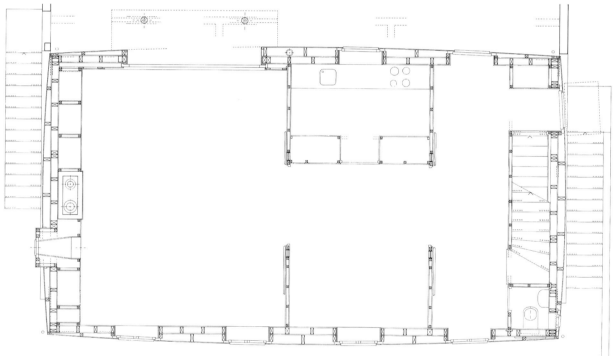

Obergeschoß und Erdgeschoß
Upper floor and ground floor

Quartierplan Cuncas, Sils i. E., Wettbewerbsprojekt 1991.

Die weißen Marmortürme begrenzen eine exakte Fläche, die eine Wiederholung der ruhigen Seeoberflächen und gemähten Wiesen der Oberengadiner Landschaft ist. Ihr besonderer Ausdruck liegt in der Gegensätzlichkeit von Ebene und Berg oder von Fläche und kristalliner Form.

Zwei Ordnungen definieren die Türme. Die äußere Form als geordnete Figur einerseits und die Anordnung der Öffnungen als ungeordnete Figur andererseits. Dieses regionale Prinzip und die relative Größe der Türme assoziiert die Engadiner Tradition der Gleichzeitigkeit von Bauernhaus und Internationalität.

Die eigentliche Aufgabe stellten die vielen Zweitwohnungen. Es kann davon ausgegangen werden, daß das Quartier Cuncas in der Zwischensaison verlassen und leer sein wird. Die Tatsache der Leere jedoch enthält noch keine Aussage über Qualität, sie ist weder schlecht noch gut. Erst ihre willentliche Behandlung führt den qualitativen Aspekt ein.

Das Thema dieses Projektes besteht nun genau aus jener Behandlung, welche die bewußte Darstellung der Leere zum Ziel hat.

Die eigens entwickelten Läden aus Marmor – bei Abwesenheit geschlossen – sind bündig mit der Marmorfassade. Auf diese Weise nehmen die Türme in der Zwischensaison eine starke Geschlossenheit an.

Plan for the Cuncas Quarter, Sils i. E., Competition Project, 1991.

The white marble towers border an exact surface that is a reiteration of the calm surfaces of the lakes and the mowed meadows of the Upper Engadine countryside. The special expression of this countryside lies in the contradiction of plain and mountain, or flat surface and crystalline form.

Two orders define the towers: the external form as an orderly figure on the one hand and the arrangement of openings as a disorderly figure on the other. This regional principle and the relative largeness of the towers creates associations with the Engadine tradition of the simultaneity of farmhouse and internationality.

The actual commission required the many second apartments. It can be assumed from this that the Cuncas quarter is abandoned and left empty during the transitional seasons. The fact of the emptiness, however, contains no statement regarding the quality – it is neither good nor bad. The qualitative aspect is introduced by the deliberate handling of the emptiness.

The theme of the project develops exactly from this handling, which has the conscious representation of emptiness as its goal.

The specially developed marble shutters – closed when no one is there – are flush with the marble façade. In this way, the towers assume a strong impermeability during the off-seasons.

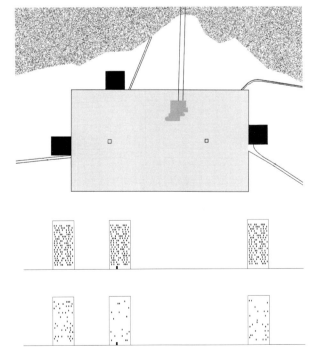

Ansicht, Farbstiftzeichnung von Mark Sasvary
 View, drawing in colored pencil by Mark Sasvary
Situation
 Situation
Fassaden mit offenen und geschlossenen Fenstern
 Façades with open and closed windows

Wiederaufbau des Souk von Beirut, Wettbewerbsprojekt, mit Frank Escher, 1994.

Der Souk von Beirut, vor dem Krieg eine dichte Ansammlung von kleinen Läden, Werkstätten und Lagerräumen, ist heute total zerstört. Unser Projekt baut auf dem alten Stadtplan auf, die ehemaligen Straßenräume werden rekonstruiert. Die Läden, Werkstätten und Lager – früher zellenartig gereiht – sind genau in die Umrisse der ehemaligen Blocks gelegt.

Jeder Laden, jede Werkstätte bildet eine Kiste. Es gibt drei verschiedene Größen von jeweils drei Meter Höhe. Zwei Wände bestehen aus Glas und zwei aus Sandstein. In horizontalen Lagen sind sie tausendfach geschichtet und gestapelt. Die Kisten sind exakt bündig mit der Außenkante des ehemaligen «Blocks», innerhalb sind sie frei und zufällig angelegt. Auf dem ersten Niveau, dem leicht abfallenden Straßenniveau, stehen sie auf einem tritthohen Sockel, in den oberen Etagen auf einer geschoßtrennenden Betonplatte. Der Souk ist ein Labyrinth von offenen Straßen und engen, gedeckten Gängen.

Das Lagern und Schichten zieht sich durch die Struktur des «Blocks», durch die Läden und Lager bis hin zu den Schaufenstern. Das Aufstellen von Ware wiederholt sich von Laden zu Laden, von Schaufenster zu Schaufenster und von Gestell zu Gestell.

Die Bilder zum Projekt sind im Computer hergestellt. Es handelt sich um rein digital-synthetische Darstellungen. Das Ziel ist, neben der volumetrischen und organisatorischen Abbildung, auch Aspekte des Materials und des Lichts zu vermitteln.

Redevelopment of the Souk of Beirut, Competition Project, with Frank Escher, 1994.

The Souk of Beirut – before the war a compressed collection of small shops, workshops and storage spaces – is today totally destroyed. Our project builds on the old city plan and the former street areas are reconstructed. The shops, workshops and storage – earlier laid out in rows of cells – are placed exactly within the contour of the former blocks.

Each shop, each workshop, forms a box. There are three different sizes, each three meters high. Two walls are of glass and two of sandstone. They are layered and stacked horizontally a thousand times over. The boxes are exactly flush with the outer edge of the former "block"; inside, they are free and randomly arranged. On the first level, the slightly inclined street level, they stand on a step-high socle, and in the upper levels, on a concrete plate that separates the floors. The Souk is a labyrinth of open streets and narrow, covered walkways.

Evidence of storing and stacking can be seen throughout the structure of the "blocks", through the storage spaces and shops, and out to the show windows. The display of goods repeats from shop to shop, from window to window, from stand to stand.

The pictures of the project are computer generated. This is pure digital synthetic representation. The goal, in addition to volumetric and organizational illustrations, is to also convey aspects of the material and the light.

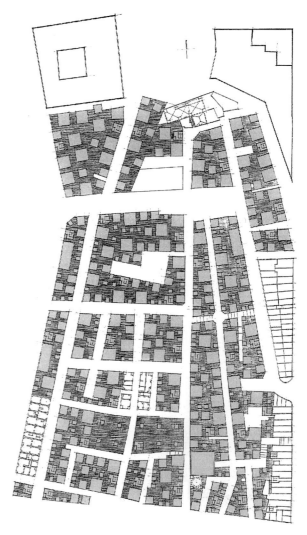

Straßengeschoß, Zustand 1973
Street level, condition 1973
Straßengeschoß, geplant
Street level, proposed

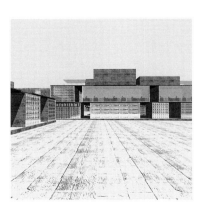

Perspektiven, Computerbilder; linke Reihe: Schema des Aufbaus
Perspectives, computer images; left row: development scheme

Biografie

Valerio Olgiati
1958 geboren.
1972-79 Gymnasium Typ C, Kantonsschule Chur, Matura.
1980-86 Architekturstudium an der ETH Zürich.
1986 Diplom bei Prof. Fabio Reinhart an der ETH Zürich.
1986/87 Assistent bei Prof. Fabio Reinhart, ETH Zürich.
1988-93 eigenes Architekturbüro in Zürich.
1993-95 Architekturbüro mit Frank Escher in Los Angeles, USA.
1994/95 Gastprofessor an der FH Stuttgart, Deutschland.
Seit 1995 eigenes Architekturbüro in Zürich.

Auszeichnungen
1993 *Anerkennung des Deutschen Architekturpreises* für das Haus Kucher, Rottenburg a. N., Deutschland.
1994 *Eidgenössisches Kunststipendium.*
1995 Auszeichnung des Hauses Kucher, Rottenburg a. N. durch die Architektenkammer Baden-Württemberg, Deutschland.
1995 *Eidgenössischer Preis für freie Kunst,* mit Frank Escher.

Werkverzeichnis

1983/84
Haus Fiala in Chur.

1988-91
Haus Kucher in Rottenburg a. N., Deutschland.

1991
Quartierplan für das Gebiet Cuncas in Sils, Engadin, Wettbewerb.

1990-92
Renovation des Großhauses von Sprecher in Luzein GR.

1992/93
Haus Dr. Hardt in Malans GR, Projekt.

1994
Wiederaufbau des Souk in Beirut, Libanon, Wettbewerb, mit Frank Escher.

1995
Korean Cultural Center (KOMA) in Los Angeles, USA, Wettbewerb, mit Frank Escher.

1988-96
Verschiedene andere Projektierungen und Wettbewerbe.

Bibliografie

Unerbittlich, in: Hochparterre, 10/1991, S. 105.
Einfamilienhaus, Rottenburg a. N., in: Architektur Jahrbuch 1992, Deutsches Architektur-Museum, Frankfurt a. M., Vittorio Magnago Lampugnani (Hrsg.), 1992, S. 154-157.
Unerbittlich genau, in: Der Architekt, 3/1992, S. 164.
Mut zur Einfachheit, in: Häuser, 6/1992, S. 44-49.
Einfamilienhaus Kucher in Rottenburg am Neckar, Architektur in Deutschland 1993, Jürgen Joedicke (Hrsg.), 1994, S. 83-85.
Haus Kucher, Rottenburg am Neckar, 1989-91, in: archithese, 5/1995, S. 10/11.
Standpunkt: Wiederaufbau von Beirut, in: archithese, 3/1995, S. 64-66.
Neue Möglichkeiten im Holzbau, in: NZZ, 6. Januar 1995, S. 57.
Polarisierte Widersprüchlichkeiten: Zur Architektur von Valerio Olgiati, in: NZZ, 3. Mai 1996, S. 68.

Biography

Valerio Olgiati
1958 Born.
1972-79 Gymnasium (high school) Typ C, Kantonsschule Chur, university entrance qualifying exam.
1980-86 Studied architecture at the ETH Zurich.
1986 Graduated from the ETH Zurich under Prof. Fabio Reinhardt.
1986/87 Assistant to Prof. Fabio Reinhart, ETH Zurich.
1988-93 Own architecture office in Zurich.
1993-95 Architecture office with Frank Escher in Los Angeles, USA.
1994/95 Visiting Professor at the Fachhochschule Stuttgart, Germany.
Since 1995 Own architectural office in Zurich.

Awards
1993 *Anerkennung des Deutschen Architekturpreises* for the Kucher House, Rottenburg on the Neckar, Germany.
1994 *Eidgenössisches Kunststipendium.*
1995 *Auszeichnung* of the Kucher House, Rottenberg on the Neckar, by the Architektenkammer Baden-Württemberg, Germany.
1995 *Eidgenössischer Preis für freie Kunst,* with Frank Escher.

List of Works

1983/84
Fiala House in Chur.

1988-91
Kucher House in Rottenburg on the Neckar, Germany.

1991
Plan for the Cuncas Quarter in Sils, Engadine, Competition.

1990-92
Large Sprecher house, renovation, Luzein.

1992/93
Residence of Dr. Hardt, Malans, project.

1994
Redevelopment of the Souk in Beirut, Lebanon, competition, with Frank Escher.

1995
Korean Cultural Center (KOMA), Los Angeles, USA, competition, with Frank Escher.

1988-96
Various other projects and competitions.

Bibliography

Unerbittlich, in: Hochparterre, 10/1991, p. 105.
Einfamilienhaus, Rottenburg a. N., in: Architektur Jahrbuch 1992, Deutsches Architektur-Museum, Frankfurt on the Main, Vittorio Magnago Lampugnani, Ed., 1992, pp. 154-7.
Unerbittlich genau, in: Der Architekt, 3/1992, p.164.
Mut zur Einfachheit, in: Häuser, 6/1992, pp. 44-9.
Einfamilienhaus Kucher in Rottenburg am Neckar, in: Architektur in Deutschland 1993, Jürgen Joedicke, Ed., 1994, pp. 83-5.
Haus Kucher, Rottenburg am Neckar, 1989-91, in: archithese, 5/1995, pp. 10/11.
Standpunkt: Wiederaufbau von Beirut, in: archithese, 3/1995, pp. 64-6.
Neue Möglichkeiten im Holzbau, in: NZZ, January 6, 1995, p. 57.
Polarisierte Widersprüchlichkeiten: Zur Architektur von Valerio Olgiati, in: NZZ, May 3, 1996, p. 68.

Manfred Schafer
Fribourg

Mitarbeiterinnen und Mitarbeiter
Collaborators
- Peter Bäriswyl
- Jean-Daniel Dubosson
- Martin Eisenring
- Michel Graber
- Roman Jungo
- Juan-Carlos Millan
- Christoph Nägeli
- Thomas Radczuweit
- Hervé Romanens
- Konrad Schafer
- Philippe Schaller
- Fréderic Schmutz
- Markus Thomann
- Susanne Zimmermann

Wohnüberbauung Cité du Grand-Torry | Housing Superstructure | Fribourg, 1990–95

Mehrfamilienhaus | Multi-family House | Düdingen, 1992–94

Unterstand Riedener | Riedener Shelter | Schmitten, 1993

Wohnsiedlung Buechlihubel | Buechlihubel Housing Development | Schmitten, 1983–86

Manfred Schafer

Bauen am Rande des «Röstigrabens».

Es ist wohl kein Zufall, daß Manfred Schafer Freiburg als einen zweisprachigen Kanton schildert, wobei sich immer wieder französische Wörter in seinen Freiburger Dialekt mischen. Schafer wohnt zwar heute in seinem deutschfreiburgischen Geburtsort Schmitten, führt sein Büro aber im überwiegend französischsprachigen Fribourg. Er studierte am dortigen Technikum, an dem er später selbst im Fach Entwurf unterrichtete, nachdem er in den Jahren 1987/88 in Zürich an der ETH Assistent war: hier wiederum bei Vincent Mangeat, dem «professeur le plus romand» der Schule. Dieses Pendeln zwischen zwei Kulturräumen hat in seinem Schaffen merkliche Spuren hinterlassen.

Die vor kurzem vollendete «Cité du Grand-Torry» in Freiburg zeigt eine neomoderne Architektursprache, wie man sie sich auch jenseits der Saane vorstellen könnte: Eine Zeilenbebauung mit Laubengängen, die sich für den sozialen Wohnungsbau bewährt hat. Bei den Materialien dominieren als Stülpschalung verwendeter grauer Eternit, feuerverzinkter Stahl, Sichtbeton, grünliches Profilitglas und naturbelassene Holzwerkstoffplatten. Zusammen erzeugen diese Materialien eine kühle, elegante Stimmung, die jedoch durch zurzeit noch fehlende Farbakzente gebrochen werden soll. Geschickt nutzt die Bebauung die Hanglage aus: Im oberen, niedrigeren Teil befinden sich auf vier Geschossen Duplexwohnungen mit je einem zugehörigen Außenraum als Vorgarten oder als Dachterrasse. Auf der anderen Seite des Geländesprungs, in welchem auf zwei Geschossen ein geschützter Verbindungsgang sowie Garagen- und Kellerräume untergebracht sind, befinden sich Etagenwohnungen. Nach unten werden die Zeilen von Duplexwohnungen abgeschlossen, was eine großmaßstäbliche, fast turmartige Gestaltung der Stirnfronten ermöglicht. Die Fenster werden dabei auf zweigeschossige Loggia-Einschnitte konzentriert. Unbeschwert werden diese von Mario Botta inspirierten Öffnungen neben quadratischen Lochfenstern und horizontalen Bändern verwendet, ohne daß die Baukörper dadurch ihre Einheit verlieren würden.

Für das an karge Deutschschweizer Kost gewohnte Auge vollends überraschend ist ein zylindrischer Turm, der als große Geste den Zugang zur ganzen Siedlung markiert und von dem aus ein bogenförmig aufgespannter Betonweg scheinbar über der Wiese schwebend zum Rückgrat der Zeilenbebauung führt. Die Gestaltung des Turmes ist bescheiden und dem sozialen Wohnungsbau angemessen, doch gerade das Fehlen von Sockel und Attika und die graue Eternithülle mit ihrem regelmäßigen Muster quadratischer Fenster, das nur nach Südwesten von einem angehängten Erker unterbrochen wird, machen den Zylinder zu einem sperrigen Objekt von kruder Monumentalität: Zweifellos ein zusätzlicher identitätsstiftender Faktor für die ganze Siedlung.

Manfred Schafer hat etliche Wohnbauten abseits städtischer Zentren realisiert, meist mit den späteren Bewohnern als Bauherrschaft. Auch bei dieser bescheidenen und schwierigen Bauaufgabe gelingt es ihm, die individuellen Bedürfnisse der Nutzer zu berücksichtigen und dennoch die einzelnen Wohnungen zu charakteristischen Einheiten zusammenzufassen. Gemeinsame Elemente wie Dächer, Treppen, Lifte und Gemeinschaftsräume werden dabei als rhetorische Gesten verwendet. Sein eigenes Reihenhaus etwa ist Teil einer Zeile, bei der markant ausgebildete Kopfbauten und ein durchgängiges Tonnendach die sechs Häuser zu einem einzigen, breitgelagerten Gebäude verschmelzen lassen, bei dem sich die einzelnen Einheiten fast nur noch durch eine differenzierende Farbgebung der Fassaden abzeichnen.

Manfred Schafer löst so ein, was er mit einem Zitat von Charles Moore – als Motto seinem Leporello vorangestellt – von der Architektur fordert: «Gebäude sollten etwas erzählen – nicht einfach vom Spiel von Form und Licht, sondern auch von Dingen, die etwas bedeuten.» M. T.

Wohnüberbauung Cité du Grand-Torry, Fribourg, 1990–95
Cité du Grand-Torry housing superstructure, Fribourg, 1990–95

Building on the Edge of the "Röstigraben".

It is certainly no accident that Manfred Schafer describes Fribourg as a two-language canton; in so doing, French words mingle time and again with his Fribourg dialect. Schafer, in fact, lives today in his German Fribourg home town of Schmitten, in the canton, but runs his office from the predominantly French-speaking town of Fribourg itself. He studied, and later taught design, at the Technikum there, after which he was an assistant at the ETH in Zurich in 1987/88, and here, he was once again with Vincent Mangeat, the school's "professeur le plus romand". This pendulum swing between two cultural zones has left its mark on his work.

The recently completed "Cité du Grand-Torry" in Fribourg demonstrates a neo-modern architectural language, as one could also imagine it on the other side of the Sarine River: a linear development with external corridors that has proved successful for publicly assisted housing construction. Gray Eternit applied as a covering of overlapping boards, hot-dip galvanized steel, exposed concrete, greenish textured glass and natural wood material sheeting are dominant materials. Together, these materials produce a cool, elegant mood that is, however, to be broken by color accents yet to come. The development skillfully exploits the inclined site. Up above in the lower part, duplex apartments, each with an exterior space of its own to be used as a front garden or roof terrace, are located on four stories. Self-contained apartments are located on the other side of the gelaendesprung, in which a protected connecting passageway plus garage and cellar spaces are arranged on two stories. Down below, the lines of duplex apartments terminate, which allows for a large-scale, almost tower-like formation of the front ends. The windows are therefore concentrated on two-story cut-in loggias. Inspired by Mario Botta, these openings are lightly employed next to the single square windows and horizontal bands, without destroying the uniformity of the building unit.

For the eye accustomed to meager German-Swiss fare, the cylindrical tower that accentuates the entrance to the development with a great gesture comes as a complete surprise. A suspended bow-shaped concrete walkway leads away from the tower and seems to float over the lawn to the spine of the linear development. The formation of the tower is unpretentious and appropriate to the public housing, but it is exactly the omission of socle and roof parapet, and the gray Eternit shell with its regular pattern of square windows interrupted only on the southwest by an appended bay window, that make the cylinder into a bulky object of crude monumentality – and doubtless an additional identity-establishing factor for the whole development.

Manfred Schafer has built a few housing constructions apart from urban centers, mostly with the later inhabitants as clients. Even with this modest and difficult building problem he succeeds in taking the individual needs of the users into consideration and is still able to bring the single apartments together into a characteristic unity. Common elements like roofs, stairs, elevators and recreation rooms are thereby used as rhetorical gestures. His own attached house, for instance, is part of a row where the strikingly developed head constructions and a continuous barrel roof allow the six houses to melt together into one single spread-out building in which the separate units emerge almost entirely because of differentiated façade coloration.

Manfred Schafer thus fulfills what he demands of architecture, expressed in a quote by Charles Moore and placed by Schafer in the front of his album as a motto: "Buildings should say something – not simply about the play of form and light, but also about things that mean something." M. T.

Manfred Schafer

Wohnüberbauung Cité du Grand-Torry, Fribourg, 1990–95.

Das Wettbewerbsprogramm forderte ein exemplarisches Projekt zum Thema sozialer Wohnungsbau. Dem L-förmigen, an der Route des Bonnesfontaines angedockten Grundstück setzten wir an dieser Stelle einen runden Wohnturm als Ort des Zugangs und der Identifikation. Von hier aus führt eine Passerelle durch den alten Obstgarten zum großen Platz beim Gemeinschaftsraum und der Kinderkrippe. Die kammförmige Überbauung wird durch eine traditionelle Nord-Süd-Achse erschlossen. Die unterschiedlichen Gebäudetiefen und Hofsituationen bilden einen erlebnisreichen Parcours. Das vielfältige Wohnungs- und Nutzungsangebot, großzügige private und halböffentliche Außenräume sowie eine kostengünstige Erstellung machen Torry zu einem attraktiven Wohnort.

Cité du Grand-Torry Housing Superstructure, Fribourg, 1990–95.

The competition program demanded an exemplary project for the publicly assisted housing construction. The L-shaped plot of land sits directly on the Route des Bonnesfontaines. On just this spot, we have set a round housing tower as entry and identification point. A passageway leads from here through the old fruit garden to the large plaza by the recreation room and day care center. The comb-formed superstructure is opened up through a central north-south axis, where varying building depths and courtyard situations form a richly interesting route. The multiple possibilities for living and utilization, generous private and semi-public exterior spaces as well as a reasonably-priced construction make Torry an attractive place to live.

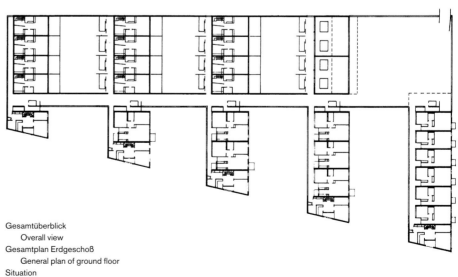

Gesamtüberblick
  Overall view
Gesamtplan Erdgeschoß
  General plan of ground floor
Situation
  Situation

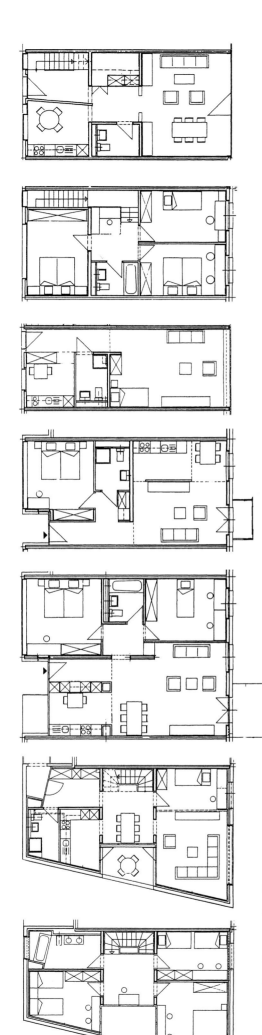

Eingangsgeschoß, 4½-Zimmer-Wohnung
 Entrance level, 4½ room apartment
Obergeschoß der Duplexwohnung
 Upper floor of duplex apartment
1½-Zimmer-Wohnung
 1½ room apartment
2½-Zimmer-Wohnung
 2½ room apartment
3½-Zimmer-Wohnung
 3½ room apartment
Eingangsgeschoß, 5½-Zimmer-Wohnung
 Entrance level, 5½ room apartment
Obergeschoß der Duplexwohnung
 Upper floor of duplex apartment

Blick in einen öffentlichen Hofraum
 View into open courtyard
Die mit privaten Gärten unterteilten Höfe
 Courtyards divided into private gardens
Die Haupterschließung der Wohnüberbauung entlang der Geländekante
 The main access way through the development along the raised edge of land

Manfred Schafer

Mehrfamilienhaus in Düdingen, 1992–94.

Eine Wohnbaugruppe erwarb für ihre eigenen Bedürfnisse ein Grundstück an der Peripherie der Gemeinde Düdingen. Entstanden sind je vier Etagen- und Duplexwohnungen im Stockwerkeigentum. Das Gebäude sucht den Süden, die freie Sicht über die Nachbarbauten hinweg. Der teilweise verglaste nördliche Laubengang dient der Erschließung und Abschottung gegenüber der nahen Autobahn. Ein zweigeschossiger Gemeinschaftsraum öffnet sich zur Ankunft und zum vorgelagerten Spielplatz.

Multi-family House in Düdingen, 1992–94.

A housing construction group acquired for their own needs a plot of land on the periphery of the Municipality of Düdingen. Four self-contained and duplex apartments have each been built as one-story condominiums. The building looks to the south – to the free view over the neighboring buildings. The partially glazed external corridor on the north serves as an accessway and a protection against the nearby freeway. A two-story recreation room opens towards the entrance and the play area directly in front.

Westfassade und Südfassade
West façade and south façade

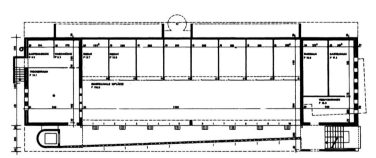
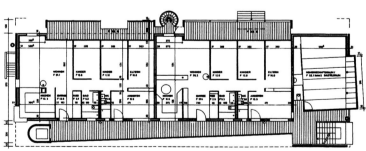
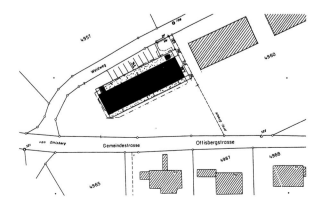

Situation
Situation

Sockelgeschoß mit offenem Unterstand
Basement level with open shelter
Erstes und zweites Obergeschoß mit Gemeinschaftsraum
First and second floors with recreation room
Drittes Obergeschoß (Eingangsgeschoß)
Third floor (entrance level)
Dachgeschoß
Attic floor
Querschnitt
Cross section

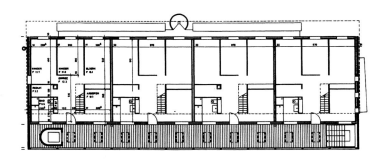
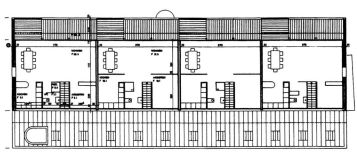
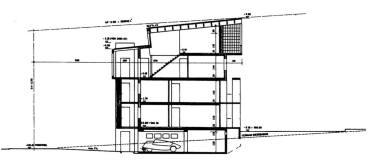

Manfred Schafer

Unterstand Riedener, Schmitten, 1993.

Die orthogonale Ausrichtung der bestehenden Gebäude und der schräg dazu verlaufende Waldrand ergaben die Grundrißgeometrie des Unterstandes. Hofseitig verbindet ein transparentes, rundumlaufendes Vordach Alt und Neu. Waldseitig beschränkt sich das lange Gebäude auf eine nach innen gekippte Lattenrostfassade. Diese schützt vor der Witterung, und der Bezug zum Wald bleibt weitgehend erhalten.

Riedener Shelter, Schmitten, 1993.

The orthogonal orientation of the existing buildings and the oblique approach of the forest resulted in the floor plan geometry of the shelter. A transparent canopy runs along the courtyard side and connects the old with the new. On the forest side, the long building is restrained with a duckboard façade which slants toward the inside. This offers protection against the weather while preserving to a great extent the relation to the forest.

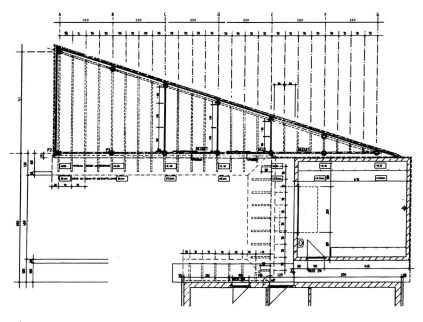

Ansichten Zufahrt und Rückseite
　Views of driveway and rear side
Grundriß und Querschnitt
　Floor plan and cross section
Situation
　Situation

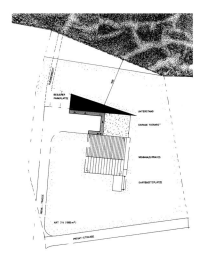
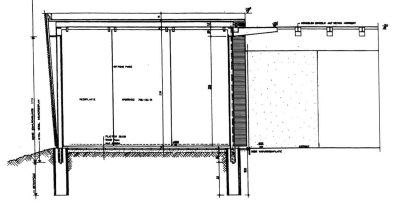

Wohnsiedlung Buechlihubel, Schmitten, 1983–86.

Der Osthang wurde anfangs der achtziger Jahre erschlossen. Auf der Hügelkuppe sollte mittels verdichteter Bauweise das zu erwartende Zersiedlungsbild beruhigt werden. Das langgestreckte Haus mit sechs den individuellen Bedürfnissen angepaßten Wohneinheiten wird von den markanten Kopfbauten (Verankerungen) und dem überspannenden Tonnendach geprägt. Die filigranen Längsfassaden (Pfosten-Riegelbau) sorgen für helle Innenräume und freie Sicht auf eine herrliche Landschaft.

Buechlihubel Housing Development, Schmitten, 1983–86.

The eastern slope was developed at the beginning of the 1980s. On the rounded hilltop, the expected urban sprawl was curtailed with a more compressed construction. The long house with living units, suiting six individual needs, is characterized by a prominent head construction (anchoring) and the barrel roof spanning the length. The filigreed long façades (post-tie beam) ensure bright interior spaces and a free view of the marvelous landscape.

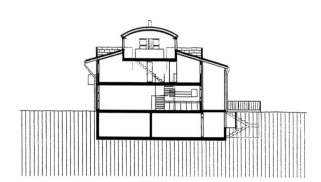

Querschnitt
  Cross section
Nordost-Fassade
  Northeast façade
Untergeschoß mit Gemeinschaftsräumen
  Basement level with commonrooms
Erdgeschoß (Eingangsgeschoß)
  Ground floor (entrance level)
Obergeschoß mit Dachgeschoß über den
vier mittleren Einheiten
  Upper floor with attic above the
  four center units
Situation
  Situation

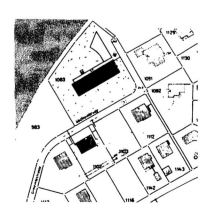

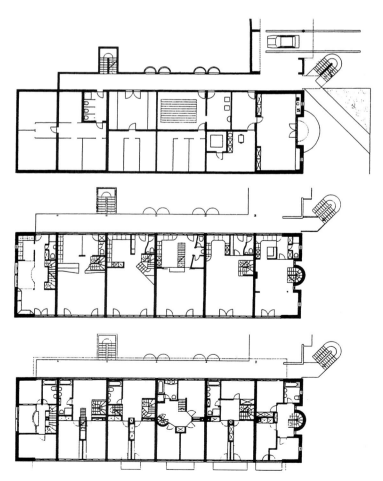

Biografie

Manfred Schafer
1952 geboren in Schmitten FR.
1969-72 Hochbauzeichnerlehre.
1973-76 Architekturstudium an der HTL Freiburg.
1976-80 Mitarbeit bei der kantonalen Denkmalpflege, Freiburg. Diverse Studienreisen.
1987/88 Assistent bei Prof. Vincent Mangeat an der ETH Zürich.
1989-94 Dozent für Entwurf an der HTL Freiburg.
1993-95 Experte im Bundesamt für Wohnungswesen.

Seit 1980 eigenes Architekturbüro in Freiburg.

Ausstellungen, Vorträge

1994 *Silence et révolte,* GSMBA-Ausstellung Sektion Freiburg, im Museum für Kunst und Geschichte Freiburg.
1995 *Economie des moyens,* Jean Pythoud und acht Freiburger Architekten, Kunsthalle Freiburg.

1995 Vortrag im Architektur Forum Zürich.

Werkverzeichnis

1981
Wohnhaus Schafer in Düdingen FR.

1982
Pfarreizentrum und Aufbahrungsgebäude in Schmitten FR.

1983
Umbau Bauernhaus Gremaud in Montévraz FR.

1984
Bankgebäude Raiffeisenbank in Schmitten FR.

1985
Umbau Mehrfamilienhaus Estermann in Freiburg.

1986
Wohnsiedlung Buechlihubel in Schmitten FR.

1987
Wohnhaus Raemy in Freiburg.

1988
Wohnsiedlung Diezig / Hurni / Nowak in St. Ursen FR.

1989
Wohnsiedlung Eberhard / Niggli / Hubmann in Schmitten FR.

1990
Wohnhaus Brügger in Wünnewil FR.
Verwaltungsgebäude in Wünnewil FR, Wettbewerb, Ankauf.
Subventionierter Wohnungsbau Cité du Grand-Torry in Freiburg. Wettbewerb, erster Preis, ausgeführt 1990-95.

1992
Schulhaus in Plaffeien FR, Wettbewerb, erster Preis.

1993
Um- und Ausbau der Tierarztpraxis Riedener in Schmitten FR.

1994
Mehrfamilienhaus in Düdingen FR.

1995
Geschäftszentrum und Altersresidenz in Muri BE, Wettbewerbseinladung.
Masterplan «Place des Nations», UNO Genf, internationaler Wettbewerb, Einladung.

1996
Umbau Bauernhaus Monney in Ependes FR.
Doppelwohnhaus Lehmann/Marbach in Tafers FR.

Bibliografie

Umbau Bauernhaus in Montévraz FR, in: as 2/1985.
Raiffeisenbank in Schmitten FR, in: as, 4/1985.
Richard Quincerot, *Six maisons à Schmitten,* in: Habitation, 5/1988.
Sigrid Hanke, *Gemeinsam individuell wohnen,* in: Atrium, 2/1989.
Werner Lehmann, *Modern und doch voller Poesie,* in: Das Einfamilienhaus, 6/1989.
Benedikt Loderer, *Schmitten: Ein gewöhnlicher Sonderfall,* in: Hochparterre, 11/1990.
Archipress, *Reihenhaus St. Ursen: Eine Lösung – drei Häuser,* in: Arch+ 98, 1/1991.
Werner Lehmann, *Angemessene Architektur,* in: Raum und Wohnen, 2/1992.
Sonnenenergie-Fachverband Schweiz, Drei Häuser unter einem Dach, in: Solare Architektur – ein neues Selbstverständnis.
Christoph Allenspach, *Experiment Mehrfamilienhaus,* in: Hochparterre, 6/1995.
Martin Tschanz, *Cité du Grand-Torry,* in: Bauwelt, 7/1995. Unter dem Titel *Bauen am Rande des Röschtigrabens,* in: NZZ, 2. Juni 1995.
Archipress, *Cité du Grand-Torry: Ein Stück Stadt,* in: Arch+ 118, 1/1996.
Marianne Kürsteiner, *Leben mit den Nachbarn, Wohnbaugruppe Düdingen,* in: A+T, 2/1996.
Genève – Concours international Place des Nations, Département des Traveaux Publiques et de l'Energie, Jurybericht, Verlag Birkhäuser 1996.

Biography

Manfred Schafer
1952 Born in Schmitten.
1969-72 Architectural drafting apprenticeship.
1973-76 Studied architecture at the HTL Fribourg.
1976-80 Worked at the Canton Preservation of Monuments, Fribourg. Diverse study trips.
1987/88 Assistant to Prof. Vincent Mangeat at the ETH.
1989-94 Lecturer in design at the HTL Fribourg.
1993-95 Expert at the Federal Department of Housing.

Since 1980 own architectural office in Fribourg.

Exhibitions, Lectures
1994 *Silence et révolte,* GSMBA Exhibition Section Fribourg, at the Museum for Art and History, Fribourg.
1995 *Economie des moyens,* Jean Pythoud and eight Fribourg architects, Art Museum, Fribourg.

1995 Lecture at Architektur Forum in Zurich.

List of Works

1981
A. Schafer Residence in Düdingen.

1982
Rectory center and lying-in-state chamber, Schmitten.

1983
Gremaud Farmhouse, conversion, Montévraz.

1984
Raiffeisen Bank building, Schmitten.

1985
Estermann Multi-family House, Fribourg.

1986
Buechlihubel Housing Development, Schmitten.

1987
Raemy Residence, Fribourg.

1988
Diezig/Hurni/Nowak Housing Development in St. Ursen.

1989
Eberhard/Niggli/Hubmann Housing Development, Schmitten.

1990
Brügger Residence, Wünnewil.
Administration building, Wünnewil, competition, purchase.
Cité du Grand-Torry, subsidized construction housing development, competition, first prize, executed 1990-95.

1992
Schoolhouse in Plaffeien, competition, first prize.

1993
Riederer veterinary practice, conversion and expansion, Schmitten.

1994
Multi-family house, Düdingen.

1995
Business center and senior residence, Muri, competition invitation.
Masterplan «Place des Nations», UNO Geneva, international competition, invitation.

1996
Monney Farmhouse, conversion, Ependes.
Lehmann/Marbach Double Residence, Tafers.

Bibliography

Umbau Bauernhaus in Montévraz FR, in: as 2/1985.
Raiffeisenbank in Schmitten FR, in: as 4/1985.
Richard Quincerot, *Six maisons à Schmitten,* in: Habitation, 5/1988.
Sigrid Hanke, *Gemeinsam individuell wohnen,* in: Atrium, 2/1989.
Werner Lehrmann, *Modern und doch voller Poesie,* in: Das Einfamilienhaus, 6/1989.
Benedikt Loderer, *Schmitten: Ein gewöhnlicher Sonderfall,* in: Hochparterre, 11/1990.
Archipress, *Reihenhaus St. Ursen: Eine Lösung – drei Häuser,* in: Arch+ 98, 1/1991.
Werner Lehrmann, *Angemessene Architektur,* in: Raum und Wohnen, 2/1992.
Sonnenenergie-Fachverband Schweiz, *Drei Häuser unter einem Dach,* in: Solare Architektur – ein neues Selbstverständnis.
Christoph Allenspach, *Experiment Mehrfamilienhaus,* in: Hochparterre, 6/1995.
Martin Tschanz, *Cité du Grand-Torry,* in: Bauwelt, 7/1995. Under the title *Bauen am Rande des Röschtigrabens,* in: NZZ, June 2, 1995.
Archipress, *Cité du Grand-Torry: Ein Stück Stadt,* in: Arch+ 118, 1/1996.
Marianne Kürsteiner, *Leben mit den Nachbarn, Wohnbaugruppe Düdingen,* in: A+T, 2/1996.
Genève – Concours international Place des Nations, Département des Traveaux Publiques et de l'Energie, jury report, Verlag Birkhäuser 1996.

Andi Scheitlin
Marc Syfrig
Luzern

Museum «Forum der Schweizergeschichte» | Schwyz, 1989–95

Betriebsleitzentrale SBB | SBB Operations Management Centre | Luzern, 1992–95

Doppeleinfamilienhaus | Semi-detached Residence | Meggen, 1994/95

Mitarbeiterinnen und Mitarbeiter
Collaborators
- Sandra Ammann
- Matthias Baumann
- Daniel Beutler
- Johannes Drexel
- Claudia Erni
- Jacques Feiner
- Bruno von Flüe
- François Guillermain
- Stefan Häberli
- Sandra Hofmarcher
- Paolo Janssen
- Ilona Kälin
- Petra Kessler
- Felix Möller
- Benedikt Rigling
- Pia Scheitlin-Rieben
- Caroline Seiler
- Hanspeter Steiger
- Benedikt Steiner
- Lukas Steiner
- Sibylle Theiler
- Willi Voney
- Ruth Wigger
- Peter Widmer

Von den Dissonanzen der Provinz.

Die Luzerner Architekten Andi Scheitlin und Marc Syfrig wurden einem größeren Publikum durch den Umbau des ehemaligen Zeughauses zum «Forum der Schweizergeschichte» in Schwyz bekannt. Sie gehören zu der Generation der an der ETH ausgebildeten Architekten, die zunächst von der Solidität ihrer Lehrer Bernhard Hösli, Dolf Schnebli und Mario Campi geprägt wurden, gleichzeitig aber durch die kontradiktorische «Störung» von Aldo Rossis Lehrtätigkeit an der ETH in den siebziger Jahren die wichtigsten Impulse erhielten.

Die von formaler Aufrichtigkeit und der Suche nach historischer und kontextueller Analyse bestimmte Theorie erwies sich jedoch im Arbeitsalltag als schwer umsetzbar. «Die Praxis verlangte von uns Antworten, auf die wir nicht gefaßt waren», so Marc Syfrig heute. «Vor allem die Zusammenarbeit im Wohnungsbau mit einer Generalunternehmung zwang uns, von formalen Idealvorstellungen Abschied zu nehmen.»

Scheitlin und Syfrig betonen, daß es ihnen heute eher um die Suche nach neuen Bildern als um die Analogie zu Vorbildern aus der Geschichte geht. Diese Bilder finden sie in der anonymen und alltäglichen Architektur der Vorstädte und wenig signifikanten Agglomerationen. «Diese Fülle an Ideen und Formen sind für uns deshalb so interessant, weil sie ohne große Geste Lösungen anbieten, die einen logischen Bezug zur Besonderheit des Ortes und zur Aufgabe aufweisen.» Nahezu folgerichtig scheint es, daß Scheitlin und Syfrig vermehrt zu Aufgaben herangezogen werden, in denen es um die Verbindung von alter Bausubstanz mit neuen Nutzungen geht. Das ist auch das Thema der Umgestaltung des «Forums der Schweizergeschichte», die von 1992 bis 1994 von ihnen realisiert wurde (Mitarbeit: Hans Steiner). Dabei wurden vom ehemaligen Zeughaus in Schwyz die Mauern und der Dachstuhl im alten Zustand belassen, im Inneren jedoch eine völlig neue Struktur injiziert. Das mehrgeschossige Gerüst nimmt mit seinen Ebenen zwar die Struktur des alten Gebäudes auf, es ist jedoch in dieses hineingestellt und betont auch mit seinen Kirschbaumverkleidungen den Gegensatz zur den weißgestrichenen Außenmauern. Ebenso bildet der gesamte Einbau mit seinem trichterförmigen Treppenhaus einen bewußten Dialog mit der Typologie des alten Gebäudes. Aus solchen Gegensätzen eine «synthetische Architektur» zu entwickeln ist das Anliegen von Syfrig und Scheitlin. Zwar war es einerseits die schnelle Entwicklung von Bauvorschriften, Vorstellungen der Bauherrn und die Eigenheit der Baumaterialien, die diesen Weg bestimmten, zugleich ist es aber auch die bewußte Aufnahme der Dissonanzen der Provinz, die ihnen wichtiger sind als die Referenz der klassischen Prototypen großer Architekten. Dabei versuchen sie klar Stellung zu beziehen, ohne durch das Eingehen auf den Ort und den Geschichtsbezug als Entwurfsgrundlage eine Eigendynamik entstehen zu lassen. Diese Haltung brachte ihnen in dem spektakulären Wettbewerb für das Kultur- und Kongreßzentrum in Luzern immerhin den vierten Preis ein. Allerdings «nur» den vierten Preis; ihr Projekt schlug damals bereits den begründeten Abriß des Kongreßhauses von Armin Meili vor, bevorzugt wurden seinerzeit jedoch jene Projekte, die den denkmalschützenden Erhalt des Gebäudes vorsahen. Mittlerweile hat sich die Stadt für den Abriß des alten Kongreßhauses entschieden.

In der Erwartung, an größeren kulturellen Aufgaben mitzugestalten, verlegten sich Scheitlin und Syfrig, wie viele ihrer Alters- und Arbeitskollegen auch, zunächst auf die präzise Formulierung und gezielte Verwendung des Materials. Die spezifischen Eigenschaften des Materials, seine Auswahl und seine Konstruktionsmethoden schaffen die Möglichkeit, den Bezug zum Ort auszudrücken, wie Marc Syfrig es nennt. Dieses Bemühen verdeutlichen ihre Projekte – und ganz besonders einer der größten öffentlichen Aufträge bisher, das «Forum der Schweizergeschichte». Durch die Reduktion auf das Wesentliche und die genaue Umsetzung des Inhalts entsteht eine Eindringlichkeit, die nicht reproduzierbar ist und die in Schwyz nur durch den Dialog des neuen Kerns mit der historischen Hülle entstehen konnte.

Das Erstreben größtmöglicher Präzision und die Liebe zur Reduktion der Teile ist sinnbildlich für Scheitlin und Syfrig und mit ihnen für viele ihrer Kollegen derselben Generation. Darin liegt für sie aber auch der Bezug zur bildenden Kunst begründet, die sie zurzeit stark beeinflußt. Sie scheint heute mehr denn je der Ort zu sein, an dem sich Modernität noch radikal abspielt, vielleicht nicht zuletzt deshalb, weil sie frei von den beschriebenen Zwängen ist: «Die Suche nach der Verwandtschaft der Bilder von Donald Judd mit der verwitterten Holzverkleidung einer Scheune mag symbolisch für das stehen, woran wir glauben: an die Schönheit und das Gute in den Dingen.» J.C.B.

Wohnhaus in Ruopigen, Littau, 1990-93
Housing block in Ruopigen, Littau, 1990-93

From the Dissonance of the Provinces.

Lucerne architects Andi Scheitlin and Marc Syfrig became known to a wider public with their conversion of the former arsenal in Schwyz into the "Forum der Schweizergeschichte", the Forum for Swiss History. They belong to the generation of architects educated at the ETH Zurich and influenced first and foremost by the competence of their teachers Bernhard Hösli, Dolf Schnebli and Mario Campi, but also at the same time receiving the most important impulses through the contradictory "disorder" of Aldo Rossi's teachings at the ETH in the 1970s.

The theory, defined by a formal sincerity and the search for historical and contextual analysis, proved to be difficult to put into practice. "The practice required answers from us that we were not prepared to give," says Marc Syfrig today. "Above all, the collaboration with a general contractor in housing construction forced us to depart from formal conceptual ideals."

Scheitlin and Syfrig emphasize that today they are more concerned with the search for new images than with the analogy to models from history. They find these images in the anonymous everyday architecture of the suburbs and insignificant agglomerations. "This abundance of ideas and forms are so interesting for us because they offer, without large gestures, solutions that present a logical relation to the specific quality of the site and to the problem." It appears almost logical that Scheitlin and Syfrig are increasingly drawn into problems that deal with the connection between old building substance and new uses. That is also the theme of the redesigning of the "Forum der Schweizergeschichte", which they actualized between 1992 and 1994 (collaboration: Hans Steiner). There, the huge walls and the roof framework of the former Schwyz arsenal were left in their old condition, while a completely new structure was injected into the interior. Although the multi-storied steel frame took on with its own planes the structure of the old building, it is only set inside the building and emphasizes even with its cherry wood surfacing the contrast to the whitewashed outer walls. In the same way, the whole installation, with its funnel-shaped stairwell, creates a conscious dialogue with the typology of the old building. Developing a "synthetic architecture" out of such contrasts is Scheitlin and Syfrig's intent. Although, on the one hand, it was the quick development of building specifications, ideas from the clients, and the uniqueness of the building material that determined this path, at the same time it is also the conscious integration of the dissonance of the provinces that is more important to them than the reference to classical prototypes of great architecture. They are clearly trying to assume a position here without letting their own dynamic develop from the response to the site and the relation to history as a basis for design. This posture after all brought them fourth price in the spectacular competition for the Kultur- und Kongresszentrum (Cultural and Convention Center) in Lucerne. Certainly, "only" fourth prize: their project proposed already then the justifiable demolition of Armin Meili's Convention Center, while at that time, any project was preferred that provided monument conservation protection for the building. In the meantime, the city has decided to demolish the old Convention Center.

With the expectation of being involved in the design of larger cultural commissions, Scheitlin and Syfrig, like many colleagues from their work and age group, initially took to the precise formulation and purposeful application of material. The specific characteristic of material, its selection and its construction method create the possibility to express the relation to the site, as Marc Syfrig calls it. These efforts distinguish their projects – and especially one of the largest public commissions so far, the "Forum der Schweizergeschichte". Through both the reduction to the essential and the exact realization of content, a force emerges that is not reproducible and which, in Schwyz, could only have developed through the dialogue of the new core with the historical outer shell.

The aim towards the greatest possible precision and the love of reducing the elements is symbolic of Scheitlin and Syfrig, and with them, for many of their colleagues of the same generation. In this, too, though, lies a grounded relation to the fine arts, which influences them strongly at present. Art appears more than ever to be the playground of radical modernity, maybe not least because it is free from the described compulsion: "The search for the kinship between paintings by Donald Judd and the decaying wooden shell of a barn may be symbolic for what we believe: in beauty and the goodness in things." J. C. B.

Museum «Forum der Schweizergeschichte», Schwyz, zusammen mit Hans Steiner, 1989–95.

Das «Forum der Schweizergeschichte» enthält eine feste Ausstellung zur Geschichte der Schweiz vom 13. bis ins 18. Jahrhundert sowie im Untergeschoß einen Raum für Wechselausstellungen. Die bestehenden Stützen und Decken des ehemaligen Zeughauses wurden entfernt und durch einen zusammenhängenden, dreigeschossigen, möbelartigen Einbau ersetzt. Die sanierte Gebäudehülle mit der freigelegten durchgehenden Wandfläche im Süden verdeutlicht den Eingriff und wird selbst zum Ausstellungsobjekt. Der trichterförmige, geschlossene Treppenkörper verbindet die Geschoßebenen und ist zugleich ein vertikal betonter Ausstellungsraum. Die neuen Einbauten nehmen den konstruktiven Raster der ehemaligen Struktur auf und verstärken gleichzeitig mit ihrer Verkleidung aus Kirschbaumholz den Kontrast zur alten, weißgestrichenen Gebäudehülle.

"Forum der Schweizergeschichte" Museum, Schwyz, in collaboration with Hans Steiner, 1989–95.

The "Forum der Schweizergeschichte" (Forum for Swiss History) contains a permanent exhibition on the history of Switzerland from the 13th to the 18th Century, as well as a room on the ground floor for temporary exhibitions. The existing supports and roofs of the former arsenal were removed and replaced by a connected, three-story furniture-like installation. The renewed and upgraded building shell with continuous exposed southern wall surface clarifies the operation and itself becomes an exhibition object. The closed, funnel-shaped stairway unit connects the floors with one another and is simultaneously a markedly vertical exhibition room. The new installations integrate the constructive grid of the former structure and, with its cherry wood surfacing, simultaneously reinforce the contrast to the old whitewashed building shell.

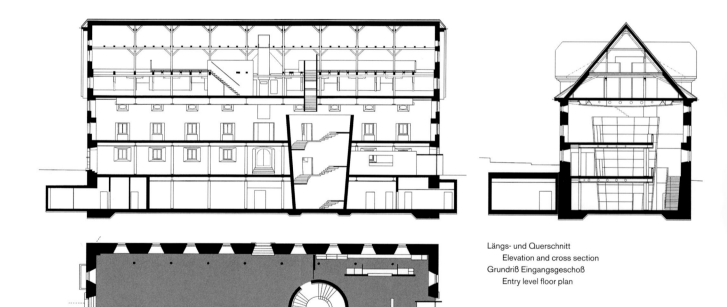

Längs- und Querschnitt
Elevation and cross section
Grundriß Eingangsgeschoß
Entry level floor plan

Die massive, freigestellte Wand des bestehenden Gebäudes und die möbelartigen Einbauten
The massive, freestanding wall of the existing building and the furniture-like installation

Andi Scheitlin, Marc Syfrig

Betriebsleitzentrale SBB, Luzern, 1992–95.

Eine Betriebsleitzentrale, ein technischer Apparat mit geheimnisvollem Inhalt, eine Mischung aus Bürogebäude und Riesencomputer, war an das bestehende Stellwerk im Geleisefeld des Luzerner Bahnhofes anzubauen: Eine Komposition mit dem Bestehenden, ein Anhänger mit einer schwarzen Schachtel beladen, glatt verschalt, sein Inneres nicht preisgebend, minimal im Detail, maximal im Ausdruck, mit schwarzeloxiertem Aluminium und fassadenbündigen Gläsern verkleidet, hingestellt auf einen Untersatz aus Beton, wie ein Verstärker, der überall stehen könnte.

SBB Operations Management Centre, Lucerne, 1992–95.

An operations management centre, a technical mechanism with secret contents, a mixture of office building and gigantic computer, was to be annexed to an existing switch tower in the railroad yard of the Lucerne Railway Station: a composition with the existing building, a trailer laden with a black box, sleekly encased, its interior not betrayed, minimal in detail, maximal in expression, clothed with black Eloxal and façade-bound glazing, placed on a concrete pedestal, like an amplifier, no matter where it stands.

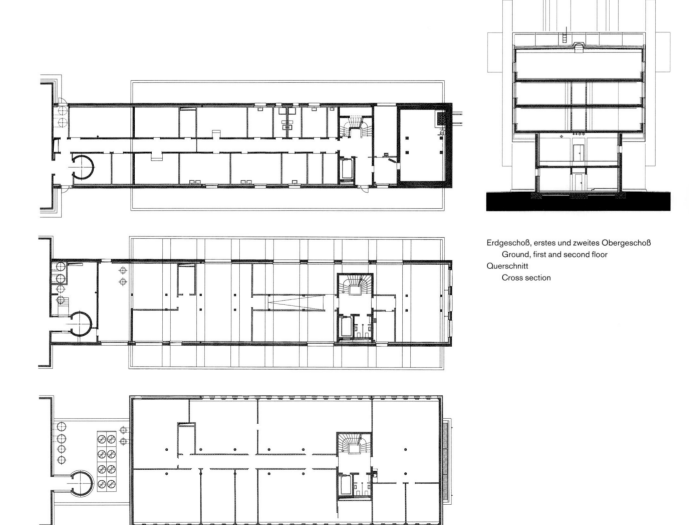

Erdgeschoß, erstes und zweites Obergeschoß
  Ground, first and second floor
Querschnitt
  Cross section

Die Betriebsleitzentrale mit dem bestehenden Stellwerk
The operations management center with the existing switch tower

Andi Scheitlin, Marc Syfrig

Doppeleinfamilienhaus Erb-Huwiler, Meggen, 1994/95.

Das Haus befindet sich in einer Einfamilienhausgruppe an bester Lage über dem Küßnachter Becken des Vierwaldstättersees. Aufgrund der wundervollen Aussicht und der Südorientierung war es selbstverständlich, möglichst viele Räume an diesen Qualitäten teilhaben zu lassen. Der Wohnbereich im Obergeschoß besteht aus einer hinteren Schicht mit Eingang, Küche und Bad und einer vorderen mit Wohnraum und Terrasse. Das vordere, sehr flach geneigte Pultdach verdeutlicht die Orientierung der Haupträume. Die hintere Schicht mit dem durchlaufenden Oberlichtband gegen Süden dient in den Übergangszeiten als Wärmespeicher. Im rotbraunen Sockel unter dem weißen Körper der Wohnräume befinden sich je drei Zimmer mit direkter Beziehung zum Außenraum. Mit seiner formalen Erscheinung steht dieses Haus in der Tradition der einfachen Villen der vierziger und fünfziger Jahre rund um den Vierwaldstättersee. Zwei in ihrer Größe bescheidene Wohneinheiten werden architektonisch zu einer großzügigen Villa zusammengefaßt. Dadurch nehmen beide Familien trotz bescheidenem Baubudget an einem Lebensgefühl teil, das heutiges Wohnen selten mehr vermitteln kann.

Erb-Huwiler Semi-detached Residence, Meggen, 1994/95.

The house is located in a group of detached one-family homes on the best site above the Küssnacht basin of the Vierwaldstättersee, or Lucerne Lake. Because of the wonderful view and the southern exposure, it was understood that the plan would allow as many rooms as possible to benefit from this situation. The living area in the upper floor is formed from a back layer, containing entrance, kitchen and bath, and a front layer, with living room and terrace. The front, very flatly inclined shed roof makes plain the orientation of the main rooms. The back layer, with the continuous skylight band facing south, serves as a heat accumulator in the transition seasons. In the reddish-brown basement under the white body of the living spaces are three rooms, each with direct contact to the outer room. Its formal appearance places this house in the tradition of simple villas from the 1940s and 50s in the area around the Vierwaldstättersee. Two modest units of that size are architectonically united into one generous villa. In this way, the two families, despite a modest building budget, can share in a feeling of life that today's living situations can seldom convey.

Eingangsgeschoß und Untergeschoß
  Entry and basement levels
Querschnitt und Ostfassade
  Cross section and east façade

Ansicht Südfassade
View of south façade

Andi Scheitlin, Marc Syfrig

Biografien

Andi Scheitlin
1952 geboren in Luzern.
1974-80 Architekturstudium an der ETH Zürich.
1980 Diplom bei Professor Dolf Schnebli an der ETH Zürich.
1980 Mitarbeit im Büro Livio Vacchini in Locarno.
1981/82 Mitarbeit im Büro Hans-Peter Ammann und Peter Baumann in Zug.
1982/83 Mitarbeit im Büro Joachim Ganz und Walter Rolfes in Berlin.
1983/84 Mitarbeit im Büro Arge Indermühle-Roost-Dähler in Bern.

Marc Syfrig
1952 geboren in Luzern.
1973-79 Architekturstudium an der ETH Zürich.
1979 Diplom bei Professor Dolf Schnebli an der ETH Zürich.
1979-81 Mitarbeit im Büro Daniel Gerber und Xaver Nauer in Zürich.
1981-85 Mitarbeit im Büro Walter Rüssli in Luzern.
1983-86 Assistent bei Professor Dolf Schnebli an der ETH Zürich.

Seit 1985 gemeinsames Büro in Luzern.

Auszeichnung
1995 *Auszeichnung guter Bauten im Kanton Luzern,* für Wohn- und Geschäftshaus Emmenbaum.

Werkverzeichnis

1985
Umbau zweier Altstadthäuser am Weinmarkt in Luzern, teilweise ausgeführt 1985/86.
Landwirtschafts- und Bäuerinnenschule in Schüpfheim LU, Wettbewerb, fünfter Preis.

1986
Wohn- und Geschäftshaus Emmenbaum in Emmenbrücke LU, ausgeführt 1986-88.
Stadthaus Areal in Luzern, Wettbewerb, zweiter Preis.

1987
Umbau SBB Reisebüro in Luzern, ausgeführt 1987/88.

1988
Umbau Lagerhaus Martin in Luzern, ausgeführt 1988/89.
Konstruktion von vier Tunnelportalen für die Transjuranne, Wettbewerb, dritter Preis.

1989
Museum «Forum der Schweizergeschichte» in Schwyz, in Zusammenarbeit mit Hans Steiner, Schwyz, Mitarbeit: Benedikt Rigling, Paolo Janssen, ausgeführt 1989-95.
Wohnhaus A3 in Ruopigen in Littau LU, ausgeführt 1989/90.
Wohnüberbauung Schlößlihalde in Luzern, Wettbewerb, Ankauf.
Wohnüberbauung Ober-Sörenberg in Flühli, Wettbewerb, Ankauf.
Kulturzentrum am See in Luzern, Zweistufiger Wettbewerb, vierter Rang/zweiter Preis.

1990
Wohnhaus E in Ruopigen in Littau LU, ausgeführt 1990-93.
Schulhauserweiterung in Rickenbach SZ, Wettbewerb, zweiter Preis.
Alterswohnungen in Baar ZG, Wettbewerb, zweiter Preis.

1991
Wohn- und Geschäftshaus Hertensteinstrasse in Luzern, ausgeführt 1991-96.
Überbauung Meier Möbel in Sursee LU, Wettbewerb, erster Preis.
Verwaltungsgebäude Schweizerischer Bankverein in Ittigen BE, Wettbewerb, dritter Preis.

1992
SBB Betriebsleitzentrale Luzern, Mitarbeit: Hanspeter Steiger, ausgeführt 1992-95.
Umbau Coiffeursalon Hanin in Luzern.
Erweiterung Kantonsschule in Pfäffikon SZ, in Zusammenarbeit mit Hans Steiner, Schwyz, Studienauftrag, erster Rang.
Wohnüberbauung Rosengartenhalde in Luzern, Studienauftrag, erster Rang.

1993
Erweiterung Schulanlage Nottwil LU, Projekt in Ausführung 1993-96.
Überbauung Schachen in Aarau, Wettbewerb, dritter Preis.

1994
Umbau Praxis Dr. Grüter in Luzern, ausgeführt.
Doppeleinfamilienhaus Erb-Huwiler in Meggen LU, Mitarbeit: Willi Voney, ausgeführt 1994/95.
Erweiterung ETH Lausanne, in Zusammenarbeit mit Hans Cometti, Alexander Galliker und Dieter Geissbühler, Luzern, Wettbewerb, fünfter Preis.
Alterswohnungen in Vitznau, Wettbewerb, dritter Preis.

Elektronikgebäude BAMF in Buochs NW, Studienauftrag, erster Rang.
Erweiterung Kantonspolizei in Luzern, Wettbewerb, vierter Preis.
Ortskernplanung in Horw LU, Studienauftrag, erster Rang, Weiterbearbeitung.

1995
Kulturgüterschutzraum in Schwyz, in Zusammenarbeit mit Hans Steiner, Schwyz.
Umbau Altes Spital Obergrundstraße in Luzern, Städtische Verwaltung.
Kaufhaus, Hotel und Wohnhaus Türmli in Altdorf UR, Wettbewerb, zweiter Rang/erster Preis.
Studienauftrag Hotel Schweizerhof in Luzern.
Seniorenresidenz Sonnmatt in Luzern, Wettbewerb, erster Preis.
Platzgestaltung Hofmatt in Schwyz in Zusammenarbeit mit H. Steiner, Schwyz, ausgeführt 1995/96.

1996
Heizzentrale Flugplatz in Buochs NW.
Kasernenareal in Bern, Kultur- und Ausbildungszentrum, in Zusammenarbeit mit Alexander Galliker und Dieter Geissbühler, Luzern, Wettbewerb, dritter Preis.
Heilpädagogische Schule in Sursee LU, Wettbewerb, erster Preis.
Kulturzentrum in Arlesheim BL, Wettbewerb, zweiter Preis, Weiterbearbeitung.

Bibliografie

Reisebüro SBB, *Innenräume gestaltet, nicht bloss dekoriert,* in: Luzerner Neuste Nachrichten, Kultur, 28. April 1988.
Reisebüro SBB, *Eingriffe im Innern bestehender Gebäude,* in: Neue Zürcher Zeitung, Planen, Bauen, Wohnen, 6. Mai 1988.
Reisebüro SBB, *Ein Raum als Hülle,* in: Jardin des Modes, Juni 1988.
Neue Hüllen für die Kultur, in: Hochparterre, März 1989.
Wohn- und Geschäftshaus Emmenbaum, Werk-Material, Werk, Bauen + Wohnen 5/1990.
Wohn- und Geschäftshaus Emmenbaum, Architektur in der deutschen Schweiz 1980-1990, Verlag ADV, Lugano 1991.
Wohn- und Geschäftshaus Emmenbaum, Schweizer Architekturführer, 1992, Verlag Werk AG, Zürich.
Wohn- und Geschäftshaus Emmenbaum, Auszeichnung guter Bauten im Kanton Luzern 1983-1993, Katalog, Luzern 1995.
Museum Forum der Schweizergeschichte, *Einzelfälle, Neue Beispiele aus dem Schweizer Architekturschaffen,* in: Werk, Bauen + Wohnen 5/1995.
Museum «Forum der Schweizergeschichte», *Cul de Sac, Architektur und Ausstellungskonzept,* in: archithese 4/1995.
Wohn- und Geschäftshaus Emmenbaum, *Die Häuser auf dem Haus,* in: Luzerner Neuste Nachrichten, Beilage Wohnen, 13. April 1989.
J. Christoph Bürkle: *Die Autonomie des Materials,* in: Neue Zürcher Zeitung, 7. Juli 1995.

Biographies

Andi Scheitlin
1952 Born in Lucerne.
1974-80 Studied architecture at the ETH Zurich.
1980 Graduated from the ETH Zurich under Professor Dolf Schnebli.
1980 Worked at office of Livio Vacchini in Locarno.
1981/82 Worked in office of Hans-Peter Ammann and Peter Baumann in Zug.
1982/83 Worked in office of Joachim Ganz and Walter Rolfes in Berlin.
1983/84 Worked in office of Arge Indermühle-Roost-Dähler in Bern.

Marc Syfrig
1952 Born in Lucerne.
1973-79 Studied architecture at the ETH Zurich.
1979 Graduated from the ETH Zurich under Professor Dolf Schnebli
1979-81 Worked in office of Daniel Gerber and Xaver Nauer in Zurich.
1981-85 Worked in office of Walter Rüssli in Lucerne.
1983-86 Assistant to Professor Dolf Schnebli at the ETH Zurich.

Since 1985 joint office in Lucerne.

Award
1995 *Auszeichnung guter Bauten im Kanton Luzern,* for Emmenbaum Residence and Business House.

List of Works

1985
Two houses in the old city center on Weinmarkt, conversion, Lucerne, partially completed 1985/86.
Agriculture and Women's Farming School in Schüpfheim, competition, fifth prize.

1986
Emmenbaum Residence and Business House in Emmenbrücke, executed 1986-88.
Lucerne City Hall grounds, competition, second prize.

1987
SBB Travel Office, conversion, Lucerne, executed 1987/88.

1988
Martin Warehouse, conversion, Lucerne, executed 1988/89.
Construction for four tunnel portals for the Transjuranne, competition, third prize.

1989
Museum «Forum der Schweizergeschichte» in Schwyz, in collaboration with Hans Steiner, Schwyz, assistance: Benedikt Rigling, Paolo Janssen, executed 1989-95.
Residence A3 in Ruopigen in Littau, executed 1989/90.
Schlössihalde housing superstructure, Lucerne, competition, purchase.
Ober-Sörenberg housing superstructure, Flühli, competition, purchase.
Kulturzentrum am See, Lucerne, competition in two stages, fourth ranking/second prize.

1990
Residence E in Ruopigen, Littau, executed 1990-93.
Schoolhouse expansion, Rickenbach, competition, second prize.
Senior apartments, Baar, competition, second prize.

1991
Residence and business house Hertensteinstrasse, Lucerne, executed 1991-96.
Meier Möbel superstructure, Sursee, competition, first prize.
Swiss Union Bank administration building, Ittigen, competition, third prize.

1992
SBB operations management center, Lucerne, assistance: Hanspeter Steiger, executed 1992-95.
Coiffeursalon Hanin, conversion, Lucerne.
Kantonschule (Canton school), expansion, Pfäffikon, in collaboration with Hans Steiner, Schwyz, commissioned study, first ranking.
Rosengartenhalde housing superstructure, Lucerne, commissioned study, first ranking.

1993
School complex, expansion, Nottwil, project in execution, 1993-96.
Schachen superstructure, Aarau, competition, third prize.

1994
Practice of Dr. Grüter, conversion, Lucerne, executed.
Erb-Huwiler semi-detached residence house, Meggen, assistance: Willi Voney, executed 1994/95.
ETH Lausanne, expansion, in collaboration with Hans Cometti, Alexander Galliker and Dieter Giessbühler, Lucerne, competition, fifth prize.

Senior apartments, Vitznau, competition, third prize.
BAMF Electronic building, Buochs, commissioned study, first ranking.
Kantonspolizei Lucerne, expansion, fourth prize.
Village center planning, Horw, commissioned study, first ranking, continued work.

1995
Cultural assets shelter, Schwyz, in collaboration with Hans Steiner, Schwyz.
Old hospital, Obergrundstrasse, conversion, Lucerne, urban administration.
Türmli department store, hotel and residence, Altdorf, competition, second ranking, first prize.
Hotel Schweizerhof, commissioned study, Lucerne.
Sonnmatt senior residence, Lucerne, competition, first prize.
Hofmatt plaza design, Schwyz, in collaboration with H. Steiner, Schwyz, executed 1995/96.

1996
Airport central heating system, Buochs.
Kasernenareal, Bern, Cultural and Educational Center, in collaboration with Alexander Galliker and Dieter Geissbühler, Lucerne, competition, third prize.
Therapeutic Pedagogy School, Sursee, competition, first prize.
Cultural Center, Arlesheim, competition, second prize, further work.

Bibliography

SBB Travel Office, *Innenräume gestaltet, nicht bloss dekoriert,* in: Luzerner Neuste Nachrichten, Kultur, April 28, 1988.
SBB Travel Office, *Eingriffe im Innern bestehender Gebäude,* in: Neue Zürcher Zeitung, Planen, Bauen, Wohnen, May 6, 1988.
SBB Travel Office, *Ein Raum als Hülle,* in: Jardin des Modes, June 1988.
Neue Hüllen für die Kultur, in: Hochparterre, March 1989.
Wohn- und Geschäftshaus Emmenbaum, Werk-Material, Werk, Bauen + Wohnen 5/1990.
Wohn- und Geschäftshaus Emmenbaum, Architektur in der deutschen Schweiz 1980-1990, Verlag ADV, Lugano 1991.
Wohn- und Geschäftshaus Emmenbaum, Schweizer Architekturführer, 1992, Verlag Werk AG, Zurich.
Wohn- und Geschäftshaus Emmenbaum, Auszeichnung guter Bauten im Kanton Luzern 1983-1993, catalogue, Lucerne, 1995.
Museum Forum der Schweizergeschichte, *Einzelfälle, Neue Beispiele aus dem Schweizer Architekturschaffen,* in: Werk, Bauen + Wohnen 5/1995.
Museum «Forum der Schweizergeschichte», *Cul de Sac, Architektur und Ausstellungskonzept,* in: archithese 4/1995.
Wohn- und Geschäftshaus Emmenbaum, *Die Häuser auf dem Haus,* in: Luzerner Neuste Nachrichten, supplement on living, April 13, 1996.
J. Christoph Bürkle: *Die Autonomie des Materials,* in: Neue Zürcher Zeitung, July 7, 1995.

Thomas Schregenberger
Zürich

Mitarbeiterinnen und Mitarbeiter
Collaborators
    Alexandra Gübeli
    Andrea Krupski
    Lorenz Peter
    Caspar Schärer
    Maja Scherrer
    Paolo Tognola

«Metamorphose»: Anbau Haus Maurer | Maurer House Annex | Zuzwil, 1989–93

«Variation»: Wohnung für eine Graphologin | Apartment for a Graphologist | Zürich, 1992

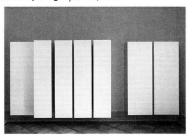

«Fabric»: Wettbewerb Fabrik am Wasser | Fabrik am Wasser, Competition | Zürich, 1995

«Flächen im Park»: Überbauung Rehbühl | Rehbühl Superstructure | Uster, 1996

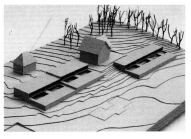

Thomas Schregenberger

Erlebbare Konzepte.

Thomas Schregenberger verfolgt eine stark konzeptionelle Arbeitsweise, bei der die Themen im Konkreten der Situation und der Entwurfsaufgabe verwurzelt sind. Die Analyse von Programm und Ort führt dabei nicht auf direktem Weg zu einer architektonischen Lösung. Aus ihr werden vielmehr zunächst Themen herausdestilliert, die später neu interpretiert dem ganzen Entwurfsprozeß zugrunde gelegt werden. Ihre Auswahl erfolgt nach subjektiven Kriterien. Es kann ebenso ein konstruktives Prinzip, ein Material oder ein Bild von Interesse sein wie ein Aspekt des Programms oder des Ortes. So wurde zum Beispiel im Wettbewerbsbeitrag von Roos & Schregenberger für die Wohnüberbauung Rütihof in Zürich-Höngg (1991) der Begriff der Dachlandschaft wörtlich genommen. Die Silhouette der gestaffelten Zeilen reflektiert dabei in einer sanften Wellenform der Dächer ein Charakteristikum von Topographie und Horizont dieses spezifischen Ortes. Thomas Schregenberger spricht in diesem Zusammenhang vom Entwerfen als einem Wahrnehmbar-Machen dessen, was durch eine aufmerksame und subjektive Wahrnehmung entdeckt wurde.

Bei einem aktuellen Projekt für die Erweiterung eines Bürogebäudes am Rande der Altstadt von Zug wird das Thema Weiterbauen inszeniert. Ein Reitergebäude wird dabei rittlings über den modernen Anbau an ein Haus aus der Gründerzeit gestellt. Konsequent wird die Konstruktion von außen nach innen entwickelt. Die Stützen und horizontalen Träger bilden eine in sich steife Rahmenkonstruktion, an welche Holzelemente mit durchscheinenden und durchsichtigen Gläsern angeschlagen werden: Der Fassadenvorhang wird innen eingehängt. Die Stahlkonstruktion paßt sich einerseits den bestehenden Bauten in Achsmaß und Höhenkoten an, betont andererseits die Eigenständigkeit des Neuen. So werden etwa die Dachlinien des Altbaus weitergeführt, jedoch nicht als Geschoßeinteilung. Die horizontalen Träger verwischen vielmehr mit ihrem engen Abstand, der sich für die Montage der Fenster eignet, die Lesbarkeit der Geschosse und damit des Maßstabes. Aus einem einfachen konstruktiven Prinzip entsteht so ein die Wahrnehmung irritierendes Gebilde. Immer wieder werden in den Arbeiten solche Mehrdeutigkeiten gesucht, die aus dem konsequenten Verfolgen eines Prinzips entstehen. Das mag auch mit der Aussage gemeint sein, es interessiere eine «Architektur, die Fragen stellt und die Begriffe auf ihre Bedeutung hin untersucht». Die Resultate, die bei dieser interpretierenden Arbeitsweise entstehen, sind spezifisch. Es erstaunt daher nicht, daß sie sich nicht mit ein paar Schlagworten erfassen lassen. Eine formale Trademark gibt es nicht und wird auch nicht angestrebt.

Die Suche nach Entscheidungsgrundlagen beim Entwerfen führte Thomas Schregenberger 1975 nach einer Lehre als Hochbauzeichner an die Städelschule nach Frankfurt, wo er den späteren langjährigen Partner Harry Roos in der gleichen Situation antraf. Weiterführende Studien an der AA in London bei Nigel Coates 1981–84 beeinflußten das konzeptuelle Denken maßgeblich, hier wurde die Wahrnehmung des Alltäglichen geschärft und die Möglichkeit erprobt, daraus architektonische Konzepte zu entwickeln. Zurück in Zürich hat der britische Titel «dipl. Arch. AA/RIBA» wohl manche Mißverständnisse befördert. Schnell war das Verdikt «Dekonstruktivismus» gefällt, besonders nach der Publikation eines Studios an der Bucheggstraße in Zürich, das einige modische Schrägen aufweist; leicht wurde dabei seine konstruktive Konzeption übersehen.

Ein besonderes Interesse von Thomas Schregenberger gilt den verwendeten Materialien. Oft werden bekannte, ja banale Produkte durch eine ungewohnte Verwendung oder eine bescheidene Manipulation uminterpretiert, allerdings nicht als Selbstzweck, sondern im Dienst des architektonischen Ganzen. Zum Beispiel werden bei der Erweiterung eines Einfamilienhauses in Zuzwil kunstharzgetränkte Papierplatten als Fassadenverkleidung verwendet, wie sie normalerweise als unsichtbarer Kern für laminatbeschichtete Elemente in Bädern und anderen feuchten Räumen eingesetzt werden. Damit wird nicht nur eine neue Anwendungsmöglichkeit für ein an sich gewöhnliches Material erschlossen, seine Verwendung ist in der konkreten Situation auch angemessen. Das Billigprodukt paßt mit seiner rotbraunen, leicht unregelmäßigen Farbigkeit hervorragend zum dunklen Backstein, zu Kupfer und Ziegel des bestehenden Hauses, ohne sich anzubiedern. Es reflektiert zudem das minimale Budget, das für den Bau zur Verfügung stand.

Seit 1994 arbeitet Thomas Schregenberger allein. In den Arbeiten, die seither entstanden sind, läßt sich eine gewisse Tendenz zu einer Vereinfachung der Formen feststellen, die man als Prozeß der Konzentration deuten möchte. Die konzeptuelle Arbeitsweise, in welcher Experimentierfreudigkeit im Denken mit Respekt vor den pragmatischen Anforderungen der Baupraxis zusammenkommt, wird dabei weitergeführt. M.T.

Büroeinbau KPMG-FIDES, Zug, 1990/91
KPMG-FIDES office installment, Zug, 1990/91

Concepts to Experience.

Thomas Schregenberger follows a strongly conceptual working method in which the themes are rooted in the actuality of the situation and the design problem. Yet the analysis of program and site do not lead directly to an architectonic solution. It is much more the case that themes are first of all distilled from the analysis and reinterpreted later to lay the basis for the entire design process. Their selection is the result of subjective criteria that can just as easily be a construction principle, a material or an interesting image as an aspect of the program or the site. This is how, for example, in Roos & Schregenberger's contribution to the competition for the Rütihof housing superstructure in Zürich-Höngg (1991), the concept of a "rooftop landscape" came to be taken literally. The silhouette of the staggered lines reflects a characteristic of the topography and horizon of this particular site in the soft waving form of the roofs. In this connection, Thomas Schregenberger speaks of design as a "making perceptible" which is discovered through attentive and subjective observation.

The theme of building expansion was played out in a current project for the extension of an office building on the rim of the old city center of Zug. A mounted building is placed astride the modern annex to a house from the economic boom years of the early 1870s. Consequently, the construction is developed from the outside in. The supports and horizontal beams form a rigid frame construction on which wooden elements with translucent and transparent glass are fastened. The façade curtain is hung inside. The steel construction, on the one hand, fits to the existing constructions in unit spacing and spot heights, while on the other it emphasizes the autonomy of the new. The roof lines of the old building, for instance, were carried on in the same way, although not as dividers between the stories. Rather, the horizontal beams obliterate with their narrow spacing, which suits the fitting of the windows, the readability of the stories, and with that, the scale. Thus from a simple construction principle, an image emerges that irritates the perception. Again and again, such ambiguities are sought in works where they arise as a logical consequence of a principle. That may also be what is meant by the statement that what is interesting is "architecture that asks questions and examines concepts for their meaning". The results arising from this interpretive method of working are specific. It is not astounding, therefore, that they cannot be summarized in a couple of catchwords. There is no formal trademark and none is aspired to.

The search for the foundations upon which to make decisions during the design process led Thomas Schregenberger in 1975, after his apprenticeship as an architectural drafter at the Städelschule, to Frankfurt, where he chanced to meet Harry Roos, who was to be his partner for many years and who was at that time in the same situation as himself. Continuing studies at the AA in London under Nigel Coates from 1981–84 decisively influenced his conceptual thinking; here, perception of the ordinary and the everyday was sharpened and the possibility of developing architectural concepts from them was tested. Back in Zurich, the British title "dipl. Arch. AA/RIBA" certainly led to misunderstandings. The verdict of "deconstructivism" was quickly pronounced, especially after the publication of a studio on Bucheggstrasse in Zurich that featured some fashionable diagonals; his constructive conception was easily disregarded in the process.

A special interest of Thomas Schregenberger is the employment of materials. Familiar, even banal, products are often reinterpreted through an unusual application or decisive manipulation, certainly not as an end in itself but rather in the service of the architectonic whole. The expansion of a one-family residence in Zuzwil is an example. Paper plating saturated with synthetic resin was used as façade surfacing, while it normally would be found as an invisible core for laminated elements in baths and other damp rooms. With this, not only was a new possible use for an ordinary material developed, its application also suited the concrete situation. The inexpensive product, with its red-brown, slightly irregular coloring, fits superbly to the dark red brick, copper and tile of the existing house while retaining its own properties. It reflects moreover the minimal budget that was allocated for the construction.

Since 1994, Thomas Schregenberger has worked alone. In the works erected in that period of time, a certain tendency towards simplification of form can be detected; this might suggest a process of concentration. The conceptual working method, in which the joyful experimentation of thought comes together with respect for the pragmatic requirements of the practice of building, will nevertheless continue. M. T.

Thomas Schregenberger

«Metamorphose»: Anbau Haus Maurer, mit Harry Roos, Zuzwil, 1989–93.

Der neue Anbau bewirkt eine Veränderung in der Wahrnehmung des Gebäudes. Die vorgefundenen Eigenschaften des bestehenden Einfamilienhauses, ein Konglomerat von Formen und Gebäudeteilen, werden kultiviert, Materialien und Farben in den Anbau einbezogen und verarbeitet. Damit wird das Bestehende kommentiert und über diese Art des Dialogs eine neue Einheit geschaffen. Dieser Dialog verändert die Wahrnehmung des Gebäudes im Sinne einer Metamorphose.

Das Raumprogramm des Anbaus umfaßt einen Wintergarten, die Erweiterung des Wohnraums und einen Schlafraum. Der Wintergarten bildet eine klimatische Hülle, die aus einem Betondach und einer seitlichen Einfachverglasung besteht und sich in großformatigen HPL-Platten im Schlafbereich fortsetzt. In diese Hülle wurden die isolierten Wohnräume eingeschoben. Da der Anbau sehr preisgünstig sein sollte, bestand die Maxime in der möglichst unbehandelten Verwendung der Baustoffe. Für die innenliegenden Wände wurden großformatige Porenbetonsteine verwendet, die statische und isolierende Funktionen übernehmen und nur noch gestrichen werden mußten. In den Wohnräumen wurde die Betondecke mit in Bitumen verlegten Schaumglasplatten isoliert. Die dampfdichten und festen dunklen Platten konnten dank dieser Eigenschaften unbehandelt belassen werden.

"Metamorphosis": Maurer House Annex, with Harry Roos, Zuzwil, 1989–93.

The new annex effects a change in the perception of the building. The given characteristics of the existing one-family residence, a conglomeration of forms and building parts, are cultivated, materials and colors in the annex incorporated and processed. This comments on the existing building, and through this kind of dialogue a new unity is created that transforms, or rather metamorphoses, one's perception of the building.

The room program of the annex encompasses a winter garden, the expansion of the living room, and a bedroom. The winter garden forms a climatic case made up of a concrete roof and single-layer glazing on the side, and is continued in large format HPL sheets in the area of the bedroom. The insulated living areas are set into this case. Because the annex was to be reasonably priced, the majority of the building is done in the least treated material possible. For the interior walls, large format concrete building blocks were used, which function in a constructive and insulating capacity and only required painting. In the living rooms, the concrete ceiling is insulated with foam glass plates laid with bitumen. Thanks to their vapor-tightness and compactness, the dark plates could be left untreated.

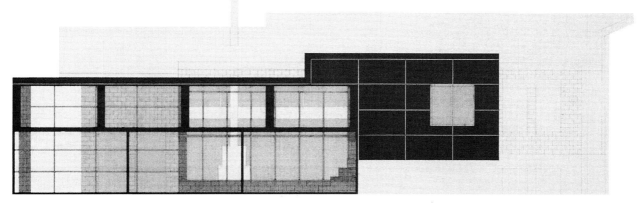

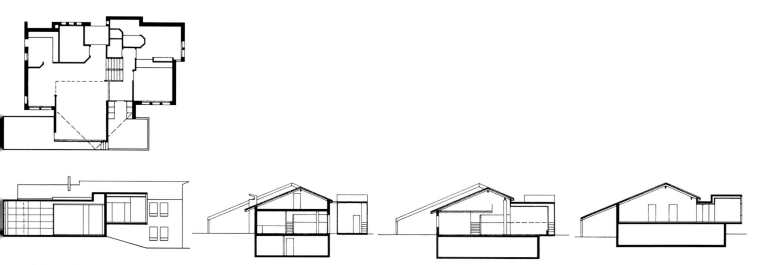

Erdgeschoß, Längsschnitt und Querschnitte
Ground floor, elevation section and cross section

Gartenansicht
View from garden
Innenansichten Wintergarten und Wohnzimmer
Interiors, winter garden and living room

Thomas Schregenberger

«Variation»: Wohnung für eine Graphologin, mit Harry Roos, Zürich, 1992.

Die hier vorgestellten Schrankeinbauten beschriften die Wohnräume einer Graphologin. Sie bestehen aus einzelnen Elementen, die aneinandergereiht ähnlich wie Buchstaben Schriftzüge bilden. Rhythmus und Betonung, wesentliche Charakteristika der Handschrift, prägen auch die einzelnen Schrankgruppen. Sie variieren dementsprechend und werden so zu einer Analogie individueller Schrifttypen: Einen kontrolliert sachlichen für das Arbeitszimmer, einen leidenschaftlich emotionalen für das Schlafzimmer, einen einladend offenen für das Wohnzimmer und einen zurückhaltend ruhigen für das Gästezimmer.

Dreiundzwanzig gleichförmige Schrankelemente von 180 × 40 × 60 Zentimeter sind 30 Zentimeter über dem Parkett in unterschiedlichen Abständen längs- beziehungsweise breitseitig an die Wand montiert. Sie sind im neutralen Weiß RAL 9010 gespritzt und völlig detaillos. Ihre Funktion variiert von Raum zu Raum.

"Variation": Apartment for a Graphologist, with Harry Roos, Zurich, 1992.

The cabinet installations presented here inscribe the living spaces of a graphologist. They are composed of single elements which, placed next to one another in rows, form characters similar to letters. Rhythm and stress, essential characteristics of handwriting, also characterize the individual cabinet groups. They vary accordingly and thus become an analogy of individual writing types: a controlled, matter-of-fact type for the study; a passionate, emotional type for the bedroom; an inviting, open type for the living room; and a reserved, calm type for the guest room.

Twenty-three similarly formed cabinet elements of 180 × 40 × 60 centimeters are mounted on the wall 30 centimeters above the parquet in varying intervals, lengthwise or broadside, respectively. They are sprayed with neutral white RAL 9010 and are completely without detail. Their function varies from room to room.

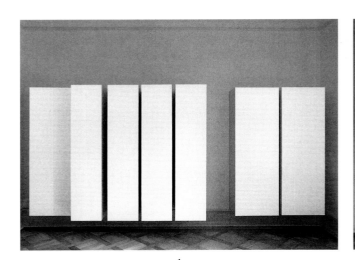

1

2

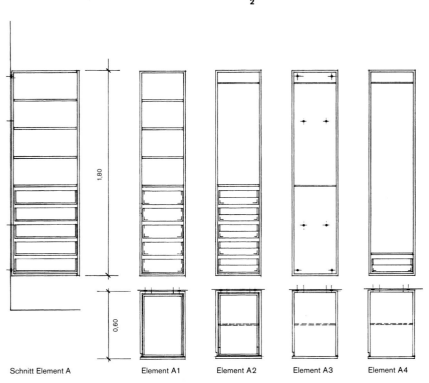

Schnitt Element A — Element A1 — Element A2 — Element A3 — Element A4

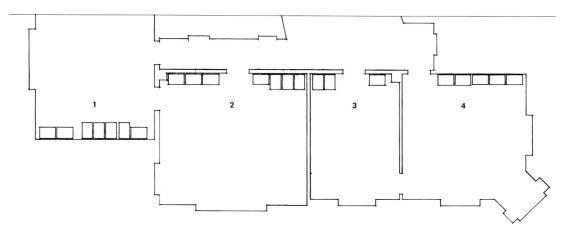

Wohnungsgrundriß: 1 Schlafzimmer, 2 Wohnzimmer, 3 Gästezimmer, 4 Arbeitszimmer
Apartment floor plan: 1 bedroom, 2 living room, 3 guest room, 4 study

3

4

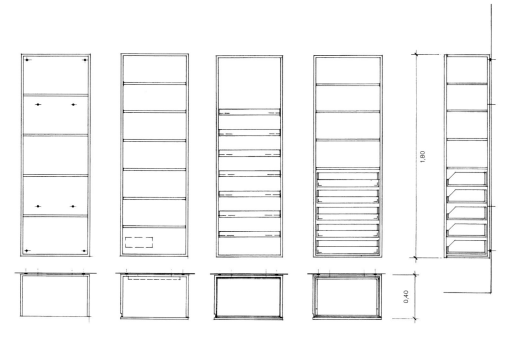

Schrankelemente, Schnitte und Grundrisse
Cabinet elements, section and plan

Element B4   Element B3   Element B2   Element B1   Schnitt Element B

Thomas Schregenberger

«Fabric»: Projektwettbewerb Fabrik am Wasser, mit Lorenz Peter, Zürich, 1995.

Die Fabrik am Wasser, eine ehemalige Seidenweberei, die aber auch ein bedeutendes Industriedenkmal aus dem 19. Jahrhundert darstellt, wurde 1992 durch einen Brand weitgehend zerstört. Aufgabe des Wettbewerbs war es, für die fast ganz niedergebrannten Shedhallen Ersatzbauten zu projektieren, in denen eine Volksschule und Wohnungen untergebracht sind.

Der englische Terminus *fabric* bedeutet Stoff, Gebilde, Gefüge, Struktur, System und verweist auf das Konzept der dargestellten Arbeit. Ausgehend von der ehemaligen Fabrikanlage wurde eine neue Struktur destilliert, welche die Neubauten organisiert und zusammen mit den noch bestehenden Bauten zu einer Gesamtanlage werden läßt. Diese neue Ordnung wird geprägt durch die Lage der Gebäude, ihre Typologie und Struktur, durch die vorgefundenen Materialien und den Charakter der alten Fabrik. Die Fabrik am Wasser unterwirft sich einem ortogonalen System, das die Ausrichtung des zugeschütteten Wasserkanals übernimmt.

Die Anlage ist streifenartig zoniert. Der erste Streifen besteht aus dem alten Fabrikgebäude, der zweite wird durch die noch bestehende Shedhalle bestimmt; der dritte Streifen vervollständigt die ehemalige Fabrikanlage, während der vierte, der leicht versetzt ist, die Erweiterung markiert. Der östliche Teil des Grundstücks sowie die Uferzone sind bestimmt von der Erinnerung an die ehemalige Kanalanlage. Zum Turbinenhaus führende, immer breiter werdende Rasenflächen, begleitet von Heckenstreifen, stellen die Wasserkraft dar und organisieren zugleich Wegnetz, Pflanzgärten und Parkplätze.

Das Muster, welches das Projekt prägt, besteht aus gleichen, sich wiederholenden Elementen. Ob Gebäude, Erschließungshof, Rasenfläche, Baumreihe oder Schulhof: Alle Teile unterwerfen sich der neuen Ordnung und transportieren die Idee der Fabrikation. Die geschlossenen Stirnfassaden der fünf Wohnbauten ergeben eine klare Ausrichtung und betonen die Einheitlichkeit der Elemente. Die Längsfassaden visualisieren noch einmal die Thematik des Webens. Geschoßhohe Gußglaselemente rhythmisieren die Horizontale der Geschoßdecken. Während sie sich im Süden gegen die Sonne öffnen, werden sie im Norden zu breiten Bahnen und verkleiden Teile des Laubengangs. Die vorgelagerten Birken zeichnen auf der matten Oberfläche ein bewegtes Bild.

"Fabric": Fabrik am Wasser, Project Competition, with Lorenz Peter, Zurich, 1995.

The Fabrik am Wasser (factory on the water), a former silk weaving mill, also represents a significant 19th Century monument to industry that was extensively destroyed in a fire in 1992. The task of the competition was to project a replacement construction for the almost completely devastated roof frame. An elementary school and apartments are to be housed within the new construction.

The English term "fabric" (cousin to *Fabrik*, the German term for factory) connotes textile, pattern, texture, structure, system, and refers to the concept of the work represented in this project. Beginning with the former factory complex and working out from that, a new structure was distilled which organized the new construction and allowed it to become a united complex together with the existing buildings. This new order is determined by the building site, its topology and structure, by the given materials and character of the old factory. The Fabrik am Wasser acquiesces to an orthogonal system that appropriates the orientation to the filled-in canal.

The complex is zoned in strips. The first strip is composed of the old factory building, the second is defined by the still existing roof frame; the third strip completes the former factory complex, while the fourth, slightly displaced, marks the expansion. The eastern part of the property as well as the river bank zone are defined by the memory of the former canal system. Grassy areas that lead to the turbine house, widening as they go and accompanied by rows of hedges, represent the hydraulic power and at the same time organize the system of paths, the garden and the parking lot.

The pattern formed by the project is composed of identical repeating elements. Whether building, access courtyard, grassy lawn, row of trees or school yard, all the parts submit to the new order and transmit the idea of manufacture. The closed end façades on the five housing units result in a clear orientation and emphasize the uniformity of the elements. The long façades once again make the theme of weaving visible. Cast glass elements at the height of one story set a rhythm for the horizontality of the story ceilings. While they open toward the sun in the south, in the north they become wide lanes covering parts of the exposed corridor. The birches in the front draw a moving picture on the matte surfaces.

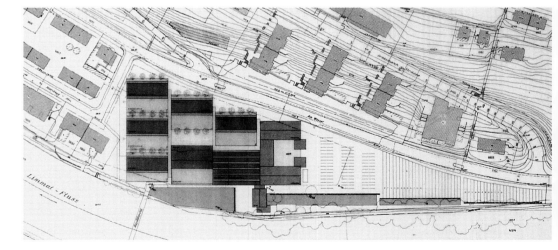

Modell und Situation
Model and situation

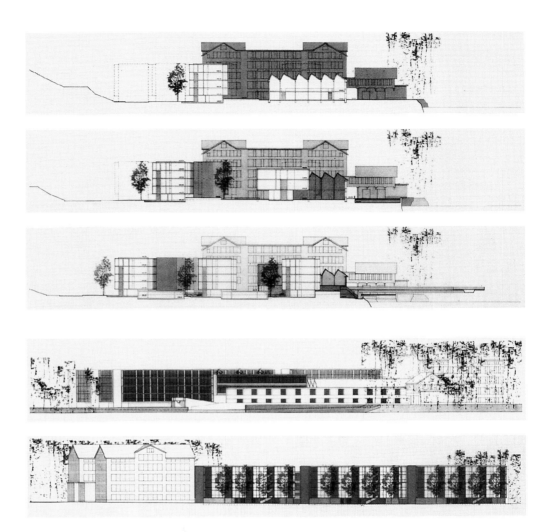
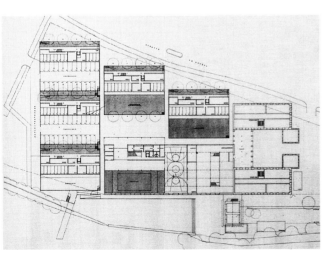
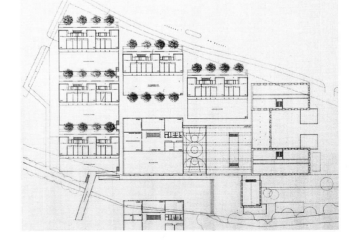

Grundrisse Eingangs- und Obergeschosse
　Floor plans of entrance and upper floors
Schnittsequenz
　Section sequence
Ansicht Limmatseite
　View from the Limmat
Ansicht Straßenseite
　View from the street

Thomas Schregenberger

«Flächen im Park»: Überbauung Rehbühl, Uster, 1996.

Der Park ist die Gartenanlage der Villa Rehbühl, die in den Park gelegten «Flächen» die geplanten Wohnhäuser. Die Anlage mit der Villa und dem Gärtnerhaus, 1920 vom Textilfabrikanten Balthasar Trüb erbaut, repräsentiert einen Teil der gesellschaftspolitischen Geschichte der Stadt Uster, die projektierten Wohnhäuser die veränderten Lebensformen von heute. Der Park ist ein Zeitdokument, die Liegenschaft ein Potential für attraktives, zentrumsnahes Wohnen. Ziel dieses Projektes ist es, die Parkanlage und die geplanten Wohnbauten zu einem neuen Ensemble zusammenzufügen.

Definiert ist die bestehende Anlage durch ihre Geometrie und durch die Topographie des Ortes; die neu in den Park gelegten, flachen Baukörper unterwerfen sich einerseits der bestehenden Geometrie, zeichnen aber auch, die Topographie abstrahierend, in ihrer Ansicht die Höhenkurven des abfallenden Geländes nach. So entspricht die Terrassierung des im Westen der Villa gelegenen neuen Baukörpers dem diagonalen Verlauf der dortigen Höhenkurven. Die dadurch in der Aufsicht entstehende Vierteiligkeit des Gebäudekomplexes erinnert aber an die Geometrie des ehemaligen Nutzgartens. Dasselbe gilt für den im Süden der Villa gelegenen zweiten Baukörper. Seine Terrassierung visualisiert nicht nur den Geländeverlauf, sondern zeichnet auch die damals mit Zierbäumen markierte ehemalige Grundstücksgrenze nach. Die Villa bleibt geometrische Ausnahme und damit Mittel- und Drehpunkt des Ensembles. Die fünfzehn introvertierten, über Atrien belichteten Wohneinheiten betonen Ausmaß und Format der Parkanlage und bilden für die Villa eine neue Plattform.

"Planes in the Park": Rehbühl Superstructure, Uster, 1996.

The park is a garden complex of the Villa Rehbühl, the "planes" in the park the proposed residence buildings. The complex with Villa and gardener's house, built in 1920 by textile manufacturer Balthasar Trüb, represents a part of the social-political history of the city of Uster, and the proposed housing the shift to the new forms of today's living. The park is a document of the times, the property a potential for attractive, centrally-located living. The aim of this project is to join together the park complex and the proposed housing construction into a new ensemble.

The existing complex is defined by its geometry and by the topography of the site; the flat buildings, new to the park grounds, surrender on the one hand to the existing geometry, but also draw on the sloping landscape of the abstracted topography's contour curves for their view. The terracing of the new building unit west of the Villa thus corresponds to the diagonal contour curves in that area, but the resulting division of the building complex as seen from above reminds one of the geometry of the former fruit and vegetable garden. The same holds true for the second building unit to the south of the Villa. Its terracing not only makes the course of the land visible but also draws on the former border of the property, once marked by ornamental trees. The Villa remains the geometric exception and, with that, the center and fulcrum point of the group. The fifteen introverted housing units, illuminated over atriums, emphasize the dimensions and format of the parking complex and create a new platform for the Villa.

Villa mit Gärtnerhaus
Villa with gardener's house

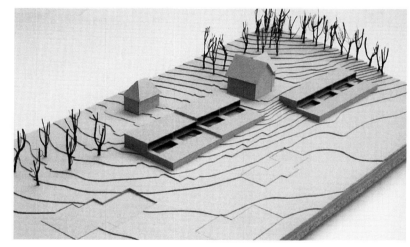

Situationsmodell
Situation model

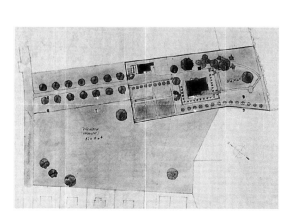

Bestehende Gartenanlage
Existing garden complex

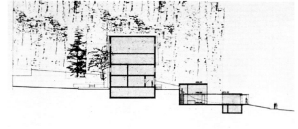
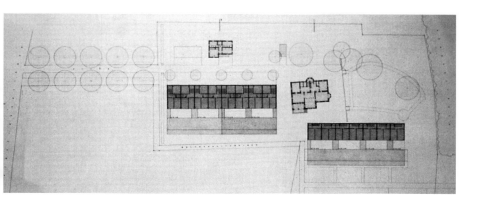
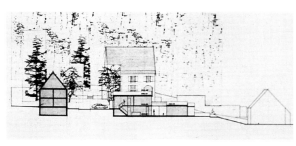
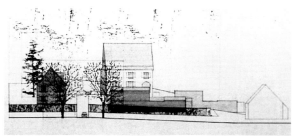
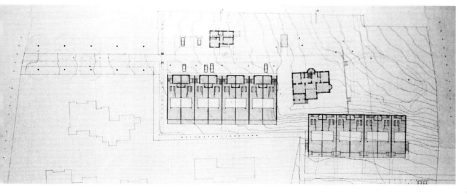
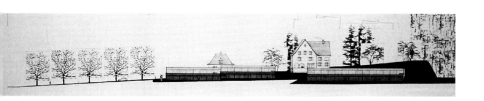

Grundrisse Ober- und Erdgeschoß
Floor plans, upper and ground floors
Ansicht Süd-West
View from the southwest

Schnittsequenz
Section sequence

Biografie

Thomas Schregenberger
1950 geboren in St. Gallen.
1968-72 Lehre als Hochbauzeichner.
1975-78 Architekturstudium an der Staatlichen Hochschule für Bildende Künste, Städelschule, in Frankfurt am Main.
1978 Diplom an der HBK Frankfurt a. M.
1981-84 Architekturstudium an der AA (Architectural Association) in London.
1984 AA Diplom und RIBA (Royal Institut of British Architecture) part 1 + 2, London.
1985-94 Architekturbüro mit Harry Roos (Roos & Schregenberger) in Zürich.
Seit 1994 Architekturbüro Thomas Schregenberger in Zürich

Werkverzeichnis

1985
Liegenschaft «Zur Steinernen Traube» in Stein am Rhein SH, Restaurierung 1985-87.*

1986
Ausbau und Erweiterung der Liegenschaft Bucheggstraße 41/43 in Zürich, ausgeführt 1986-88.*
Erweiterung und Renovation der Liegenschaft «Schweizerhof» in Richterswil ZH, ausgeführt 1986-88.*

1987
Peat Marwick, Büroeinbau, Sitz Zug, ausgeführt 1987/88.*
Liegenschaft «Frösch» in Zofingen AG, Restaurierung 1987/88.*
Verwaltungs- und Wohngebäude Röschbachstraße, Zürich, Projekt.

1988
Pestalozzi-Bibliothek in Zürich-Albisrieden, Projekt.

1989
Impuls Travel, Reisebüro in Zürich, ausgeführt 1989/90.*
Überbauung Augarten in Rheinfelden, Sanierung von 6 Wohnhochhäusern (Ciba-Geigy), Projekt.*

1990
KPMG Fides, Büroeinbau, Sitz Zug, Wettbewerb (auf Einladung), erster Preis, ausgeführt 1990/91.*
Hochhaus Gutstraße in Zürich (Architekt: Karl Egender), Projekt Restaurierung.*
Überbauung des Zentrums Horgen, Wettbewerb, fünfter Preis.*
Kathedrale Lausanne, Wettbewerb, dritter Preis.*
Überbauung Röntgenareal Zürich, Wettbewerb, sechster Preis.*
Alterssiedlung Arbon, erster Ankauf.*

1991
Bernhard Rothfos AG, Büroeinbau, Sitz Schweiz in Zug, ausgeführt 1991/92.*
Um- und Ausbau Haus Mathers in Oberwil ZG, ausgeführt 1991/94.*
Wohnüberbauung Rütihof Zürich, Wettbewerb (auf Einladung), fünfter Preis.*
Wohnüberbauung Fehr in Buchberg ZH, Projekt.*

1992
Wohnung für eine Graphologin in Zürich, ausgeführt 1992.*
Wohnhaus auf Korfu, Griechenland, ausgeführt 1992/93.*
Kantonales Laboratorium St. Gallen, Wettbewerb, zweiter Preis.*

1993
Erweiterungsbau Haus Maurer in Zuzwil SG, ausgeführt 1993.*
Wohnüberbauung Baslerstraße in Brugg AG, Projekt.
Parkhaus in Rümlang ZH, ausgeführt 1993/94.*

1994
Überbauung Dammweg in Zürich, Projekt.
Verwaltungsgebäude Poststraße 4 in Zug.

1995
Fabrik am Wasser Zürich, mit Lorenz Peter, Lukas Schweinegruber (Landschaftsarchitekt), Wettbewerb, vierter Preis.
KPMG, Umbau Hauptsitz Zürich, Wettbewerb (auf Einladung), erster Preis.

1996
Wohnüberbauung «Rehbühl» in Uster ZH, Projekt.
Gartenanlage in Lija, Malta, Ausführung 1996/97.
KPMG, Umbau Eingangs- und Konferenzbereich Hauptsitz Zürich.
KPMG, Gesamterneuerung Hauptsitz Zürich, Projekt.
KPMG, Umbau Specialized Services Zürich, Projekt.

* Architekturbüro Roos & Schregenberger

Bibliografie

Charles Jencks, *Representational Orders* (Studie), in: AD Architectural Design 1/2, 1982.
Nigel Coates, *Getto und Globus* (Albien, Body-Park), in: archithese 5/1983.
Nigel Coates, *Ghetto & Globe* (Albien, Body-Park), in: AA-Files 5/1984.
Nigel Coates, *City of Nomads* (STAL-Airport), in: AA Review 1984.
Günter Bock, *Das Detail als Kommentar* (Bucheggstraße), in: archithese 6/1990.
Schilling/Lichtenstein, *Architektur in Zürich, 1980-1990* (Bucheggstraße), in: Museum für Gestaltung, Stadt Zürich 1990.
Anton Herrmann, *z. B. Stein am Rhein* (Zur Steinernen Traube), in: archithese 2/1991.
James Salazar, *Restructuration of a court* (Zur Steinernen Traube), in: Quaderns Q199, Barcelona.
James Salazar, *Annex for a Studio* (Bucheggstraße Zürich), in: Quaderns Q199, Barcelona.
Martin Tschanz, *Hauptsächlich eine Wand* (KPMG Zug), in: archithese 5/1993.
Robert Huber/Lucas Schwarz, *Feindbild Hochhaus* (Hochhaus «Im Gut»), in: Architektur Forum Zürich 1993/94.
R+S, Hubeli/Luchsinger, *Drei Fragen an Architekten* (Haus Maurer, Zuzwil), in: Werk, Bauen + Wohnen 3/1994.
Martin Tschanz, *Erlebbare Konzepte,* Zur Architektur von Thomas Schregenberger, in: Neue Zürcher Zeitung 82/1995.
André Bideau, *Stimmungsvolle Höfe* (Fabrik am Wasser), in: Werk, Bauen + Wohnen 6/1995.
Peter Omahen, *Viel Hoffnung – wenig Durchblick* (Fabrik am Wasser), in: archithese 3/1995.
Martin Tschanz, *Sanfte Pervertierungen* (KPMG Zug), in: Daidalos 56/1995.
Ursula Suter, *Anpacker und Ausreißer*, in: db, deutsche bauzeitung 9/1995.
Helmut Lerch, *Wohnhauserweiterungen* (Haus Maurer), in: Alexander Koch Verlag.

Eigene Veröffentlichungen
Ein Quartier lebt auf, Westernkwartier Delft, in: Werk und Zeit 9/10, 1975.
Die Pioniere und ihre Erben, Hellerhofsiedlung Ffm., in: Werk und Zeit 3/1976.
Weniger ist langweilig, Venturi & Rauch, in: Tages-Anzeiger-Magazin 10/1979.
Die Säulen des Architekten, über die GSMBA, in: archithese 1/1980.
Rossi und nochmals Rossi, in: archithese 1/1980.
Von Tigerman bis Tesar, in: archithese 6/1980.
Venedig 1980, in: archithese 1/1981.
Englisches in der neuen englischen Architektur, in: archithese 5/1983.
Zeit – Geist, in: archithese 5/1983.
Z. B. Stein am Rhein, in: archithese 2/1991.
Drei Fragen an Architekten, in: Werk, Bauen + Wohnen 3/1994.
Farbe als Material, in: archithese 6/1994.
Farbe als Bedeutungsträger, in: archithese 6/1994.

Biography

Thomas Schregenberger
1950 Born in St. Gallen.
1968-72 Apprenticeship as architectural drafter.
1975-78 Studied architecture at the Staatlichen Hochschule für Bildende Künste, Städelschule, Frankfurt on the Main.
1978 Graduated from the HBK, Frankfurt on the Main.
1981-84 Studied architecture at the AA (Architectural Association), London.
1984 Graduated AA and RIBA (Royal Institute of British Architecture), parts 1 + 2, London.
1985-94 Architecture office with Harry Roos (Roos & Schregenberger), Zurich.
Since 1994 architecture office Thomas Schregenberger, Zurich.

List of Works

1985
"Zur Steinernen Traube", building and property, Stein am Rhein, restoration 1985-87.*

1986
Bucheggstrasse 41/43, building and property, development and expansion, Zurich, executed 1986-88.*
"Schweizerhof", building and property, expansion and renovation, Richterswil, executed 1986-88.*

1987
Peat Marwick, office installation, Zug, executed 1987/88.*
"Frösch" building and property, Zofingen, restauration executed 1987/88.*
Röschbachstrasse administration and residence building, Zurich, project.

1988
Pestalozzi Library, Zurich-Albisrieden, project.

1989
Impuls Travel, travel office, Zurich, executed 1989/90.*
Augarten superstructure, renewal and upgrade of six high-rise residences (Ciba-Geigy), Rheinfelden, project.*

1990
KPMG Fides, office installation, Zug, competition (upon invitation), first prize, executed 1990/91.*
Gutstrasse high-rise, Zurich (architect: Karl Egender), project restoration.*
Central superstructure, Horgen, competition, fifth prize.*
Cathedral, Lausanne, competition, third prize.*
Röntgenareal superstructure, Zurich, competition, sixth prize.*
Arbon senior community, first purchase.*

1991
Bernhard Rothfos AG, office installation, Zug, executed 1991/92.*
Mathers House, conversion and development, Oberwil, executed 1991-94.*
Rütihof housing superstructure, Zurich, competition (upon invitation), fifth price.*
Fehr housing superstructure, Buchberg, project.*

1992
Apartment for a graphologist, Lunastrasse, Zurich, executed 1992/93.*
Residence on Corfu, Greece, executed 1992/93.*
Canton laboratory, St. Gallen, competition, second prize.*

1993
Maurer House, expansion, Zuzwil, executed 1993.*
Baslerstrasse housing superstructure, Brugg, project.
Parking garage, Rümlang, executed 1993/94.*

1994
Dammweg superstructure, Zurich, project.
Poststrasse 4 administration office, Zug.

1995
"Fabrik am Wasser", Zurich, with Lorenz Peter, Lukas Schweinegruber (landscape architect), competition, fourth prize.
KPMG, conversion, main office, Zurich, competition (upon invitation), first prize.

Bibliography

1996
"Rehbühl" housing superstructure, Uster, project.
Garden complex, Lija, Malta, execution 1996/97.
KPMG, conversion of entrance and conference area, main office, Zurich.
KPMG, total renovation, main office Zurich, project.
KPMG, Specialized Services, conversion, Zurich, project.

* Architecture office Roos & Schregenberger

Charles Jencks, *Representational Orders* (study), in: AD Architectural Design 1/2, 1982.
Nigel Coates, *Ghetto and Globus* (Albien, Body-Park), in: archithese 5/1983.
Nigel Coates, *Ghetto and Globe* (Albien, Body-Park), in: AA-Files 5/1984.
Nigel Coates, *City of Nomads* (STAL-Airport), in: AA Review 1984.
Günter Bock, *Das Detail als Kommentar* (Bucheggstrasse), in: archithese 6/1990.
Schilling/Lichtenstein, *Architektur in Zürich, 1980-1990* (Bucheggstrasse), in: Museum für Gestaltung, City of Zurich 1990.
Anton Herrmann, *z. B. Stein am Rhein* (Zur Steinernen Traube), in: archithese 2/1991.
James Salazar, *Restructuration of a court* (Zur Steinernen Traube), in: Quaderns Q199, Barcelona.
James Salazar, *Annex for a Studio* (Bucheggstrasse, Zurich), in: Quaderns Q199, Barcelona.
Martin Tschanz, *Hauptsächlich eine Wand* (KPMG Zug), in: archithese 5/1993.
Robert Huber / Lucas Schwarz, *Feindbild Hochhaus* (Hochhaus "Im Gut"), in: Architektur Forum Zürich 1993/94.
R+S, Hubeli/Luchsinger, *Drei Fragen an Architekten* (Maurer House, Zuzwil), in: Werk, Bauen + Wohnen 3/1994.
Martin Tschanz, *Erlebbare Konzepte,* Zur Architektur von Thomas Schregenberger, in: Neue Zürcher Zeitung 82/1995.
André Bideau, *Stimmungsvolle Höfe* (Fabrik am Wasser), in: Werk, Bauen + Wohnen 6/1995.
Peter Omahen, *Viel Hoffnung – wenig Durchblick* (Fabrik am Wasser), in: archithese 3/1995.
Martin Tschanz, *Sanfte Pervertierungen,* (KPMG Zug), in: Daidalos 56/1995.
Ursula Suter, *Anpacker und Ausreißer,* in: db, deutsche Bauzeitung 9/1995.
Helmut Lerch, *Wohnhauserweiterungen* (Maurer House), in: Alexander Koch Verlag.

Publications by the Architect
Ein Quartier lebt auf, Westernkwartier Delft, in: Werk und Zeit 9/10, 1975.
Der Pioniere und ihre Erben, Hellerhofsiedlung Ffm., in: Werk und Zeit 3/1976.
Weniger ist langweilig, Venturi & Rauch, in: Tages-Anzeiger-Magazin 10/1979.
Die Säulen des Architekten, about the GSMBA, in: archithese 1/1980.
Rossi und nochmals Rossi, in: archithese 1/1980.
Von Tigerman bis Tesar, in: archithese 6/1980.
Venedig 1980, in: archithese 1/1981.
Englisches in der neuen englischen Architektur, in: archithese 5/1983.
Zeit – Geist, in: archithese 5/1983.
z. B. Stein am Rhein, in: archithese 2/1991.
Drei Fragen an Architekten, in: Werk, Bauen + Wohnen 3/1994.
Farbe als Material, in: archithese 6/1994.
Farbe als Bedeutungsträger, in: archithese 6/1994.

Jakob Steib
Zürich

Mehrfamilienhaus Weizacker | Weizacker Multifamily Housing | Winterthur, 1988–92

Mehrfamilienhaus Hinterfeld | Hinterfeld Multifamily Housing | Zwingen, 1993–95

Wohnüberbauung Dättnau | Dättnau Housing Superstructure | Winterthur, 1995

Wohnheim für Behinderte | Residence Home for the Disabled | Niederhasli, 1996/97

Mitarbeiterinnen und Mitarbeiter
Collaborators
- Eric Alles
- Michel Gübeli
- Benjamin Leimgruber
- Fabio Lüthi
- Peter Meyer
- Barbara Neff
- Andrea Roth
- Mischa Spoerri

Weitere Mitarbeiterinnen und Mitarbeiter
Further collaborators
- Beatrix Bencseky
- Silvia Benelli
- Jacques Feiner
- Christian Fierz
- Michael Gruber
- Verena Klump
- Anja Krasselt
- Roberto Lüder
- Max Micelli
- Joos Mutzner
- Thomas Nemeth
- Andreas Wirz
- Cornelia Zoller

Jakob Steib

Wohnbauten im Vorort.

Der in Basel aufgewachsene und zurzeit in Zürich praktizierende Jakob Steib interessiert sich speziell für den Wohnungsbau, der in der Schweiz mittlerweile «eine eigene Richtung eingeschlagen hat». 1992 fiel Steib mit dem Wohnhaus an der Weizackerstraße in Winterthur auf, kürzlich wurde das Mehrfamilienhaus in Zwingen realisiert. Mit beiden Arbeiten versuchte Steib räumliche Experimente umzusetzen, diese mit unterschiedlichen Bildwelten zu verknüpfen und dabei das Objekthafte der Bauten zu steigern, ohne sogleich programmatische Position zu beziehen. Damit beteiligt sich Steib ganz bewußt an dem Diskurs der architektonischen Themen, die für junge Architekten in der Schweiz zurzeit von Interesse sind. Der 1959 in Basel geborene Jakob Steib studierte an der ETH Zürich, war danach in verschiedenen Zürcher Büros tätig und hat sich 1987 mit einem eigenen Büro selbständig gemacht. Ihn interessiert es, speziell im Wohnungsbau «Systeme auszuklügeln», wie er es nennt, und optische Wirkungen mit räumlichen Qualitäten möglichst sinnfällig zu verbinden. Mit dem Wohnhaus an der Weizackerstraße in Winterthur entstand ein freistehendes Reihenhaus, das einerseits die Zeile eines Siedlungsbaus assoziiert, andrerseits sich als Solitär in eigenständiger Form von der typischen Bebauung des Winterthurer Außenquartiers abhebt. Damit wird an traditionelle Typologien zwar angeknüpft, zugleich werden diese aber auch hinterfragt zugunsten eines durchaus auf Irritation angelegten Baukörpers, der mit den der Hanglinie folgenden, abgetreppten Wohneinheiten sich an konventionellen Hangbebauungen orientiert, zugleich aber mit einem durchgezogenen Dachabschluß eine kontrakompositorische Zäsur setzt, die dem Gebäude erst die signifikante, bildhafte Eigenständigkeit verleiht.

Mit dem Mehrfamilienhaus Hinterfeld in Zwingen, einer Vorortgemeinde von Basel, knüpft Jakob Steib an die eigene Typologie direkt an. Die Wohneinheiten haben einen eindeutigen Seriencharakter, wirken gleichsam angedockt und sind doch als individuelle Wohneinheiten klar erfahrbar.

Die Grunddisposition der fünfzehn Wohnungen setzt sich aus drei unterschiedlichen Geschossen mit jeweils fünf gleichen Wohnungstypen pro Geschoß zusammen: Die fünf Zweizimmerwohnungen im Dachgeschoß, von einem Laubengang aus erschlossen, die Dreizimmerwohnung im Erdgeschoß und die darüberliegenden Wohnungen im ersten Obergeschoß teilen sich jeweils ein gemeinsames Treppenhaus. Die Kopfwohnungen im Westen sind direkt von außen zugänglich, alle Wohnungen sind nach Süden orientiert. Im Erd- und ersten Obergeschoß sind sie L-förmig um ihren jeweils eigenen zweigeschossigen Außenraum angeordnet. In ihrer Raumzuordnung sind diese Wohnungen mit dem in der Mitte eingestellten Küchenabteil äußerst präzise durchdacht und aufgeteilt. Mit unterschiedlich in die Tiefe entwickelten Grundrissen und entsprechend zurückgestaffelten Außenräumen sind sie seriell aneinandergereiht, so daß abwechslungsweise Vor- und Rücksprünge entstehen, die das kubische Erscheinungsbild der Südseite prägen.

Auf Brüstungshöhe des zweiten Obergeschosses bindet ein weit auskragendes Vordach die Volumen der Südfassade zu einer Gesamtform zusammen und verleiht dieser eine ausgeprägte horizontale Wirkung. Mit dieser Maßnahme und dem linearen, zurückversetzten und in die Dachsilhouette eingebetteten Attikageschoß entsteht das eindeutige Erscheinungsbild eines Wohnblocks, obwohl der Bau zugleich das synthetische Gleichgewicht zwischen einem Reihenhaustypus und einem Mehrfamilienhaus thematisiert.

Durch die ungewöhnlich hohe Lage der Brüstungen entsteht zudem für die Innenräume des ersten Obergeschosses die Möglichkeit, sehr hohe Wohnräume zu schaffen. Diese Überhöhe wird schließlich nochmals durch große Fensteröffnungen markiert. Die unmittelbare Nähe von kleinen Fenstern läßt ein bildhaftes Spiel mit der Maßstäblichkeit entstehen, das durch die außenliegende, die Flächigkeit betonende Verglasungsebene noch verstärkt wird. Durch die generell hochgehaltenen, in die kubische Auflösung integrierten massiven Brüstungen wird der Bezug von Flächenwirkung und Wandaufbau ebenfalls thematisiert. Im Gegensatz zur kubischen Südseite zeichnet sich die rückseitige Nordfassade durch ihre Flächigkeit und durch ihre einheitliche, ruhige Gesamterscheinung aus. Zwei Fensterformate, ein schmales, stehendes Rechteck und ein Quadrat, werden als modulare Felder präzis in die Fläche des Klinkermauerwerks gesetzt und unmerklich variiert. Auch in dieser Komposition wird ein Zusammenwirken von serieller Addition und Einheit des Ganzen angestrebt.

Trotz des präzisen kalkulierten Einsatzes von Raumwirkung und Material betont Jakob Steib, daß der Entwurf auch aus der Empfindung heraus entstanden ist und bildhafte Assoziationen beispielsweise von Arbeiten Frank Lloyd Wrights aufnimmt. «Zwar ist es im Trend, daß Material und Detail jede Ecke im Haus bestimmen», so Jakob Steib, dennoch soll das «Wohnen im Vorort» in erster Linie durch eine klare architektonische Sprache definiert sein.

J. C. B.

Mehrfamilienhaus Hinterfeld, Zwingen, 1993-95
Hinterfeld multi-family residence, Zwingen 1993-95

Housing in the Suburbs.

Jakob Steib grew up in Basle and is practicing today in Zurich. He has a special interest in apartment construction, which has in the meantime "struck off in its own direction" in Switzerland. In 1992 Steib attracted attention with the residence on Weizackerstrasse in Winterthur; a multi-family house was built only recently in Zwingen. In both works, Steib attempted to actualize spatial experiments and to tie these in with various constellations of images, thereby heightening the object-ness of the building while at the same time not taking a programmatic position. In this way, Steib is very consciously taking part in the discourse on architectural themes which is currently of great interest to young architects in Switzerland. Born in Basle in 1959, Jakob Steib studied at the ETH Zurich, after which he worked with a variety of Zurich architects, and by 1987 he had set up his own office. He is especially interested, in the realm of apartment construction, in "contriving systems", as he calls it, and in connecting optical effects with spatial qualities as strikingly as possible. For the housing on Weizackerstrasse in Winterthur, a freestanding row of attached houses was built that, on the one hand, calls up associations of a line in a housing tract, while on the other, sets itself apart from the typical development in the outer quarters of Winterthur as a solitary unit with its own individual form. This in fact creates a connection with traditional typologies, but at the same time these typologies are critically questioned in favor of a building thoroughly aimed at irritation. The stepped housing units follow the line of the slope and are oriented according to conventional incline development; the continuous line of the roof edge, meanwhile, sets a caesura counter to the composition, and only then does the building assume a significant pictorial individuality.

With the multi-family house in Hinterfeld in Zwingen, a suburb of Basle, Jakob Steib went on in a direct continuation of his own typology. The housing units have a clearly serial character – they rather give the impression of being parked next to one another – and yet it is still possible to experience them as individual units.

The basic layout of the fifteen apartments comprises three different floors, each with five identical apartment types per floor: the five two-room apartments on the attic floor, accessible through an exposed corridor, the three-room apartment on the first floor, and the apartments above them on the second floor all share a common stairwell. The head apartments in the west can be entered directly from the outside. All the apartments face south. On the first and second floors, they are L-shaped, each organized around its own two-story-high outside space. The arrangement of rooms in these apartments, with kitchen compartment placed in the middle, is very precisely thought out and the rooms accordingly distributed. With floor plans variously developed along their depth and exterior spaces correspondingly recessed, the apartments are set next to one another in a series that alternates projections and recessions, giving the building its characteristic cubic appearance on the south side.

At the level of the parapet on the third floor, a widely projecting canopy unites the volumes of the south façade into a general form and gives it a distinctive horizontal effect. These measures, plus the linear roof parapet story, set back and embedded in the silhouette of the roof, leads to the clear appearance of a housing block, although the building simultaneously deals with the theme of the synthetic balance between an attached housing block as a type and a multi-family residence.

Because of the unusual height of the parapet, it becomes possible to create very high living areas in the interior spaces of the second floor. This superelevation is ultimately once again marked by huge window openings. The direct proximity of the small windows plays a pictorial game with scale that is reinforced by the accentuated flatness of the outer glazed panes. The theme of the reference between surface effect and wall development is also played out through the generally high placement of the massive parapets, which have been integrated into the cubic solution. In contrast to the cubic south side, the rear north side distinguishes itself by its general appearance of calmness and unity. The two window formats – one narrow, standing rectangle and one square – are set precisely into the surfaces of the clinker masonry as modular fields and are imperceptibly varied. This composition also strives toward an interplay of serial addition and unity of the whole.

Despite the precise, calculated employment of spatial effect and material, Jakob Steib emphasizes that the design has also developed out of sensibility and integrates pictorial associations from, for example, Frank Lloyd Wright. "Although it is a trend for the material and detail to define every corner in the house," says Jakob Steib, "suburban living" should nevertheless be defined above all by a clear architectural language. J. C. B.

Jakob Steib

Mehrfamilienhaus Weizacker, Winterthur, 1988–92.

In der offenen Umgebung eines typischen Winterthurer Außenquartiers schmiegt sich die Wohnzeile an den Hang. Durch die rhythmisierende Abtreppung der Wohnungen und das zurückgesetzte dunkle Dachgeschoß vermag der Neubau gegenüber den umgebenden Wohnbauten eine neue Maßstäblichkeit zu etablieren, was ihm aus der Ferne eine gewisse Entrücktheit verleiht. Die zeichenhafte Behandlung der Erschließung durch einen Liftturm, eine offene Außentreppe und einen Laubengang sowie die ruhige Dachlinie und die spezielle Kopfausbildung am Hangfuß wirken identitätsbildend und binden die seriell gereihten, sich abtreppenden Elemente zu einer Gesamtform zusammen.

Die Disposition von zwei übereinanderliegenden Maisonettewohnungen wird im Fassadenaufbau sichtbar. Die beiden Schlafgeschosse liegen als Ruhezonen zwischen den beiden Wohngeschossen. Die Anordnung wird dort sichtbar, wo der Verputz der Schlafgeschoße an den Beton des Sockelgeschosses und der Dachterrasse stößt. Die vorspringende Betonplatte der Dachterrasse erzeugt eine eigene Surrealität, indem sie den Traufabschluß gegenüber dem Attikageschoß bildet und durch ihre Abtreppung wie eine vom Boden abgehobene, schwebende Straße wirkt. Der graugestrichene Dachaufbau ist mit einer hinterlüfteten Holzschalung verkleidet. Durch die Raumüberlappung erhält die Dachwohnung eine perspektivische Ausdehnung vom Wohn- zum Schlafgeschoß. Der spiralförmige Grundriß impliziert ein kontinuierliches dynamisches Raumerlebnis. Betritt man die Wohnung, öffnet sich der Blick gegen Süden auf die Terrasse. Der Wohnraum bildet die Mitte der Wohnung und wird durch die Wegführung und die Niveauunterschiede in mehrere Bereiche zoniert. Er ist nicht nur räumliches, sondern auch architektonisches Zentrum.

Die Böden sowie die Simsabdeckungen bestehen aus graublauem Kalkstein, die Wände und die Decken sind weiß verputzt. Die Türöffnungen im Schlafgeschoß sind als optische Raumerweiterung auf der Südseite bis an die Decke gezogen, damit die Südsonne tief in die Wohnung dringt. So wird trotz der Einschränkungen, welche den Mietwohnungsbau beherrschen, ein Optimum an räumlicher Qualität erreicht.

Weizacker Multifamily Housing, Winterthur, 1988–92.

In the open environs of a typical outlying quarter of Winterthur, the row of attached houses nestles against the hillside. In comparison to the housing construction in the area, the new building, with its rhythmical stepping zigzag of the apartments and its dark recessed roof story, is able to establish a new scale which, when seen from a distance, gives a certain sense of vanishing. The graphic handling of access to the building with an elevator tower, an open exterior staircase and an exposed corridor, together with the smooth roof line and the special head construction at the foot of the hillside, act as identity-formers and bind the stepped series of elements into one total form.

The arrangement of two maisonette apartments placed one above the other is made visible in the construction of the façade. The two floors reserved for sleeping are quiet zones between the two floors for living. The arrangement becomes visible where the plastering of the sleeping floor pushes against the concrete of the basement and the roof terrace. The projecting concrete plate of the roof terrace exhibits its own surreality, in that it forms the end of the eaves across from the roof parapet story and, with its stepped form, looks like a floating street that has been lifted off the ground. The gray painted roof construction is covered with a ventilated wood shuttering. The overlapping of the space gives the roof apartment a perspective elongation from living to sleeping floor. The spiral floor plan implies a continuous, dynamic experience of space. When one enters the apartment, the view opens up toward the south on the terraces. The living space forms the center of the apartment and becomes a zone in each of several other areas as it leads away and changes levels. It is not only the spatial, but also the architectonic, center.

The floors and the sill coverings are out of gray-blue limestone; the walls and ceiling are plastered white. The door openings on the sleeping floor are optical space extenders up to the ceiling on the south side, so that the southern sun penetrates deep into the apartment. Thus, despite the limitations that dominate rental apartment construction, optimal spatial quality is achieved.

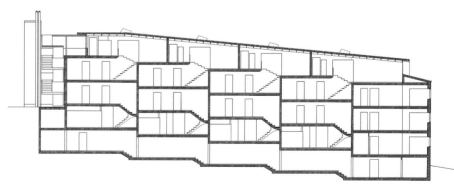

Längsschnitt
Elevation section
Ansicht Südfassade
View of south façade

Dachaufbau und Wohnzimmer im Dachgeschoß
  Roof construction and living room on attic floor
Dachgeschoß
  Attic floor
Zweites Obergeschoß
  Second floor
Erstes Obergeschoß
  First floor
Erdgeschoß
  Ground floor

Jakob Steib

Mehrfamilienhaus Hinterfeld, Zwingen, 1993–95.

Zwingen ist durch den Kantonswechsel von Bern zu Baselland zu einer beliebten Vorortsgemeinde mit guten Verkehrsverbindungen zu Basel geworden. Wohnungen sind dort zurzeit Mangelware. Das in der Birsebene gelegene Gebiet Hinterfeld ist zum Teil von älteren ansprechenden Arbeiterhäusern der Papierfabrik Zwingen überbaut. Die Aussicht auf die Birs und den bewaldeten Hang ist zwar nicht spektakulär, aber wenigstens angenehm. Die Höhenzüge ringsum bieten gute Erholung. Trotz dieser recht attraktiven Voraussetzung muß eine Mietwohnung in Zwingen deutlich mehr bieten als in der Stadt oder in einem größeren Zentrum.

Aufgrund der aus einem Wettbewerb hervorgegangenen Gesamtplanung von Michael Alder, Basel, galt es, das Mietwohnhaus als einfachen, langgestreckten Baukörper zu gestalten. Der dreigeschossige Bau ist kubisch aufgelöst und durchstrukturiert. Auf diese Weise erhalten alle fünfzehn Wohnungen eine unverwechselbare Identität. Jede Wohnung besitzt einen ungestörten Außenraum als erweiterte Wohnzone. Dem «Wohnen im Vorort», das weder städtisch noch ländlich ist, wird damit auf eine neue Art Form gegeben. Für die Nordfassade wurde Klinker im Binder-Läufer-Verband und für die Südfassade rotes Zedernholz verwendet.

Hinterfeld Multifamily Housing, Zwingen, 1993–95.

In the course of its change from being part of the Canton of Bern to the Canton of Basle (countryside), Zwingen has become a popular suburb community with good commuting connections to Basle. Apartments there are scarce commodities these days. The region of Hinterfeld that lies in the Birs River plain is built up in part of old, attractive houses once belonging to the workers at the paper factory in Zwingen. The view over the Birs and the forested hillside is in fact not spectacular, but it is at least agreeable. The range of hills that rings the area is relaxing. Despite this truly attractive situation, a rental apartment in Zwingen clearly has to offer more than an apartment in the city or in a large center.

On the basis of the overall planning (Michael Alder, Basle) arising from a competition, it was necessary to design a long, simple building for the rental apartment. The three-story construction is reduced to cubes and structured so throughout. In this way, all fifteen apartments acquire an unmistakable identity. An undisturbed and peaceful outside space belongs to each apartment as an extended living zone. "Suburban living", in neither city nor country, is thus given a new type of form. For the north façade, clinker is used in the running header band and, for the south façade, red cedar wood.

Südfassade
South façade
Terrasse im ersten Obergeschoß
Terrace on first floor

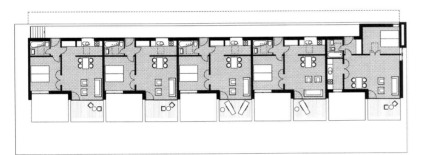
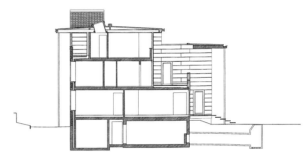

Wohnraum im ersten Obergeschoß
  Living room on first floor
Zweites Obergeschoß
  Second floor
Erstes Obergeschoß
  First floor
Erdgeschoß
  Ground floor
Querschnitt im Bereich der eingezogenen Terrassen
  Cross section in the area of the retracted terraces

Jakob Steib

Wohnüberbauung Dättnau, Winterthur, 1995.

Da der bestehende Weiler mit seiner idyllischen Ausstrahlung möglichst unangetastet bleiben soll, wird die zu planende neue Baumasse als eigenständige, kompakte Anlage am gegenüberliegenden Hang angesiedelt.

Eine Parallelenschar von einfachen, schlichten Baukörpern mit ruhiger Dachaufsicht unterstützt die topografische Hauptrichtung des Tals und bettet sich ganz selbstverständlich in die Landschaft ein. Vier parallel zum Hang liegende längliche Wohnhäuser bilden zwei langgestreckte öffentliche Hofräume, auf die hin primär gewohnt wird. Von hier aus erfolgt auch die Erschließung der Wohnungen. Das Wohnungssystem beruht auf einem linearen Querschotenprinzip. Je nach Bedarf kann eine Wohnung um halbe oder ganze Querschotenabschnitte erweitert werden. Der Zutritt zu den Wohnungen erfolgt über eine große Veranda, die sich in den kalten Jahreszeiten leicht zu einem Wintergarten umbauen läßt.

Eine Besonderheit ist der große, durchgehende, loftartige Gemeinschaftsbereich, der die räumliche Mitte der Wohnung bildet und von dem aus sämtliche Zimmer erschlossen werden. Damit können unnötige Verkehrsflächen vermieden werden. Zudem ist es auf diese Weise möglich, die Individualräume groß (jedes Zimmer eignet sich als Elternschlafzimmer), die gesamte Wohnfläche dagegen klein zu dimensionieren. Das shedartige Dach ermöglicht im zweiten Obergeschoß weitere räumliche Dispositionen. Es entsteht so eine belichtete Mittelzone, die als Arbeitsnische, Eßecke oder Spielfläche zwischen zwei Schlafzimmern genutzt werden kann. Zusätzlich vermittelt die spezielle Lichtführung eine Atelieratmosphäre.

Das einfache Querschotenprinzip ermöglicht große Flexibilität. Veränderungen können ohne großen Aufwand vorgenommen werden. Diese Struktur ermöglicht im Erdgeschoß große Gartenwohnungen, Kleinwohnungen (die sich auch als Alterswohnungen eignen) und separate Einzelzimmer, im ersten und zweiten Obergeschoß mittelgroße und kleine Wohnungen. Die Großwohnungen können in zwei kleinere umgewandelt werden.

Dättnau Housing Superstructure, Winterthur, 1995.

Because the existing hamlet with its idyllic charm is to remain as untouched as possible, the new planned building mass is to be settled as a compact, independent complex on the opposite hillside.

A group of simple, modest, parallel building units with a smooth and calm overhead view supports the main topographical direction of the valley and nestles naturally into the landscape. Four housing blocks lying lengthwise, parallel to the slope, form two long public courtyard spaces where much of the living takes place. The apartment access way also leads out from here. The apartment system is based on a linear diagonal pod principle. According to need, each apartment can be expanded by one-half or one whole diagonal pod segment. The entrance to the apartments leads over a large veranda which, in the colder months, is easily converted into a winter garden.

A special feature is the large, continuous loft-like communal area that forms the spatial center of the apartment and is accessed by all the rooms, thereby avoiding unnecessary traffic surfaces. This setup moreover makes it possible for the individual rooms to be big (every room is appropriate as a master bedroom), while the total floor space is comparatively reduced. The shed-like roof allows for further spatial organization on the third floor. An illuminated middle zone between the bedrooms develops from this that can be used as a work niche, an eating corner, or a play area. In addition, the special control of light conveys an atelier atmosphere.

The simple diagonal pod principle allows for a large amount of flexibility. Changes can be made without a great deal of trouble. This structure makes large garden apartments on the ground floor possible, as well as small apartments (suitable as senior apartments) and separate individual rooms; on the second and third floors, medium-sized and small apartments can be made, as the large apartments can be transformed into two smaller apartments.

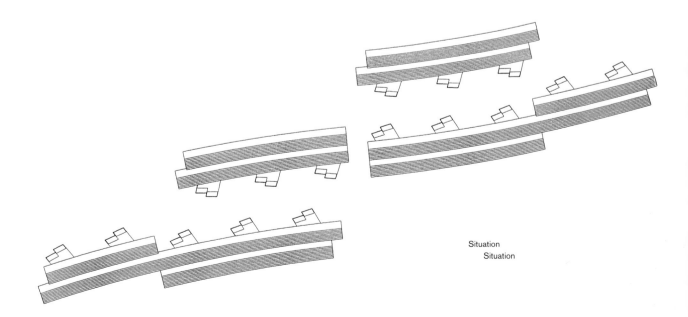

Situation
Situation

| 2 Zimmer | 3 Zimmer | 4½ Zimmer | 5½ Zimmer | evtl. 6½ Zimmer | Einzelzimmer |

Modellfoto eines Hofraums
    Model photo of courtyard
Gesamtanlage
    Overall situation
Wohnungstypen
    Apartment types
Grundstruktur
    Basic structure

Wohnheim mit Beschäftigungsmöglichkeit für Behinderte, Niederhasli, 1996/97.

Das Grundstück befindet sich in einem «Hofraum», der durch die bestehenden Nachbarhäuser definiert wird. In diesen Hofraum erstreckt sich die zweigeschossige neue Anlage. Das niedrige Gebäude weist eine mit Oberlichtbändern versehene Dachlandschaft auf, die begrünt werden kann. Das L-förmige, nach Süden geöffnete Gebäude schafft eine geschützte, jedoch nicht vollständig abgeschlossene Innenwelt. Die öffentliche Erschließung erfolgt über die Spitzstraße. Entlang der Ostfassade befinden sich der Haupteingang, der Spitex-Eingang und die Anlieferung. Für die Betriebsfahrzeuge ist ein abgeschlossener Werkhof mit gedeckten Parkplätzen vorgesehen, dem Personal und den Besuchern stehen ungedeckte Autoabstellplätze zur Verfügung.

Durch die zweigeschossige Konzeption entstehen zusammenhängende, hindernisfreie Flächen, die den Bewohnern große Bewegungsfreiheit ermöglichen. Die Zweigeschossigkeit erlaubt die einfache Trennung in ein Erdgeschoß mit Arbeits- und Gemeinschaftsräumen sowie in ein Obergeschoß, das dem Wohnen vorbehalten ist. Das Erdgeschoß zeichnet sich durch eine große zentrale Halle aus, die sich zum Garten hin öffnet und mit ihrem gedeckten Sitzplatz zum Verweilen einlädt. Sämtliche Heimbereiche (Therapie, Wohngruppen, Eß- und Sitzungsraum, Verwaltung, Spitex) werden von ihr aus übersichtlich erschlossen.

Die Gartenhöfe erlauben eine gute Belichtung des Therapiebereichs und bieten attraktive Außenräume. Das Obergeschoß wird von einem kompakten Zimmerkranz L-förmig umgeben. Darin eingebettet entfaltet sich eine vielfältige Wohnlandschaft, die den Bewohnern Schutz und Geborgenheit bietet und das eigentliche Herz der Anlage darstellt. In jeder einzelnen Wohngruppe bilden die Wohn- und Eßbereiche den Schwerpunkt und evozieren so eine familiäre Stimmung.

Die Oblichtbänder lassen eine größere Gebäudetiefe zu und bringen Südlicht in die weniger gut orientierten Zimmer. Über zwei weitläufige Sonnenterrassen haben die Wohngruppen einen direkten Bezug zum Außenraum. Großzügige Freitreppen führen vom Wohngeschoß in den Garten.

Residence Home with Occupational Possibilities for the Disabled, Niederhasli, 1996/97.

The property lies in a "courtyard area" which is defined by the existing neighboring houses. The new two-story complex extends across this courtyard. The low building features a roof landscape, designed with bands of overhead skylighting, that can be planted with greenery. The L-shaped building, opening toward the south, creates a protected, yet not completely closed off, inner world. Public access is by way of Spitzstrasse. Along the length of the east façade is the main entrance, the Spitex entrance for home care facilities, and the delivery. Vehicles for the operation of the home are provided with a closed work yard with covered parking places; for staff and visitors, uncovered parking places are available.

The two-story conception gives rise to interconnected, obstacle-free surface areas on which the residents can move with freedom. It also allows for the simple separation into one ground floor, where there are work and recreation rooms, and one upper floor, reserved for living. The ground floor is distinguished by a large central hall that opens onto a garden and invites one to linger in its covered patio area. All the areas of the home (therapy, living groups, dining and sitting rooms, administration, Spitex) are all clearly accessed from here.

The garden courtyards allow good lighting of the therapy areas and offer attractive outside spaces. The upper floor is surrounded by a compact L-shaped room cornice. Embedded inside, a multifarious housing landscape unfolds, which offers the residents protection and security and which represents the actual heart of the complex. In each living group, the living and dining areas form the central point and thus evoke an intimate and familiar atmosphere.

The bands of skylights allow a greater depth in the construction of the building and carry southern light into the less fortunately oriented rooms. The living groups have direct contact to the outside areas over two extensive sun terraces. Generous outer staircases lead from the residence floor to the garden.

Begrünbare Dachlandschaft mit Oberlichtbändern
Plantable roof landscape with skylight bands

Modellfoto Nord-West-Fassade
Model photo of northwest façade

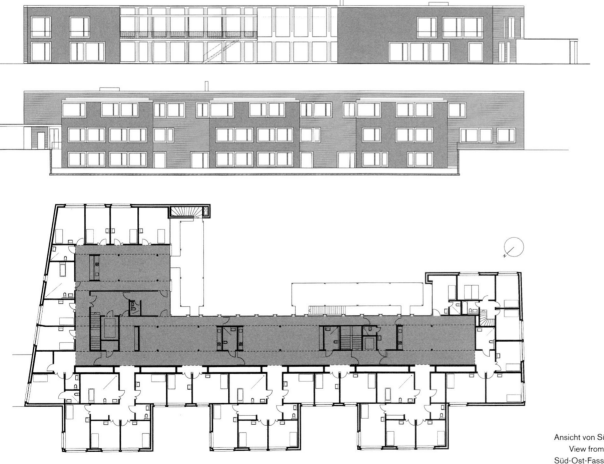

Ansicht von Süden, Modell
 View from the south, model
Süd-Ost-Fassade
 Southeast façade
Nord-West-Fassade
 Northwest façade
Erstes Obergeschoß
 First floor

Biografie

Jakob Steib

1959 geboren in Basel.
1978-83 Architekturstudium an der ETH Zürich.
1983 Diplom bei Prof. Dolf Schnebli an der ETH Zürich.
1983 Auslandsemester an der Harward Graduate School of Design bei Prof. G. Kallmann.
1981-84 Praktikum in verschiedenen Zürcher Architekturbüros (E. Studer, B. Bétrix und E. Consolascio).
1986-89 Assistent an der ETH Zürich bei Prof. K. Steib und Prof. A. Rüegg, daneben angestellt bei Stücheli Architekten für Projekte für Landis und Gyr.
1994 Diplomassistent bei Prof. A. Rüegg an der ETH Zürich.
Seit 1995 Mitglied des Bundes Schweizer Architekten (BSA).
Seit 1987 eigenes Architekturbüro in Zürich, enge Zusammenarbeit mit W. und K. Steib, Basel, besonderes Interesse für Wohnungsbau.

Werkverzeichnis

1988

Mehrfamilienhaus Weizacker, Winterthur (11 Wohnungseinheiten), Mitarbeit: Hans Krieg und Silvia Benelli, ausgeführt 1988-92.
Wohnüberbauung Dalbe-Dych im Gellert, Basel, Ideenwettbewerb (auf Einladung), für W. + K. Steib.
Überbauung der Areale der Schöller Hardturm AG, Zürich, Projektwettbewerb (auf Einladung), für W. + K. Steib.
Gemeindesaal mit Bibliothek und Restaurant, Wädenswil ZH, Projektwettbewerb (öffentlich), fünfter Rang.

1989

Wohnüberbauung Luzernerring, Basel, Projektwettbewerb (auf Einladung), für W. + K. Steib, erster Ankauf.
Regierungsviertel St. Pölten, Österreich, Ideenwettbewerb (öffentlich für Europa), mit R. Bader.

1990

Geschäftshaus Ilge, Frauenfeld, mit E. Dubler (Geschäftshaus mit Kombibüros), ausgeführt 1990-94.
Neubau Geschäftshaus «Ilge» der Elvia-Versicherung, Frauenfeld TG, Wettbewerb (auf Einladung), mit E. Dubler, erster Preis.
Arealüberbauung, Röntgenareal, Zürich, Projektwettbewerb (öffentlich), mit B. Neff und P. Meyer.
Überbauung Eßlingerdreieck für Basler und Hofmann Eßlingen ZH, Projektwettbewerb (auf Einladung), für W. + K. Steib, zweiter Preis.
Geschäftshaus Rudolfstraße, für Basler und Partner, Winterthur ZH, Projektwettbewerb (auf Einladung), für W. + K. Steib, zweiter Preis / dritter Rang.

1991

Umbau und Erweiterung Waffenplatz Brugg AG, Ideen-/Projektwettbewerb (auf Einladung), für W. + K. Steib, erste Runde: erster Preis, zweite Runde: ausgeschieden.
Erweiterung Technikum Rapperswil SG, Projektwettbewerb (öffentlich), vierter Preis.
Turnhalle auf dem Areal «Sandgrube», Basel, Projektwettbewerb (auf Einladung).

1992

Wohnüberbauung «Melchrüti», Wallisellen ZH, Ideenwettbewerb (auf Einladung), mit P. Meyer, zweiter Preis.
Erweiterung der Schulanlage «Bützi», Egg ZH, Projektwettbewerb (auf Einladung), zweiter Preis.
Dienstleistungs- und Verkaufszentrum Theaterstraße, Winterthur ZH, Projektwettbewerb (auf Einladung), für W. + K. Steib, dritter Preis / vierter Rang.

1993

Mehrfamilienhaus Hinterfeld, Zwingen (15 Wohnungseinheiten), Projektleitung: Barabara Neff, ausgeführt 1993-95.
Wohnüberbauung «Rännenfeld», Uster ZH, Projektwettbewerb (öffentlich), für W. + K. Steib, erster Ankauf.
Schulanlage «Storebode», Möhlin AG, Projektwettbewerb (öffentlich), für W. + K. Steib.

1994

Wohnüberbauung für die Keller AG, Dättnau bei Winterthur ZH, Projektwettbewerb (öffentlich), erster Preis.
Kirche und Wohnungen für die Freie Evangelische Gemeinschaft, Riehen BS, Studienauftrag für W. + K. Steib, erster Preis.
Wohnheim mit Beschäftigung für behinderte Menschen, Niederhasli ZH, Projektwettbewerb (auf Einladung), erster Preis.

1995

Wohnüberbauung Dättnau, Winterthur (90 Wohnungseinheiten, Umstrukturierung des alten Weilers), Planungsarbeiten.
Überbauung des Beutlerareals, Winova AG, Willisau LU, Studienauftrag für W. + K. Steib, erster Preis.
Kantonalbank Schwyz, Geschäftssitz, Einsiedeln SZ, Projektwettbewerb (öffentlich).
Schulheim «Zur Hoffnung» für behinderte Menschen, Riehen BS, Projektwettbewerb (öffentlich), dritter Preis.
Krankenhaus Berlin-Kaulsdorf, Berlin Deutschland, Projektwettbewerb (auf Einladung), für W. + K. Steib, Ankauf.

1996

Wohn- und Geschäftszentrum «Winova», Willisau (Läden, Büros und 26 Wohnungseinheiten).
Wohnheim mit Beschäftigung für Behinderte, Niederhasli (Wohnheim mit integrierter Gemeindebibliothek), Projektleitung: Barbara Neff.
Überbauung «Chli Sottike», Willisau, Gestaltungsplan, Projekt.
Kaserne Zürich, Projektwettbewerb in zwei Stufen (auf Einladung).

Bibliografie

Basler Experiment, in: Hochparterre, Dez./1989.
Mehrfamilienhaus Weizacker, Winterthur, in: Werk, Bauen + Wohnen, 4/1993.
Wohnsiedlung, Dättnau-Winterthur, Aktuelle Wettbewerbs Scene, 6/1994.
Mehrfamilienhaus Hinterfeld, Zwingen, in: archithese, 4/1996.
Mehrfamilienhaus Hinterfeld, Zwingen, in: Werk, Bauen + Wohnen, 8/1996.

Biography

Jakob Steib
1959 Born in Basle.
1978-83 Studied architecture at the ETH Zurich.
1983 Graduated from the ETH Zurich under Prof. Dolf Schnebli.
1983 Semester abroad at the Harvard Graduate School of Design under Prof. G. Kallmann.
1981-84 Practicum in various Zurich architecture offices (E. Studer, B. Bétrix, and E. Consolascio).
1986-89 Assistant to Prof. K. Steib and Prof. A. Rüegg at the ETH Zurich, worked at the same time at Stücheli Architekten on projects for Landis und Gyr.
1994 Graduate assistant to Prof. A. Rüegg at the ETH Zurich.
Since 1995 Member of the Bund Schweizer Architekten (BSA).
Since 1987 own architecture office in Zurich, close collaboration with W. and K. Steib, Basle, special interest in apartment construction.

List of Works

1988
Weizacker Multifamily residence, Winterthur (11 apartment units), assistance: Hans Krieg and Silvia Benelli, executed 1988-92.
Dalbe-Dych im Gellert housing superstructure, Basle, idea competition (upon invitation), for W. + K. Steib.
Superstructure on the Schöller Hardturm AG grounds, Zurich, project competition (upon invitation), for W. + K. Steib.
Community hall with library and restaurant, Wädenswil, project competition (open), fifth ranking.

1989
Luzernerring housing superstructure, project competition (upon invitation), for W. + K. Steib, first purchase.
St. Pölten governmental district, Austria, idea competition (open to Europe), with R. Bader.

1990
Ilge business building, Frauenfeld, with E. Dubler (business building with combination offices), executed 1990-94.
Elvia Insurance, new "Ilge" business building, Frauenfeld, competition (upon invitation), with E. Dubler, first prize.
Röntgenareal superstructure, Zurich, project competition (open), with B. Neff and P. Meyer.
Esslingen triangle superstructure, for Basler und Hofmann, Esslingen, project competition (upon invitation), for W. + K. Steib, second prize.
Rudolfstrasse business building, for Basler und Partner, Winterthur, project competition (upon invitation), for W. + K. Steib, second prize / third ranking.

1991
Waffenplatz Brugg AG, conversion and expansion, idea and project competition (upon invitation), for W. + K. Steib, first round: first prize, second round: eliminated.
Technikum Rapperswil, expansion, project competition (open), fourth prize.
Gymnasium on the "Sandgrube" grounds, Basle, project competition (upon invitation).

1992
"Melchrüti" housing superstructure, Wallisellen, idea competition, with P. Meyer, second prize.
"Bützi" school complex, expansion, Egg, project competition (upon invitation), second prize.
Theaterstrasse service and shopping center, Winterthur, project competition (upon invitation), for W. + K. Steib, third prize/fourth ranking.

1993
Hinterfeld Multifamily residence, Zwingen (15 apartment units) project supervision: Barbara Neff, executed 1993-95.
"Rännenfeld" housing superstructure, Uster, project competition (open), for W. + K. Steib, first purchase.
"Storebode" school complex, Möhlin AG, project competition (open), for W. + K. Steib.

1994
Dättnau housing superstructure, for Keller AG, Winterthur, project competition (open), first prize).
Free Evangelical Congregation church and apartments, Riehen, commissioned study for W. + K. Steib, first prize.
Residence home with occupational possibilities for the disabled, Niederhasli, project competition (upon invitation), first prize.

1995
Dättnau housing superstructure, Winterthur (90 apartment units, restructure of the old hamlet), planning work.
Beutlerareal superstructure, Winova AG, Willisau, commissioned study, for W. + K. Steib, first prize.
Kantonalbank Schwyz, business seat, Einsiedeln, project competition (open).
"Zur Hoffnung" school home for the disabled, Riehen, project competition (open), third prize.
Berlin-Kaulsdorf Hospital, Berlin, Germany, project competition (upon invitation), for W. + K. Steib, purchase.

1996
"Winova" housing and business center, Willisau (shops, offices and 26 apartment units).
Residence home with occupational possibilities for the disabled (residence home with integrated community library), project supervision: Barbara Neff.
"Chil Sottike" superstructure, Willisau, design plan, project.
Kaserne (barracks), Zurich, project competition in two stages (upon invitation).

Bibliography

Basler Experiment, in: Hochparterre, Dec./1989.
Mehrfamilienhaus Weizacker, Winterthur, in: Werk, Bauen + Wohnen, 4/1993.
Wohnsiedlung, Dättnau-Winterthur, Aktuelle Wettbewerbs Scene, 6/1994.
Mehrfamilienhaus Hinterfeld, Zwingen, in: archithese, 4/1996.
Mehrfamilienhaus Hinterfeld, Zwingen, in: Werk, Bauen + Wohnen, 8/1996.

Fotonachweis | Photo credits

Fotos ohne Nachweis stammen vom jeweiligen Architekturbüro
Fotos showing no credit, have been supplied by the respective architect's office

Althammer, Hochuli
    Christian Kerez (Corum, Seiten 28, 29)
    Guido Baselgia (Corum, Seite 30/31)
Angélil, Graham, Pfenninger, Scholl
    Michael Arden
    Hewitt/Garrison Photographers
    Eduard Hueber
    Martin Siegenthaler
    Rainer Zimmermann
Bauart Architekten
    Christine Blaser
Clavuot
    Ralph Feiner (Haus Dr. Heinz)
    Christian Kerez (Unterwerk Prättigau)
Consoni
    Tanja Schindler (Haus Sonderegger)
    Markus Baumgartner (alle übrigen Fotos)
Ehrenbold, Schudel
    Franz Rindlisbacher (Verandaausbau)
    Amt für Bundesbauten, Bern (Luftaufnahme City West)
Grego, Smolenicky
    Andrea Berclaz (Ballettsaal, Modellfoto)
    Julien Vonier (Jockey/Vollmoeller)
Knapkiewicz, Fickert
    Heinrich Helfenstein (Seite 126 links, Seite 133)
    Alexander Troehler (Seite 131 unten rechts)
Miller, Maranta
    Ruedi Walti (Seiten 17, 138, 140-145)
Olgiati
    Alberto Piovano (Haus Kucher)
Schafer
    Ives Eigenmann (Cité du Grand Torry)
Scheitlin, Syfrig
    Remy Markowitsch (Seite 21)
    Christoph Eckert (Seiten 176, 183)
    Heinrich Helfenstein (Seite 179)
    Stefan Wicki (Seite 181)
Schregenberger
    Felix Schregenberger
Steib
    Nick Spoerri/Regards (Seite 23)